1

A Wider Range

A Wider Range

Travel Writing by Women in Victorian England

Maria H. Frawley

Rutherford ● Madison ● Teaneck
Fairleigh Dickinson University Press
London and Toronto: Associated University Presses

1 — 3138

Associated University Presses
440 Forsgate Drive
Cranbury, NJ 08512

Associated University Presses
25 Sicilian Avenue
London WC1A 2QH, England

Associated University Presses
P.O. Box 338, Port Credit
Mississauga, Ontario
Canada L5G 4L8

The paper used in this publication meets the requirements of the American National Standard for Permanence of Paper for Printed Library Materials Z39.48-1984.

Library of Congress Cataloging-in-Publication Data

Frawley, Maria H., 1961–
    A wider range : travel writing by women in Victorian England /
Maria H. Frawley.
        p. cm.
    Includes bibliographical references (p.   ) and index.
    ISBN 0-8386-3544-X (alk. paper)
    1. Travelers' writings, English—Women authors—History and
criticism.   2. English prose literature—19th century—History and
criticism.   3. Women and literature—Great Britain—History—19th
century.   4. Voyages and travels—Historiography.   5. British—
Travel—Historiography.   6. Women—Travel—Historiography.
7. Travel in literature.   8. Women travelers.   I. Title.
PR778.T72F7   1994
820.9'355—dc20   92-55127
                                                                      CIP

PRINTED IN THE UNITED STATES OF AMERICA

Contents

Preface

THE idea for this book emerged out of the last graduate seminar that I took while enrolled in the Ph.D. program at the University of Delaware. The seminar was titled "Victorian Nonfiction Prose," and in it we read and studied works by the standard luminaries, among them Macaulay, Carlyle, Newman, Mill, Ruskin, Arnold, Huxley, and Pater, using as our primary sourcebook William E. Buckler's *Prose of the Victorian Period.*[1] The absence of women writers in this textual landscape was both conspicuous and confusing; after all, women writers seemed in some ways to dominate other Victorian genres. Skimming through Victorian periodicals—a favorite pasttime of mine—didn't resolve any of my questions. Women's nonfiction was there, and in abundance. Victorian women *seemed* to have written nonfiction as prolifically as they wrote fiction.

Months later Virginia Woolf rejuvenated my interest. Rereading one of the lesser known chapters of *A Room of One's Own,* I came upon the following passage:

> If the male is still the voluble sex, it is certainly true that women no longer write novels solely. There are Jane Harrison's books on Greek archaeology; Vernon Lee's books on aesthetics; Gertrude Bell's books on Persia. There are books on all sorts of subjects which a generation ago no woman could have touched. There are poems and plays and criticism; there are histories and biographies, books of travel and books of scholarship and research; there are even a few philosophies and books about science and economics.[2]

"The natural simplicity, the epic age of women's writing may have gone," Woolf concluded. "Reading and criticism may have given her a wider range, a greater subtlety" (83). Although Woolf's comments were based in part on her reading of turn-of-the-century and early modern women writers, they helped me to rethink how women's writing changed in nineteenth-century England. I began to suspect that in our zest to usher in a new canon of Victorian literature that reflected more accurately women's participation in private and public modes of writing we had overlooked something. Despite—or perhaps because of—the success of influential works such as Elaine Showalter's *A Literature of Their Own: British Women Novelists from Brontë to Lessing,* we became focused almost exclusively on fictional and poetic traditions.[3]

Back then I dreamed of writing a book about Victorian women's nonfiction. My early surveys of the literature suggested easy chapter divisions: I would have a chapter on art criticism, a chapter on history writing, a chapter on sociological writing, a chapter on biography, a chapter on travel writing, and so forth. What I discovered very soon was that the material was simply too vast to condense into simple summaries and too interesting to reduce to description. More important, I recognized that much of what seemed to be art criticism, or history, or sociology, *also* looked curiously like travel writing. The art criticism was about visiting museums in Venice; the history was about traveling through Middle Eastern lands; the sociology was about the character of Americans. My thesis—that many Victorian women used their travel experiences to establish authority to write in areas traditionally outside of women's sphere—was born.

My understanding of Victorian women's travel writing has changed much since then and, indeed, is still taking shape. Although I continue to believe that a great deal of the interest of women's travel writing derives from its investment in beliefs about professional identity and about cultural legitimacy, I have come to appreciate that the conjunctions between Victorian women, travel, and writing are much more complicated than I at first imagined. I find a certain degree of solace in my confidence that women's travel writing has much yet to offer to cultural studies of Victorian England, studies that continue to shape our understanding of its literature. Feminist scholarship has to date played a crucial role in the evolution of Victorian cultural studies. One thing I have learned from reading in this vast body of literature is the need to recognize that the appeal of Victorian literature—its multiple viewpoints and seemingly deliberate contradictions—is also its challenge. Underwriting this multiplicity is ideological instability that results in what Mary Poovey so appropriately described as "uneven developments."[4] This unevenness represents itself not only in the period's literature but also in its institutions and social relations.

What follows, then, should not be read as a study of the "evolution" of "the Victorian woman traveler" that purports to be either definitive or comprehensive, for such a reading would gloss the "uneven developments" met along the textual terrain of Victorian women's travel writing. My title in some ways suggests both my scope and its inevitable limits. *A Wider Range* plays not only on Virginia Woolf's celebratory recognition of the achievements of the period in *A Room of One's Own* but also on Martha Vicinus's important study of Victorian women and institutions, aptly titled *A Widening Sphere: Changing Roles of Victorian Women*.[5] Both works from their different positions and in their different ways underscore the need of feminists to recognize and celebrate historical evidence of women challenging the institutional and ideological boundaries of their society, a need that continues to drive feminist scholarship today. I was prompted by the same sense of need to undertake this project.

Many people and institutions helped me along the way. I want to acknowledge the support of a fellowship from the Huntington Library in San Marino, California, and a Grant-in-Aid from the University of Delaware's College of Arts and Science, both of which enabled me to spend an uninterrupted period reading and writing at a crucial stage in the development of this book. I thank my colleagues at Elizabethtown College, especially my chairperson Dr. John Campbell, for their support during revision of the manuscript.

I also want to thank the editor of *Nineteenth-Century Contexts* for permission to reprint in revised form portions of my "Desert Places/ Gendered Spaces: Victorian Women in the Middle East," the editor of *Annals of Scholarship* for permission to reprint in revised form portions of my "'Fair Amazons Abroad': The Social Construction of the Victorian Adventuress," and the editor of *The Victorian Newsletter* for permission to reprint in revised form portions of my "Harriet Martineau in America: Gender and the Discourse of Sociology." Full citations for these articles are included in the bibliography.

I owe thanks to many people for helping me make sure that the manuscript finally did take shape. Barbara Gates long ago introduced me to the fascinating extremes of Victorian literature and to the delights of reading literature by and about Victorian women. The energy Barbara has thrown into her own work—and the confidence she has shown in mine—has inspired and challenged me on countless occasions and in numerous ways. Other colleagues at the University of Delaware provided encouragement and advice; I owe special thanks to Jerry Beasley, Michael Cotsell, and Ann Ardis. Offering both wisdom and wit in a generous reading of the entire manuscript, Sally Mitchell from Temple University served as my model feminist, scholar, and teacher.

I owe thanks of another sort to my family. My sisters especially were stable sources of laughter, and my parents, Barton and Sabrena Hinkle, have provided inspiration and emotional support in many ways. That I found Victorian women travelers so inviting in the first place owes something to my husband, William Frawley, with whom I have traveled in so many ways since we met. Finally, I thank my son Christopher Barton Frawley who, though born while this work was in progress, seems always to have been in my life.

A Wider Range

1

Voyagers Out: Victorian Women Abroad

In 1902, Constance Larymore traveled with her husband to northern Nigeria. Recalling the end of her tour in *A Resident's Wife in Nigeria* (1908), Larymore wrote:

> I had ridden over 3000 miles, learnt a new language, made thousands of new friends in the animal and flower world, as well as valued human ones. I felt as if I had "enlarged my borders" mentally, and had certainly begun to know and love Africa with a deep affection that, I think, is never lost by those who once acquire it.[1]

The passage reflects much of the confidence, freedom of spirit, and sense of accomplishment felt by Victorian women who traveled abroad. This is a study of what it meant for Victorian women to cross distances, learn languages, and enlarge borders. Distance, discovery, and borders are all part of the special language with which Victorian women travelers experienced and recorded the world outside of England. For Constance Larymore, travel to Africa was taken as "a step in the darkest dark" where "no Englishwoman yet had gone."[2]

Although Larymore did traverse many hundreds of miles through the interior of Nigeria, Mary Anne Barker, Lucie Duff Gordon, Amelia Edwards, and Mary Kingsley are just a few of the Victorian women who traveled to Africa before her. Nor were they by any stretch of the imagination the only English women to travel to regions of the world remote from England. Florence Dixie and Constance Gordon Cumming visited South America; Mary Seacole and Florence Nightingale ventured to the Crimea; Isabella Bird Bishop chose as one of her many destinations Japan; Annie Taylor explored Tibet; and Annie Brassey sailed around the world. Destinations less exotic enticed Victorian women travelers as well. Frances Trollope, Harriet Martineau, Emily Faithfull, and Beatrice Webb were among the many Victorian women who went to the United States; Anna Jameson rambled in Canada. Charlotte Eaton, Mary Shelley, Frances Power Cobbe, Frances Elliot, and Vernon Lee spent extended periods of time in

Italy. Victorian women traveled. Whatever their destination, though, these women shared both a determination to leave home and a sense—however misguided—that they were going where "no Englishwoman yet had gone."

Once beyond the boundaries of England, many of these Victorian women felt compelled to write about their experiences away from home. At the close of the first volume of *Diary of an Idle Woman in Italy* (1871), the Victorian travel writer Frances Elliot observes:

> I had, during the last few hours, felt, admired, and examined so much, my mind was oppressed by the weight of recollections. On returning home I caught up a pen in *furore*, determined to convey on paper, however faintly, some idea of the variety offered by one day's sight-seeing at Rome.[3]

The intensity with which Elliot takes up her pen in an attempt to record her thoughts suggests much about the complex position of a Victorian woman abroad. After a day of intense intellectual stimulation, Elliot initially appears to write simply to purge her cluttered mind of its thoughts. Yet the resolute tone with which she approaches pen and paper implies that she is desperate to preserve on paper what she has seen and learned. Like most Victorian women who traveled, Frances Elliot was anxious to record her experiences because she believed that experiences worthy of being recorded, preserved, and made public would stop once she returned to England. Other Victorian women who traveled shared her sense of urgency. Isabella Bird, for instance, kept ink warming on the stove while in the Rocky Mountains for fear that if it froze she would be unable to write. In her diary of her experiences in America, Barbara Leigh Smith (later Bodichon) admits: "I write as much as I can without blinding myself" (122). And at the end of *Diary of an Idle Woman in Italy,* Elliot laments: "I am suddenly called back to England, and 'the Idle Woman' (not so very idle after all) lays down her pen and becomes 'the woman of the period,' with *really* nothing to do!"[4]

Elliot here alludes to the kind of woman paid homage to in the popular essays of Eliza Lynn Linton—the woman whose experiences were carefully circumscribed by the boundaries and borders of a domestic sphere within which there was much for a woman to be but little for her to do.[5] For Elliot, as for many other Victorian women who chose to leave home for extended periods, travel was first and foremost a way of getting outside of those boundaries to a place where one could do more. What is noteworthy about her comment is that she implicitly equates the activity of travel with that of writing:

Both occur in conjunction with one another and are necessary to one another; and both are intimately connected to the writer's sense of her self and of her relationship to others. Both give to the writer an identity with purpose and a basis for accomplishment.

The central project of this study is to ascertain how travel and writing functioned together in nineteenth-century England to enable women to cross physical and ideological distances, to expand institutional and psychological borders. What Victorian women wrote from and about their experiences abroad is by and large nonfiction, and these nonfictional letters, essays, and books are the materials of this study's cultural interpretation. Although few are today considered canonical literary texts, these works—like much Victorian fiction—index relations of power and authority both between men and women and between women and the peoples of other cultures. Many were also enormously popular. These works written by women who traveled are hence no less a part of Victorian culture or history than are the novels, poems, plays, and essays that have been accorded the status of aesthetically or historically legitimate objects of study. To examine the place of women's travel and writing in Victorian culture is necessarily to consider how certain documents come to be privileged as representative of a literary period, a social history, a class, or a gender.

Those of us who have been initiated into Victorian culture through its fiction are familiar with the use of the wider world as an imaginative realm in which to situate narratives of adventure, conquest, and liberation. The "weight of recollections" that burden the Victorian traveler Frances Elliot at the end of her day in Rome, for example, recalls the reaction of a fictitious English visitor to the eternal city. In the 1871–72 novel *Middlemarch*, Italy plays a crucial role in the emotional liberation of Dorothea Brooke.[6] In an often-quoted passage, Eliot describes the tremendous effect that the "weight of unintelligible Rome" has on Dorothea during her honeymoon (225). Before her trip to Rome, Dorothea naively anticipates a marriage filled with learning. Contemplating life with the scholar Edward Casaubon, she thinks, "It would be like marrying Pascal. I should learn to see the truth by the same light as great men have seen it by" (51). Casaubon, though, fails to lead Dorothea down the grand path of learning that she envisions. His is a mind "weighted with unpublished matter" (230), and on their honeymoon in Rome Dorothea discovers that "what was fresh to her mind was worn out to his; and such capacity of thought and feeling as had ever been stimulated in him by the general life of mankind had long shrunk to a sort of dried preparation, a lifeless embalmment of knowledge" (228–29).

In *Middlemarch*, Eliot undercuts the truth that great men have to offer by centering it initially in the effete and sickly Casaubon, whose projected *Key to All Mythologies* turns out to be a sham. It is not Casaubon but Rome that offers Dorothea the opportunity and stimulation to learn. It is not her husband but Rome that takes possession of Dorothea during the early days of her marriage; it is Rome that addresses her "great mental need" to "see the truth." Although before marriage Dorothea anticipates "a grand life here—now—in England" (51), it is significant that she must travel outside of England to begin the process of self assessment that will determine her fate once she returns home.

The paradigm of a young woman yearning to "see the truth by the same light as great men," established early on in *Middlemarch*, is found also in *The Mill on the Floss* (1860), *Romola* (1863), and *Daniel Deronda* (1876). Like these works by George Eliot, many Victorian novels condition us to associate women with the "hidden life" that Dorothea will eventually lead, one in which access to a perceived body of knowledge and culture is either restricted, prohibited, or—still worse—absent. The hidden life to which Eliot consigns Dorothea is one unaffecting and almost unaffected by the world in which the novel's ardent public men participate. *Vanity Fair* (1848), of course, opens with Becky Sharp triumphantly pitching her copy of Johnson's dictionary out the window of her carriage, but most Victorian heroines do not derive as much pleasure rejecting the learning associated with male culture. The similar fates of Maggie Tulliver in *The Mill on the Floss* and Eustacia Vye in *The Return of the Native* (1878) are telling; their deaths suggest much about the Victorian novelist's sense of the consequences facing a young woman too eager to learn, too anxious to attach herself to a public and cultured world.

Another such woman is Rose Yorke, a marginal character in Charlotte Brontë's novel *Shirley* (1849). In an important passage in the novel one of the central heroines, Caroline Helstone, finds Rose reading from Ann Radcliffe's *The Italian* (1796), and the two women discuss their impressions of the novel. To Rose, the novel pleases because "you feel as if you were far away from England—really in Italy—under another sort of sky—that blue sky of the south which travelers describe."[7] Intrepid and outspoken Rose is prompted by her reading of Radcliffe to insist to homebound Caroline: "my life shall be a life: not a black trance like a toad's, buried in marble; nor a long, slow death like yours in Briarfield Rectory" (385). *Shirley* is about the ways women both take and lose control of their lives and, like most of Brontë's work, its ending is ambiguous. Rose, the narrator informs us, becomes no more than "a lonely emigrant in some region of the southern hemisphere" (168).

More revealing than Rose Yorke's outcome, though, is the revitalizing potential that she imagines travel to have; the light she associates with "another sort of sky" suggests energy and transformation akin to that which Dorothea Brooke discovers on her honeymoon in Rome. To Rose the mere idea of travel beyond the boundaries of England implies the acquisition of meaningful identity, the making of a life something that will be other than the "black trance" she associates with woman's life in England. In *Villette* (1853), Brontë's next and last complete novel, the heroine Lucy Snowe also travels with "nothing to lose" to a foreign country. In Labassecour, Brontë's fictional name for Belgium, immersion in a foreign culture allows Lucy the freedom both to construct an identity and to embrace anonymity, to scrutinize and to retreat from self.

Both Charlotte Brontë and George Eliot understood the capacity of travel—of distance, really—to satisfy these dual needs. In a letter written in July of 1854, just prior to leaving England in the company of a married man, George Henry Lewes, Eliot wrote to her friend Sara Hennell and enigmatically explained her intent by making subtle reference to *Villette:* "I shall soon send you a good bye, for I am preparing to go to 'Labassecour.'"[8] Both Brontë and Eliot equated travel with release, adventure, the opportunity to learn, and sexual deliverance. Eliot made her sexual liaison public by traveling to Weimar with Lewes. Brontë was intellectually stimulated by and fell in love with her teacher Constantin Heger while training for a career in teaching at the Pensionnat Heger in Brussels. Although literary histories have unduly emphasized the romantic nature of these attachments, it is significant that both Eliot and Brontë established through their relationships the satisfaction of intellectual compatibility. For both, also, that satisfaction required leaving England, at least for a time. Lewes and Eliot learned languages while abroad together; in Germany he wrote his biography of Goethe while she translated Spinoza. Working closely under Heger's supervision while in Belgium, Brontë refined her command of the French language and wrote a series of essays that grappled with issues of authority, genius, and religious faith—topics that would later permeate her fiction.[9] At the same time, however, travel abroad for both writers exacerbated a painful relationship to "home" and invited longing, separation, and the misery of displacement to compete with hopefulness, satisfaction, and companionship. In their fiction—as in their lives—travel encompassed these same narrative dynamics: it enabled energy, confidence, initiation, and inquiry to create dialogue with separation, pain, and, oddly enough, immobility.

Foreign locales nearly always function as the sites that engendered these dialogues. From the beginning of her writing career, Brontë experimented with foreign location: from her creation of an imaginary West African Kingdom in her juvenilia to her last complete novel, *Villette*, Brontë imagined foreign countries as the loci for her heroines' adventures. In *Villette* foreign culture allows Brontë to highlight the depth of Lucy Snowe's interior exile and to emphasize the extent to which a woman's retreat into anonymity signified her lack of a relation to a public, male-dominated culture. Thus in *Villette* travel becomes almost entirely interiorized; in no other Victorian novel is the heroine so often represented as motionless despite movement between rooms, houses, cities, and countries.

In Victorian literature as a whole, travel frequently functions as a means to place a narrative of female energy and control somewhere outside of England. In *Daniel Deronda*, for example, readers are first introduced to Gwendolen Harleth at the gambling tables in Germany where, before being struck down by Deronda's gaze, she plays the confident and spirited adventuress, winning in a man's world. Later she travels to Italy where her monstrous husband drowns. Her return to England signals a return to domestic conformity and emotional lethargy—and the end of her story.

Instances of female adventure and energy abroad occur in lesser-known novels as well and suggest that by taking a woman outside the boundaries of England novelists opened up the scope of possibilities from which to construct narratives of identity. These narratives of adventure and identity occur throughout the nineteenth century and may have been inaugurated by the Gothic tradition. In Radcliffe's influential *The Mysteries of Udolpho*, published in 1794, a retreat in the Apennines is the place where the sexual and moral will of Emily St. Aubert is put to test. The sensational novelists picked up where earlier Gothic novelists had left off. In Mrs. Henry Wood's 1861 best-selling novel *East Lynne,* it is Lady Isobel's flight abroad that creates the sensation and introduces themes of bigamy and adultery into a novel fundamentally about the female quest for security. A similar pattern is found in Mary Braddon's enormously popular *Lady Audley's Secret*, published just one year later. Stories that equate female adventure with foreign locale occur in more traditional domestic novels as well. In Mrs. Humphry Ward's best-seller *Robert Elsmere* of 1888, the source of female interest is less with the domestic-minded, staunchly puritan, and predictable heroine Catherine Elsmere than with her sister Rose Leyburn, a "new woman" who travels to Germany to develop fully her musical talents.

Yet the female characters of Victorian literature whose lives have tended to be taken as paradigmatic of the lives of real Victorian women are the ones who never leave England—characters like Jane Eyre, Maggie Tulliver, and Eustacia Vye. In *Jane Eyre* (1847) the possibility of life in India with St. John Rivers tempts Jane only momentarily; his sisters warn her that she would be "grilled alive in Calcutta" and soon after Jane hears the mysterious voice that summons her back to Rochester and a life in England. Intellectually ambitious Maggie Tulliver never escapes the River Floss. In *The Return of the Native*, adventure-hungry Eustacia Vye fails to convince her husband to quit Egdon Heath and live in Paris. In each of these novels the absence of travel in a woman's life is as much a determinant of her outcome as in those narratives that move her from England into the wider world.

These are but a few examples of the way travel seeps into the social fabric of Victorian fiction and colors the narratives of female identity, but they accumulate to suggest something of the hold that travel—real and metaphorical—had on the imagination of fiction writers of the period. In fact, the idea of travel and, correspondingly, of access to a world outside of England influenced almost all writers of the period, permeating English culture in ways that are only partially reflected by its literature. And with good reason. After the French Revolution, commerce with and beyond Europe increased dramatically for the British. The strength of evangelical forces at home fortified missionary activity abroad. Most important, the introduction of steam locomotion and railways in the nineteenth century—and the work of travel entrepreneur Thomas Cook—radically changed how much the English middle and upper classes were able to explore cultures other than their own. The confidence with which the Victorians left home can be gauged by the remarks in 1845 of the art historian Elizabeth Rigby Eastlake, who ended a review essay on the travel writing of women with the following invocation:

> Let us . . . rejoice that the long continuation of peace, the gradual removal of prejudices, the strength of the British character, and the faith in British honesty, have not only made way for the foot of our countrymen through countries hardly accessible before, but also for that of the tender and delicate companion, whose participation in his foreign pleasures his home habits have made indispensable to him.[10]

The Victorian period in England was the first to see a large-scale

movement of its men *and* women into the wider world on both temporary and long-term bases.

Many Victorians traveled abroad on professional or commercial
ventures, making their niche in the empire as bureaucrats, traders,
missionaries, and correspondents. But as John Pemble shows in *The
Mediterranean Passion: Victorians and Edwardians in the South*, an increasing number of Victorians traveled at leisure, justifying their excursions away from home by turning their trips into pilgrimages that
sought to improve their spiritual, cultural, or physical health.[11] Pemble observes:

> Various writers diagnosed the annual exodus from England as a symptom
> of restlessness, of a perpetual desire to be somewhere else that was pecu-
> liar to the British; and this they attributed to special environmental and
> historical circumstances.[12]

The number of Victorians traveling at leisure increased steadily, Pemble reports, as a rise in wealth and a decrease in the cost of travel
made foreign vacations possible for even the lower middle classes.
Victorians moved between cities and countries at relatively fast rates
and consequently saw much more of the world than did their predecessors.

Many Victorians left home assured that their status as English men
and women would guarantee a privileged position abroad. Indeed,
some felt it their duty to elicit respect by demanding all the comforts
of home. Traveling up the Nile, for instance, Amelia Edwards insisted
on having a fresh bouquet of flowers brought on board to her daily.
Commenting on the postures adopted by Victorians seeking to find
home in abroad, Sir Charles Petrie observed:

> The impression one gets is that if the right rooms were not immediately
> forthcoming at an acceptable rate, or if the laundry failed to return in
> time, recourse would be had to the British consul without any undue
> delay, and that if speedy redress were not obtained Lord Palmerston
> would send a gunboat.[13]

Though no doubt overstated, such comments reveal an important
aspect of the way many Victorians experienced the wider world; what
they saw was from a privileged perspective, one that enabled them
to experience and record with great confidence.

Their claim to privilege was most pronounced in those places
where many traveled, where communities of English expatriates had
formed, and where English "requirements" were already known.
Switzerland, Germany, Belgium, and France throughout the century

drew a large share of English travelers, but the "blue sky of the South" held the most allure. Italy by far attracted the majority of those travelers tempted by the Mediterranean region. Victorians disenchanted with the dense urban fog of London and its environs migrated toward the sensuous south in order to soak up its climate and ambiance—what Amelia Edwards in *Untrodden Peaks and Unfrequented Valleys* describes as "the rich Italian summer, with its wealth of fruits and flowers, its intolerable heat, and its blinding brightness."[14] Victorians flocked to Rome in hordes and often moved on to spend time in Florence, Sorrento, and Naples. Travelers dotted the coast of Greece and the French and Spanish Rivieras. Egypt enticed hundreds of travelers as well, many of whom went on to the Middle East via the Sinai peninsula or to India on the "overland" (Alexandria-Suez) route.[15] Here, as Frances Power Cobbe wrote in *Cities of the Past* (1864), travelers could "give themselves the delight of beholding the spots of earth round which imagination has hovered from childhood."[16] Accounts of African travel written by Victorians are many, and they diligently documented expeditions into South America, the United States, and Canada as well. The noticeable presence of Victorians abroad is captured by Amelia Edwards in her description in 1889 of Cairo:

> Here are invalids in search of health; artists in search of subjects; sportsmen keen upon crocodiles; statesmen out for a holiday; special correspondents alert for gossip; collectors on the scent of papyri and mummies; men of science with only scientific ends in view; and the usual surplus of idlers who travel for the mere love of travel, or the satisfaction of a purposeless curiosity.[17]

As Edwards's catalog suggests, the wider world afforded a wealth of material for the inquisitive, and travel was undertaken to satisfy a multitude of yearnings.

The effects on Victorian culture of this nineteenth-century revolution in travel are many and varied. As travel became increasingly available to the middle classes, it became correspondingly more accessible to women. English women had of course traveled outside of England before the nineteenth century, but never before had so many women traveled so extensively.[18] Several travel accounts written by women and published just prior to the nineteenth century are notable both for their contemporary popularity and for the critical attention that they have garnered in recent years. Lady Mary Wortley Montagu published her *Letters Written during her Travels in Europe, Asia, and Africa* in 1763, and in 1796 Mary Wollstonecraft published a series of letters detailing her travels, *Letters Written During a Short Residence in Sweden, Norway, and Denmark*. Eighteenth-century England also produced one of the first woman explorers to be widely celebrated: Lady Hester Stanhope traveled to Mediterranean regions and never returned to England.[19]

In the early years of the nineteenth century, women traveled even more frequently, often as family members—wives and daughters—of those bureaucrats, traders, and missionaries infiltrating the British empire. As the century progressed, however, more and more women went abroad with a defined sense of personal interest and professional purpose, going abroad, for example, as members of the World's Women's Temperance Association or as lecturing members of the International Women's Congress. Others went as governesses for families on an extended holiday or in search of permanent positions as governesses abroad. Still more Victorian women traveled on their own, however, with the loosely defined goal of "learning." In 1852, Florence Nightingale wrote *Cassandra* to announce for the benefit of all women that she needed to learn; as she had once written in a letter, "I have a mind, an active nature which requires satisfaction."[20] She left soon after to work in the Crimea. Others like her found the satisfaction of learning through travel. In 1857 Elizabeth Gaskell wrote of Charlotte and Emily Brontë's decision to go to Belgium: "They wanted learning. They came for learning. They would learn."[21] Although overstated in a way befitting the hagiographic qualities of the biography, her comment captures the spirit of many Victorian women travelers and could apply to many who left England to learn about and experience the wider world.

Travel was seen by some Victorian women as a means to keep up with world events, and this in turn was seen as necessary to intellectual survival. Consider, for instance, the remarks of Frances Power Cobbe in her chapter on Palestine from *The Cities of the Past*. After encouraging other women to undertake the journey to Palestine, Cobbe writes:

> Especially does it seem desirable that women should seek by these and all other modes of study to fit themselves for their proper part in sharing the progress of human thought in our age. Too often have their limited lives, their scope of vision . . . made women the champions of antiquated prejudices, the cruel enemies of every newly-born truth.[22]

As Cobbe's remark suggests, a Victorian woman could prove her sincere interest in learning by going abroad, by enlarging her "scope of vision." Cobbe was only one of several women eager to demonstrate the knowledge she had gained through travel. On her way to America in 1834, Harriet Martineau never came on deck to socialize with other passengers without bringing her lap board and writing utensils with her. Wanting to demonstrate the seriousness of purpose and to set herself above other women on board who "idled about in sunny places," Martineau wrote in *Retrospect of Western Travel* (1838): "I had a task to do, which is a thing that should be avoided on board ship. I had a long article to write; and nothing else would I do, on a fine morning, till it was finished."[23] Martineau's trips abroad always resulted in an abundance of such articles. In *Eastern Life, Present and Past* (1848) she prides herself on the "stores of knowledge" she would bring from the Middle East back to England. Victorian women travelers were both teachers and students. Much later in the century Mary Kingsley wrote in *Travels in West Africa* (1897) of the Gold Coast locals, "They cannot but say that I was a diligent pupil, who honestly tried to learn the lessons they taught me so kindly."[24]

Many of the Victorian women who embarked on voyages of learning traveled together, as did Vernon Lee and Clementine "Kit" Anstruther-Thompson or Amelia Edwards and the unnamed female friend of *A Thousand Miles up the Nile*. Still more accompanied a married couple, at least for the passage en route, and then embarked on their own; of this group Harriet Martineau, Mary Kingsley, and Florence Nightingale are notable examples. By far, however, the large majority of Victorian women travelers traveled alone—Mary Gaunt, Lucie Duff-Gordon, and Marianne North, for example, are just a few of the most prominent women who traveled alone in Africa. In her autobiography, Frances Power Cobbe notes that when she set out on her solitary travels in 1857 such a journey was "still accounted somewhat of an enterprise for a 'lone woman.'" John Pemble corroborates her sense of her status in *The Mediterranean Passion:*

> All females abroad without male escorts, whether traveling singly, in pairs, or in groups, were classified as "unprotected," and the term carried strong connotations of eccentricity.[25]

Travel—and especially travel alone—was at least in part a means to express one's independence. As Catherine Barnes Stevenson notes, "By the latter part of the nineteenth century, women travelers began to be singled out as exemplars of the new freedom and prowess of women."[26]

More important, travel enabled women to acquire experience unlike that available to them at home, experience that could be recorded, analyzed, and published. The Victorian women who traveled discovered more than refuge, adventure, and learning abroad; they found room to write. Like Dorothea Brooke, they found that the satisfaction of a life of learning and knowledge was not to be found in England or in marriage but abroad. But unlike Dorothea, who returns to a "hidden life" of "unhistoric acts" in England, many Victorian women used their experiences outside of England to forge identities at home with the reading public—a public that consumed writing about travel and foreign culture voraciously. They kept detailed journals about their experiences and made sketches of what they saw. They read widely about the lands and cultures that they visited, and compared their findings to those of reputable historians, geologists, anthropologists, and explorers. They wrote letters, essays, articles, and books about their experiences abroad, and they gave lectures about what they learned to audiences at home.

Travel enabled many Victorian women to create a connection to and establish authority with a part of English culture that hitherto had evaded them because they lacked the education that decreed cultural authority. One way to measure Victorian women's success in winning public recognition for their achievements is suggested by the titles of those biographical reference works so prevalent in the period. Significantly, the popular reference work titled *Men of the Time* changed its title to *Men and Women of the Time* in 1891, less in response to the burgeoning feminist movements than to the increasing number of women who could be admitted on the basis of public achievement. In addition, *Men and Women of the Time* documents how much travel was increasingly thought of throughout the century as a profession. The most common professions available to women included not just "actress," "musician," "painter," and "social reformer," but also "journalist," "archeologist," "explorer," and "travel writer."

In essence, travel conferred on many Victorian women a measure of cultural competence that derived not from education but from experience. And as a mode of experience through which they gained the authority to write about culture, travel was empowering. Travel enabled many Victorian women to gain the experience necessary to win a new kind of recognition for themselves.

Domestic Ideology and Victorian Women Travelers

To a significant extent, women writers achieved a degree of public recognition for their travel writing because it was considered to be a nondomestic genre and hence by implication an unusual and risky choice for the woman writer. Whereas many of the women who wrote fiction were thought of as popular novelists—entertainers—women who wrote nonfiction demanded a different, perhaps more serious, kind of recognition. In her work on the social history of Victorian women, Jihang Park rightly emphasizes the implications of such recognition: "The problem of women's emancipation in nineteenth-century Britain was not only how to win equal rights with men, but also how to win recognition for their achievements in a man's world."[27] One way was to move their sphere for achievement out of England, into places thought to be less circumscribed by domestic ideology— by those socially constructed boundaries of public and private, male and female, felt so powerfully at home. Travel writing was for many women quite simply a way to document achievements worthy of recognition.

That their achievements abroad were assumed to be worthy of public recognition is in part due to the powerful hold of domestic ideology on the Victorian imagination and its concomitant forms of writing. The term *separate spheres* has long been used by scholars studying women and the structure of Victorian society to denote the ostensibly rigid separation of nineteenth-century social life into a private sphere of home, family, and interpersonal relations and a public sphere of work and politics.[28] Such studies focus both on the symbolic positioning of women within the private domain and on the material conditions of this domain as well as on the symbolic positioning of men within the public domain and its corresponding material conditions. More recently historians and literary scholars have questioned the entrenchment of separate spheres ideology, showing the fluidity of public/private boundaries and basing their arguments on evidence of Victorian women's participation in public activities. Victorian women's travel writing has played a crucial role in this critical reassessment. For example, in "Victorian Women, Wisdom, and Southeast Asia," Susan Morgan argues that "many women put the notion of separate spheres to public use by defining it as incomplete and therefore as an empowering rather than a disabling paradigm."[29] Morgan rightly concludes: "The question for critics now is how many exceptions we need to gather before the weight of accumulated facts will finally deflate to its proper, and modest, size this long-favored phallic truism."[30]

Nonetheless, literary historians argue that the extent to which Victorian women were at least ideologically associated with a private domestic sphere is evidenced by the representation of their social and psychological position in such works as Ruskin's treatise "Of Queen's Gardens" and Coventry Patmore's long poem "The Angel in the House," works that ostensibly exalt women by representing their moral authority within the home. Popular advice writers like Sara Ellis and Sarah Lewis had publicly advocated this position long before Patmore or Ruskin; both women frequently admonished their fellow countrywomen to restrict their influence to the "sacred precincts of home." In the 1839 treatise *Woman's Mission*, for example, Lewis argued that a woman's influence was dependent on her maternal feeling and thus must be exercised within the boundaries of home.[31] No matter how influential one believes Ellis and Lewis to have been, what clearly is important to appreciate is that many Victorian women felt both bounded by and bonded to the home. How much women responded to this conflictual position can be sensed in the words of the African explorer Mary Kingsley, who, in the years after her travels, recollected: "The whole of my childhood and youth was spent at home, in the house and garden. . . . The living outside world I saw little of and cared less for."[32] Kingsley felt compelled to explain her achievements in the public world as a consequence of and reaction against her early "rooting" in home and garden.

Feminist theorists more recently have emphasized how the categories of public and private basic to the concept of separate spheres point to societal divisions central to the structuring of gender in modern Western society, and they have argued that feminist criticism should seek to demonstrate the historical origins and evolution of those divisions others have assumed to be either natural or inevitable. One critic who has tried to do this is Mary Poovey, and in *Uneven Developments: The Ideological Work of Gender in Mid-Victorian England* she writes: "The model of binary opposition between the sexes, which was socially realized in separate but supposedly equal 'spheres,' underwrote an entire system of institutional practices and conventions at midcentury, ranging from a sexual division of labor to a sexual division of economic and political rights."[33] Poovey goes on in her work to demonstrate that though representations of gender often took the form of a binary organization of difference in Victorian culture, different Victorian institutions (e.g., medical, legal, and literary) interpreted this binary logic differently. Poovey's thesis has important applicability to women's travel writing, because it, too, reflects the complexities and "uneven developments" of gender difference or, to be more exact, representations of gender difference.

In fact, one of the ways that gender ideology is most prominently represented in travel writing by women is in their portrayals of "leaving home," which, while characteristic of travel literature in general, is more self-consciously addressed in the works of Victorian women. Given the depth of ideological connection between Victorian women and home, it is not surprising that their accounts of leaving home would be represented as monumental undertakings. The historian John Pemble writes that for all Victorians: "Abandoning Britain meant abandoning home. It therefore threatened all the cherished values that home implied—fidelity, obedience, connubial affection, and a stable and rooted existence."[34] These were of course the values for whose maintenance middle-class Victorian women were responsible, and travel away from the home thus required a great degree of initiative and willfulness on the part of women. This is perhaps what Gabriele Annan meant when she wrote of women travelers: "They had to be braver than men, socially as well as physically."[35]

Women did not undertake travel lightly, and their written accounts of journeys abroad are often replete with explanation and justification for finding a life beyond the boundaries of England. Mary Kingsley, for example, opens *Travels in West Africa* (1897) by cautiously explaining: "For the first time in my life, I found myself in possession of five or six months which were not heavily forestalled" (1). Like Dorothy in Oz, Victorian women who traveled abroad were expected to discover that there was no place like home. Those who chose to remain away for extended periods were subject to a level of moral censure that could only be counteracted by finding many opportunities to act out the duties associated with "home" in England: fidelity, obedience, affection, and stability. Lucie Duff Gordon was one such woman; she left a husband and child in England to recuperate from a respiratory ailment and found in Egypt hundreds of sick natives to attend to while she waited for her own health to improve. Her *Letters from Egypt* (1876) are full of defensive accounts of her activities and seemingly hollow yearnings to rejoin her family, even though she evidently believed her health to be jeopardized by the English climate and clearly enjoyed her new-found role as health facilitator abroad. Thus, part of the interest of travel literature like that written by Lucie Duff Gordon and many others is that it both challenged and accommodated those domestic ideals against which so many Victorian women were measured. How much they saw their work as accommodation and/or challenge varied greatly among individual women, but almost all viewed their travel writing as a public statement; that is, as a means through which to ratify their sense of themselves as public individuals with experience enough to write about the wider world.

Travel Writing and Cultural Authority

The institution through which women writers established their credibility as cultural spokespersons was the publishing industry and, for many, the periodical presses. The Victorian period was, as many have observed, the great age of periodical literature. In the preface to their study of the Victorian periodical press, Joanne Shattock and Michael Wolff observe: "The press, in all of its manifestations, became during the Victorian period the context within which people lived and worked and thought, and from which they derived their (in most cases quite new) sense of the outside world."[36] Hence it is not surprising that many women travelers chose to place their work initially in magazines and journals.[37] As the most influential of the "opinion-making" institutions within Victorian culture and the dominant medium through which people learned about the world outside of England, the periodical press was an important avenue through which women could disseminate the results of their travel. During the century, travel literature became the bread-and-butter of both the periodical presses and book publishing industry, and often replaced religious and advice books on the best-seller lists of major publishing houses. Articles and essays about foreign experience appeared regularly in nearly all of the most widely read periodicals. This plethora of travel writing can be seen as one manifestation of a variety of Victorian desires, among them the thirst for adventure, discovery, conquest, and escape. Travel writing by women adds other clearly discernible desires to this list—among them nondomestic identity, public recognition, and cultural authority.

That so much of the travel writing of the period was written by women suggests that publishing houses and editors of periodicals were willing and eager to capitalize on the ostensibly different perspective that women were able to bring to literature about the wider world. Women travelers, in turn, were eager to capitalize on the publicity that their activities abroad could bring. Often a series of travel essays published by a reputable journal would later be published in book form, as were the series of essays on Italy written by Frances Power Cobbe for *Fraser's Magazine* and later published as *Cities of the Past* by Trubner's of London. Others like Cobbe used their experience abroad to gain access to the periodical press. And many of those who did flaunted their success. In her preface to *Diary of an Idle Woman in Italy,* for example, Frances Elliot writes, "It may be well to mention that some of these chapters (now almost entirely rewritten) have appeared from time to time in some of the leading periodicals" (preface). Elliot clearly believes her periodical press publications to signify her authority on the subject, but that she had to explicitly call them to her reader's attention suggests, at the same time, something of the frailty of her conviction.

Highly germane to the discussion of how Victorian women used travel writing to create a connection to their culture is the work of the French sociologist Pierre Bourdieu, who has studied the process whereby cultural legitimacy is conferred on literary works. In *Distinction*, Bourdieu argues that all cultural "products," from movies to newspapers and magazines to political documents, reveal a kind of publicly legitimate taste and that these products are almost always created and marketed by professionals.[38] Although Bourdieu's study is not rendered from the standpoint of gender, it logically follows from his argument that by becoming producers of a highly valued cultural product—a product that appealed to the reigning tastes of their society—Victorian women helped to advance their own status as professionals. Bourdieu writes: "Every critic declares not only his judgement of the work but also his claim to the right to talk about it and judge it. In short, he takes part in a struggle for the monopoly of legitimate discourse about the work of art, and consequently in the production of the value of the work of art."[39]

Published travel accounts can thus be read as implicit statements of the right to contribute to a discourse deemed by their society to be culturally valuable. Perhaps more important, travel can be viewed as participation, as efforts on the part of women to actively help to shape their society's beliefs—about the wider world and, in some cases, about the position of women in that world. In *Independent Women*, Martha Vicinus writes, "Women are never passive participants in the larger culture but actively transform and redefine their external constraints."[40] Ironically, travel away from England facilitated this transformation on the home front, because it gave to women experience valuable to the British public. In Bourdieu's terms, it gave them the "symbolic capital" with which to compete in the culture market of Victorian society and to appeal to institutionally recognized powers—the periodical presses and publishing houses.

As the century progressed, women travelers became increasingly comfortable with their authority, expressing opinions with less hesitation, making greater claims for their own powers of observation and analysis, and less frequently justifying their decision to publish their work. Consider for comparison's sake a relatively early woman traveler, Anne Radcliffe. In her preface to *A Journey Made in the Summer of 1794 Through Holland and The Western Frontier of Germany*, published shortly after returning home from a trip taken with her husband, the self-conscious and insecure Radcliffe writes:

> The title page would . . . have contained the joint names of her husband and herself, if this mode of appearing before the Public, besides being thought by that relative a greater acknowledgement than was due to his

share of the work, had not seemed liable to the imputation of a design to attract attention by extraordinary novelty. It is, however, necessary to her own satisfaction, that some notice should be taken of this assistance.[41]

Radcliffe goes on to undercut her intellectual authority by claiming that all "economical and political" commentary was "less her own" than that of her husband. As the century progressed, such self-diminishment became increasingly less frequent, in part because more and more women had ventured into regions considered remote from England and in part because many had done so alone.

Nonetheless, even the most confident of women travelers continued to look to outside sources of authority for corroboration of their own findings. Many attempted to legitimize their own work by making frequent reference to what had already been "established" by previous (and most typically male) historians and travelers. Frances Elliot, for example, prefaces her *Diary of an Idle Woman in Constantinople* (1893) with this exhaustive listing of outside sources:

> My principal authorities have been Gibbon, von Hammer, Lamartine, Theophile Gautier, Gallenga, and Amicis, Meyer's 'Turkei und Griechenland,' a most valuable book, an article by H. E. Sir Henry Elliott on Abdul Aziz in the 'Nineteenth Century' and various Handbooks, English and German.[42]

Elliot here finds in historical scholarship the evidence she needs to authenticate her own findings. More often, however, women were compelled to position their work in relation to other travel writing, other sources of authority. That others had traveled before them could be made to seem advantageous, as is evident in Amelia Edwards's comments on a mountain in Korosko:

> We were surprised to find no account of the geology of this district in any of our books. Murray and Wilkinson pass it in silence; and writers of travels—only two of whom notice only the pyramidal shape of the hills—are for the most part content to do likewise.[43]

As Edward's comments suggest, Victorian women travelers who wanted to establish authority had both to indicate their awareness of another (male) tradition of travel writing, and to stress their differences from that tradition.

By writing about her travels in the wider world a woman writer in the Victorian period could not help but participate in a predominantly masculine tradition. Such hesitation in voicing opinions as was expressed by Frances Elliot and others was in part a manifestation of the sense that they were encroaching on another territory, another tradition. But at the same time, in her reliance on experiences abroad to establish a basis for authority—a voice—she necessarily called attention to her displacement from that tradition. The double-voiced discourse that some feminist critics believe characterizes the fiction of Victorian women writers is evident in much of the travel literature written by women in the period, but its implications are rather different. In travel writing, the authority of the author is dependent on an ability to comfortably occupy several positions displaced from but relative to the "center," which for most women travelers was England—nation and "home." Thus, rather than pointing to a divisive identity, double-voiced discourse in travel literature more often indicates a capable traveler and author, one whose experiences abroad solidify rather than cleave identity. In travel writing, then, an ability to successfully manipulate and negotiate distance becomes a barometer of competence. Victorian women made good use of their distance from English society; indeed, the concept of distance functions variously to signal their sense of cultural gaps and boundaries and their simultaneous sense of proximity to and detachment from that culture. Travel both eliminated and exacerbated the traveler's sense of cultural difference. By going abroad to the extent that they did, women became more familiar with foreign cultures; for some this lack of distance diminished their sense of wonder at the "other." For others, it merely underscored their sense that foreign populations were foreign. In addition, the heightened awareness of a wider world complicated the context from which they assessed their own society and their position as women within that society; cultural differences demanded new modes of self-awareness.

One might argue that Victorian women travelers made too good use of distance. How much Victorian women's travel writing successfully featured the traveler's distance from the mainstream can be sensed in the degree to which this literature has been left out of history, of our accounts of and claims for Victorian literature, society, and culture. That travel literature—despite its abundancy and interest—is so rarely discussed today is in part a consequence of how the Victorians themselves categorized "the woman writer" and how we continue to reify their values in our own work.

Gender and Genre

The tendency to marginalize the travel writing of Victorian women is indicative of a more general devaluation or ignorance of all nonfictional writing by women. As Carol Christ summarizes in her essay on nonfiction prose and masculinity: "There were 'lady novelists,' 'feminine poets,' and 'men of letters.' "[44] The Victorian woman writer has become, by association and almost by definition, a novelist or poet, or, more rarely, a dramatist. One explanation for the tendency to equate women with fiction can be found in the fact that throughout the period the majority of novel readers and writers were believed to be women. Such a perception was not wholly unfounded because, at least initially, women dominated the field of novel writing. In *Edging Women Out: Victorian Novelists, Publishers, and Social Change*, Gaye Tuchman and Nina Fortin argue that the very success of women novelists in the early part of the century helped to ratify the judgement of "men of letters" that the novel was an important genre and to spawn the kind of criticism that "considered 'the woman writer' in order to dismiss her potential contribution to the dominant culture."[45] They write: "By 1870 men of letters were using the term 'high culture' to set off novels they admired from those they deemed run-of-the-mill. Most of these high-culture novels were written by men."[46] One important outcome of the abundance of such criticism was to make the term *woman writer* virtually synonymous with *woman novelist* and to make "woman novelist" synonymous with producer of popular, as opposed to "high culture" novels.[47] Women hoping to break into a writing career did so well aware that popular novel writing offered the most promise of financial success.

The association of women writers with the genre of the novel and, to a lesser extent, poetry, is in turn indicative of a larger cultural tendency to identify women with the potential for the creative rather than with the analytical. As repositories of creative potential, women were "naturally" suited to novel writing. The critic George Henry Lewes was one of many influential Victorians whose work helped to perpetuate this claim. Lewes well represents mainstream Victorian thought when he condescendingly suggested in his midcentury essay "The Lady Novelists" that women writers restrict themselves to the "one subject which they have eternally at command—love," and it follows from his argument that the proper form with which to make manifest this procreative impulse is the novel, the Victorian literary genre most concerned with evincing domestic realism. Nonfiction, seeming to demand more analytical skill on the part of its author, was, by implication, male territory. Such a judgment seems to have been corroborated in practice as well. In *Edging Women Out*, Tuchman and Fortin find that contributors of nonfiction during the Victorian period were more likely to have a university degree than contributors of fiction.[48]

The tendency to associate women with the creative rather than with the rational and analytical was part and parcel of the widespread assumption of male intellectual superiority, a belief corroborated by the observation that the brain of a man had greater physical weight than that of a woman. In *Feminine Character: A Study of Ideology*, Viola Klein explains: "It was emphasized by brain anatomists that the frontal lobes—believed to be the seat of logical thought and of all higher intellectual process—were distinctly more developed in men than in women."[49]

George Eliot demonstrated the weightiness of her own frontal lobes when she defied Lewes's advice to stick to novel writing and proclaimed in an essay: "Women have not to prove that they can be emotional, and rhapsodic, and spiritualistic; every one believes that already. They have to prove that they are capable of accurate thought, severe study, and continuous self-command."[50] Making her statement in a published essay, Eliot by implication argues that nonfictional genres were avenues through which women could prove their analytic, critical abilities. But Eliot was an exceptional Victorian woman writer, one of the very few who managed to establish public credibility as a sage.

Many women, however, found what Michael Cotsell has called in his introduction to *Creditable Warriors* "a marginal sagedom" through travel writing,[51] an achievement recognized by Susan Morgan in "Victorian Women, Wisdom, and Southeast Asia" and by Linda Peterson in "Harriet Martineau: Masculine Discourse, Female Sage," both published in Thais Morgan's collection of essays titled *Victorian Sages and Cultural Discourse: Renegotiating Gender and Power.* As a popular nonfictional Victorian genre, travel writing can also be understood as what Tuchman and Fortin label a "mixed specialty," a nonfictional genre through which both men and women could distinguish themselves.[52] As a mixed specialty, travel writing was a politically expedient choice for women writers interested in moving into "high-prestige" and "male specialty" genres of nonfiction. Travel writing, in other words, offered more than an opportunity to participate in a form with great popular appeal; it also offered women the opportunity to establish or solidify their credibility in a public arena shared by men. In her work on the rise of feminine authority in the Victorian period, Nancy Armstrong observes:

Any major change in the idea of who could write literature is just one part of a much larger revision in the culture's conception of social authority. In order for female literary authority to come into being, this revision obviously must have included a redefinition of gender as well as of the powers considered appropriate for each of the sexes.[53]

Armstrong's comment provides an enticing way to see travel writing as a means of revisioning Victorian culture's distribution of social authority. Armstrong's theory is at least partially applicable to Victorian women's travel writing, but, however appealing, it does not do justice to the many diverse and complex ways that Victorian women used their work to accommodate and reaffirm, rather than revise or subvert, already existing—and largely patriarchal—forms of authority.

Deirdre David convincingly argues in *Intellectual Women and Victorian Patriarchy* that those exceptional women who did make a name for themselves as intellectuals within the male-dominated culture did so by serving an auxiliary usefulness to that culture—by fostering and implicitly ratifying its dominant political, social, and sexual ideologies and by willingly adopting for themselves an ancillary role.[54] Yet David's argument seems founded on the assumption that cultural authority belongs primarily to those overtly concerned in their works with *English* society, history, and culture. It also implicitly endorses the idea that cultural authority is a stable, even static, phenomenon that women either serve or subvert.

Recently other critics have, like David, begun to write about the relationship of Victorian women to public forms of cultural authority. Martha Vicinus's *Independent Women* and Janet Murray's *Strong-Minded Women and Other Lost Voices of the Nineteenth Century,* for instance, each pay tribute to enterprising women who implicitly sought to register complaints with their patriarchal culture and with its concomitant forms of social order.[55] Vicinus argues that single women in Victorian England organized the ideological battle for women's rights within places like church committees, sisterhoods, and women's colleges. Although valuable, these studies falsify Victorian women's history in their assumption that the so-called strong-minded Victorian women with public identities and agendas were uniformly dissatisfied with their society and with their exclusion from cultural authority.

Travel writing provides an abundance of material with which to enlarge upon, modify, and in some cases correct, the scholarship that has to date focused on the status of Victorian women writers attempting to establish cultural credibility. On one level, it counteracts the tendency to base our history of Victorian women writers so exclusively on material provided by two literary forms—the novel and the poem. On another level, it provides a way to broaden our understanding of the role of cultural authority in that history. Deirdre David claims that the cultural authority to theorize about society remained firmly in the hands of the male writer throughout the century, but travel writing provides new ways to think about how women could "theorize" about their society in nontraditional or even covert ways. Some travel writing, for example, suggests that writing about other societies enabled women to critique their own. In *Winter Studies and Summer Rambles in Canada* (1838), Anna Jameson uses the condition of American Indians to launch her attack on the position of the single English woman. Harriet Martineau studies the democratic experiment in *Society in America* to make suggestions about both American and English society. Whereas cultural criticism may have been, as David and others have contended, more explicitly a male domain, it should not be assumed that it was exclusively so. Rather, we need to expand our understanding of what cultural criticism entails to include nontraditional forms of women's writing.

Victorian women's travel writing enables us to revise our understanding of the period in yet another, equally important way. It encourages us to see that the social history of Victorian women must include activity that took place outside of England. The very title of Philippa Levine's study *Feminist Lives in Victorian England* reveals a certain one-sidedness that is almost endemic to critical studies of Victorian women; that is, that Victorian feminism evidenced itself only *in* Victorian England.[56] Work like that done by Martha Vicinus in her study of single-woman communities in Victorian England or Coral Lansbury in her work on Victorian women and the antivivisectionist movement in England contributes to this pattern as well. Although all are important to our understanding of how Victorian women empowered themselves, these studies—and many others like them—may have helped create the impression that Victorian women's only sphere for empowerment was within England. As travel writing shows so well, this process of empowerment was one that also involved leaving England and its institutions behind and finding new ways to identify one's relationship to the world.

Victorian women travelers discovered, explored, studied, and described a world beyond England. Some thought of themselves not as participants but as observers, and their works tend on the whole to be descriptive—to focus on the external. Others sought to immerse themselves in new cultures, and their works corresponding invest much in the ideal of self-development through travel. Finally, a very few Victorian women sought neither to observe nor to participate; instead, their works seek to capture the imaginative experience and appeal of travel. One extreme attempts to document abroad; the other imagines and creates it. Travel writing by Victorian women is not rigidly demarcated according to these distinctions, but the two extremes do provide competing points of perspective within the various "kinds" of travel writing that emerged during the period.

This study does not pretend to be exhaustive in its coverage. Its general intent is threefold: first, to describe the major forms of Victorian women's travel writing; second, to relate those forms to geographical regions; and third, to demonstrate how decisions about the travel account's form and the traveler's choice of region relate finally to questions of and choices about professional identity. One additional note about my process of selecting primary materials and assumptions about their organization may help. Throughout this book I assume that there is a fundamental distinction between travelers and travel writers. Although thousands of Victorian women traveled abroad on holidays and learning excursions, only a small percentage of these women sought to *publish* their works. Because a part of my thesis involves the notion of using travel writing to establish cultural authority, I felt it necessary to exclude from consideration private diaries and letters that were never published as well as works that have only recently been published, such as Florence Nightingale's *Letters from Egypt*. I also distinguish between the traveler and the temporary foreign resident. For example, whereas hundreds of Victorian women wrote about their experiences as part of missionary efforts in India or in Southeast Asia, these women thought of themselves as residents, not as travelers, and their works assume a different status than that assumed within the travel accounts studied in this book.

Although the book is organized geographically, each chapter addresses issues related to the way Victorian women travelers presented their work—whether as a published diary, a collection of letters, an ethnography, a sociology, or a history. The most typical form, not surprisingly, was what might be thought of as a straightforward travel account—the chronologically rendered, diarylike report of the woman's experience in another country. Important variations among travel accounts occur even within this standard form. Curiously, the various manifestations of the simple travel account seem to correspond in a general way to geographical locale or region. For example, the Victorian women who traveled to central and southern Europe tended on the whole to represent themselves as tourists on a cultural mission; the women who traveled to Africa and other regions considered remote from England tended to represent themselves (and be represented at home) as adventuresses. These two groups of women travelers provide by far the greatest volume of travel books and articles published during the period, and their sheer number is astonishing. Yet other women travelers began during the course of the Victorian period to redirect their travel accounts in more exceptional ways. Some of the women who traveled to Italy and other places associated with "high culture" used their experiences to write art historical studies of the place, not travel accounts. Some of the women who traveled to the Middle East rendered their works not as adventures abroad but as acts of recovery, both personal and historical. Finally, many of the women who traveled to America represented their works as sociologies of the place. How these women shaped and directed their accounts hence reveals much about the various imaginative investments that the Victorians apportioned to certain regions of the wider world. And yet it also reveals more specifically how women in particular used these imaginative investments to professional advantage, finding in different places different opportunities for self-fashioning.

Each chapter of this study also examines how a particular region and its corresponding "form" shaped the personal, professional, and cultural identities of Victorian women travelers. Chapter 2 begins with the tourist accounts written by the women who sought to establish their authority through alliance with the tradition of travel writing about places of "high culture." For Victorians, the preeminent place of high culture was Italy. This chapter includes discussion of the kind of account that explicitly sought to guide other travelers, for example, Mariana Starke's influential *Letters from Italy* (1800) and Charlotte Eaton's *Rome in the Nineteenth Century* (1822). It focuses, however, on those accounts that disavow a status as comprehensive, factual guide and instead base their appeal on the author's ability to make her rendering of the country both fresh and personal. These works include Mary Shelley's *Rambles Through Germany and Italy* (1844), Frances Trollope's *A Visit to Italy* (1842), Frances Elliot's *Diary of an Idle Woman in Italy* (1871), and Vernon Lee's *The Spirit of Rome* (1906).

Chapter 3 then examines a more exceptional kind of travel writing that emerged out of travel to Italy and other countries associated in Victorian society with repositories of "high culture." Art history and criticism was one of the most important forms of nonfiction directly related to travel experience in which women distinguished themselves. Clearly, European travel offered access to hundreds of museums, churches, and libraries housing art both familiar to and remote from the English public. Forming the basis for this chapter's discussion are the works of Victorian England's two most influential art historians: Elizabeth Eastlake, who wrote a multitude of art essays for the *Quarterly Review* and *Edinburgh Review,* and Anna Jameson, whose *Diary of an Ennuyee* (1826) and *Sacred and Legendary Art* (1848) in particular are based on her experiences abroad. This chapter also looks briefly at a later generation of women art historians and critics who, while influenced by Eastlake and Jameson, made substantial use of their own travel experiences. *Tuscan Studies* and *The Renaissance of Art in Italy* (1887) by Lucy Baxter ("Leader Scott") and the essays of Julia Ady are products of two such women.

Chapter 4 then turns to the second kind of travel account through which many Victorian women distinguished themselves—the adventure narrative. While Victorian women traveled all over the wider world, the only ones to receive sustained attention at home were the ones thought of as adventuresses. These "celebrated" women travelers included Isabella Bird Bishop, Florence Dixie, Amelia Edwards, Constance Gordon Cumming, and Mary Kingsley, among many others. Whereas cultural tourists and traveling art historians based their credibility on intellectual achievement, Victorian adventuresses constructed their identities largely on physical achievement. They chose as their spheres not the densely populated places of high culture but rather the remote regions of the world—many of which were associated with the British Empire. In this realm the adventuresses created a kind of imaginary "wild zone," one that enabled them to accomplish feats of physical endurance and courage that would be inconceivable for a middle-class woman in England. At the same time, however, they domesticated their activities abroad in ways that reveal their defensiveness and that helped them justify their presence away from home. In works such as Isabella Bird Bishop's *A Lady's Life in the Rocky Mountains* (1880) and *The Yangtze Valley and Beyond* (1899), Florence Dixie's *Across Patagonia* (1880) and *In the Land of Misfortune* (1884), Amelia Edwards' *A Thousand Miles Up the Nile* (1889), Constance Gordon-Cummings's *In the Himalayas and On the Indian Plains* (1884), and Mary Kingsley's *Travels in West Africa* (1897), the authors both exaggerate their physical, psychological, and moral distance from England and collapse that distance entirely by finding ways to translate adventure into an essentially womanly activity. This chapter does not assume that Victorian women's experiences in remote regions of the wider world were the same, and it acknowledges that material conditions and political situations in regions as diverse as, say, Africa, South America, and China were vastly different. Nor does this chapter advance comprehensive claims, for recent work on Victorian women writing about Southeast Asia or about Middle Eastern experiences has extended our understanding of the breadth and diversity of Victorian women's activities in the world. Instead, it focuses on the similarities in accounts written about these widely different regions and it suggests that the similarities have primarily to do with the kind of identity constructed by the author, an identity that capitalized on certain properties of adventure while underscoring the author's domesticity. This chapter is also concerned with how the adventuresses' identities were constructed and contested at home and with how these women used their public reputations to professional advantage.

Chapter 5 moves from the general tendencies discussed in chapter 4 to examine a related but more exceptional kind of travel account to emerge out of the experience of some adventurous Victorian women travelers in regions considered remote and unknown. It looks at two travel accounts of experience in the Middle East that represented themselves as "histories" of the region. Harriet Martineau's 1848 study *Eastern Life, Present and Past* required years of preliminary reading and research in biblical studies. While the work documents Martineau's travels across the Syrian desert and into Palestine, it also illustrates an interior journey distancing her from the conventional religion of her upbringing. A similar though less-pronounced pattern emerges in Frances Power Cobbe's collection of essays in *Cities of the Past*. For both women, the Middle East with its desert (and deserted) landscape afforded the perfect opportunity to enact a process of recovery that required adopting a receptive posture, one that stands in sharp contrast to the aggressive posture adopted by the adventuress.

Finally, chapter 6 focuses on the works written by women who represented their travel accounts as social—or sociological—study. Most of these sociologies were based on experiences in America, which was widely seen as an experimental society ripe for investigation. This chapter briefly surveys the assumptions of Frances Trollope's *Domestic Manners of the Americans* (1832), Frances Wright's *Views of Society and Manners in America* (1820), Frederika Bremer's *Homes of the New World* (1853), Isabella Bird's *The Englishwoman in America* (1856), and Marianne Finch's *An Englishwoman's Experience in America* (1853), all of which focus in some way on American society and character. But the chapter's focus is on the ways that some women transformed their travel accounts into more thoroughgoing—even rigorous—social study. It looks first, for example, at the work of Harriet Martineau, who in *How to Observe Morals and Manners* (1838) developed a theoretical approach to the sociological study of abroad and in *Society in America* (1837) and in *Retrospect of Western Travel* (1838) attempted to put into practice her own methodology. The chapter also examines in detail the sociological approach taken by Emily Faithfull, who traveled to America several decades after Martineau. It closes with a glance at the use made of America by Beatrice Webb. Webb, too, began her travel experiences in the United States, but unlike Martineau and others focused her professional work on those pockets of "foreign" society she found at home, living, for instance, in the East End of London.

This study looks by way of conclusion at the kind of travel writing most removed from the simple, chronologically rendered account: the aesthetic or impressionistic study of place. Although description still has a purpose in this genre, its effect is less to document or explain than to suggest, provoke, prompt. In *Genius Loci: Notes on Places* (1899), *The Sentimental Traveller* (1908), and *The Enchanted Woods: and Other Essays on the Genius of Places* (1905), Vernon Lee demonstrates her command of the aesthetic study of place. In her essay "The Enchanted Woods," she refuses to reveal the geographical location of the woods; instead, she writes:

> When one is in them they seem to march nowhere with reality; and after issuing one is tempted to deny their existence. For they are full of spells and of adventure without end, drawing one, up that dark, gliding river, into their hidden heart.[57]

Lee is clearly interested less in place per se than in place-as-experience. In the aesthetic study of place, interiority has the right-of-way, and distance becomes a measure of the psychological "space" between such traditional Western bipolarities as public and private, self and others, and home and abroad. In Lee's essays this sense of distance is alternately eliminated and exaggerated. Also examined briefly in this concluding chapter is the work of Alice Meynell, who in 1899 published *The Spirit of Place and Other Essays* after previously distinguishing herself as a poet and literary critic. Her work has striking similarities to that of Lee and suggests certain redirections in women's travel writing at the turn of the century.

The simple travel account with which this study begins and the aesthetic study of place with which it ends represent something of the range of approach taken by Victorian women to the study of the wider world. Although both the tourist and the adventuress chronicled their experiences on a day-to-day basis, one sought to document her encounters with the everyday, whereas the other sought to suppress the everyday and document instead what was extraordinary about her achievements. For some women, travel required an openness to experience; for others it demanded a defensive, almost aggressive, posture. Some women rendered their experiences with subtle nuances of mood and expression, calling implicit attention to the primacy of language over situation and experience; others did so with unadorned language, content that their readers would intuit their fortitude and appreciate hard-won fact. Despite their differences in approach, though, all tried to convey and share an experience of distance and to make that distance visible to others. Gabriele Annan suggests that a common feature of Victorian women travelers was their "cussedness—the determination to go to forbidden places."[58] But what seems more likely was that all of the women who wrote about their travels shared a need to ground their identity in a place distanced from "home"—England—and its associated ideologies of domesticity and gender. And for all women this distance was measured and represented in psychological as well as institutional terms. Doing so prompted even the most conservative and traditional of travelers—the Lady Eastlakes and Frances Trollopes—to rethink their country's ideology of woman.

More important, travel writing demonstrates the need to recognize the contributions Victorian women made in and to the wider world. Travel enabled them to voice opinions not just as English women but as citizens of this world, as people who were interested in and could learn from other lives, histories, and cultures—and as people who could write authoritatively about these cultures. In fact, scholars have only recently begun to recognize this dimension of Victorian history in general. The series *English Literature and the Wider World* pays tribute to the impact of travel experience on the work of the Victorian literary "greats," and the Victorian volume of the series includes essays on Elizabeth Barrett Browning and George Eliot. Although important, this series does little more than acknowledge in an introductory sentence or two the impact of Victorian women travelers in helping to shape thinking about the wider world. James Buzard's study *The Beaten Track: European Tourism, Literature, and the Ways to "Culture," 1800–1918* incorporates the work of women travelers, including Frances Trollope and Anna Jameson.[59] A handful of book-length studies have been written about the adventurous "lady travelers," but few have recognized the work done by the less celebrated, perhaps less anomalous, women. Some scholars have more recently begun to redress this imbalance. A recent meeting of the Victorians Institute was organized around the theme "The Globalized Victorian," and its opening session was devoted to the achievements of women travelers. Other scholars have recently begun to concentrate in book-length studies on connections between empire and the experience of Victorian women. Sara Mills has published an influential study *Discourses of Difference: An Analysis of Women's Travel Writing and Colonialism.*[60] Helen Callaway's work on gender, culture, and empire makes much use of Victorian women's travel writing, and Deirdre David is working on Victorian women and India. Billie Melman has surveyed 245 published travelogues in her study *Women's Orients: English Women and the Middle East, 1718–1918.*[61] Susan Morgan has published excellent essays on Victorian women's travel writing generally and on Victorian women who traveled to Southeast Asia and has edited Anna Leonowens's *The Romance of the Harem.*[62] Shirley Foster has surveyed some of Victorian travelers' activities in Italy, North America, Japan, and Tibet in *Across New Worlds: Nineteenth-Century Women Travellers and their Writings.*[63] Finally, Jane Robinson's *Wayward Women: A Guide to Women Travellers* has been published to encourage further scholarship on women travelers of all periods, all nations.[64] All of these works represent important forays into what I hope in this work to demonstrate is a vast world of material that illustrates Victorian women at their best—that is, as fascinating, vital, and complex beings who used travel writing to inscribe their selves into history.

2

Into the Temple of Taste:
Victorian Women in Italy

IN 1820, a young English woman named Charlotte Ann Eaton made the first of several visits to Italy with members of her family, and recorded her impressions in lengthy and detailed letters that she would, on returning home, submit for publication. Eaton first visited Florence and, after a few weeks, arrived in Rome. Writing of the "delight," "admiration," and "astonishment" she felt after having seen the Vatican, Eaton gushed:

> Rome has become the heir of time. Her rich inheritance is the accumulated creations of gifted genius—the best legacy that departed ages have bequeathed to the world—and here they are concentered in the treasury of the fine arts, the temple of taste, the consecrated seat of the muses![1]

The rhetoric with which she describes the treasures of the Vatican reminds one of Matthew Arnold, who later defined *culture* as "the best that is known and thought in the world." The significant assumption that Arnold and other Victorians made was that the best that could be known and thought had already been known and thought, and that the task of the critic was primarily to gather it up out of the past and call it culture. For Charlotte Eaton, as for many nineteenth-century women who followed in her footsteps to the "temple of taste," Rome offered a repository of just the sort of "culture" that middle-class Victorian society deemed so important.[2] But Arnoldian culture—rendered accessible in England through immersion in the classics and, hence, made possible only via a formal education—was largely unavailable at home in England to women like Charlotte Eaton. In Italy, on the other hand, she could freely avail herself of unlimited stores of the past and gather out of her experiences as much culture as she wanted. By writing of her impressions and experiences she became akin to the kind of critic revered in her homeland; that is, she openly demonstrated her appreciation for the "best that

43

had been known and thought" and helped to propagate the legacy that she, as a visitor to the Eternal City, had inherited.

Eaton's identification of the "legacy" which the Vatican and, in a larger sense, Rome and Italy offered was less a product of her own insight—her own judgement—than it was a reflection of the English values she inherited and reproduced. In other words, the praise that she lavished on the works of Titian and Raphael while in Florence or on the accumulated treasures of St. Peter's while in Rome pays tribute to the collective belief that had already judged those objects as legitimate objects of worship and study for the English tourist abroad. Charlotte Eaton was, after all, a tourist. In his analysis of tourism, Paul Fussell distinguishes between the explorer, the traveler, and the tourist, and identifies the latter as the individual who simply seeks "that which has been discovered by entrepreneurship and prepared for him by the arts of mass publicity."[3] As a tourist, Charlotte Eaton was both expected and prepared to seek out the objects and places in Italy deemed artistic masterpieces. Her published account of her impressions, *Rome in the Nineteenth Century* (1822), correspondingly reveals as much about her desire to affirm that which had already been judged, her right to participate in that collective affirmation, and the authority that she derived from her participation as it does about her own impressions and interpretations. The task of the tourist, like that of the critic described by Arnold, was not to interpret but rather to refine one's discriminatory powers, to cultivate taste, and, ultimately, to advance culture.

Although Charlotte Eaton traveled to Italy relatively early in the nineteenth century, she was preceded in her determination to publish an account of her impressions by such women as Mariana Starke, Lady Morgan, Lady Blessington, and Hester Lynch Piozzi. By the time the Victorian period was over many hundreds of English women had, like them, journeyed to pay homage to the natural beauties and artistic treasures of the country. Whereas some women—among them Anna Jameson and Elizabeth Eastlake—used their experiences in Italy to fashion professional identities as art historians, the majority of women who traveled there wrote about their impressions in a much more general way, commenting on everything from the landscape and climate to the markets, inns, churches, and museums. The presence of English women tourists in Italy had indeed become almost stereotypically noticeable. Indeed, the presence of *all* English tourists was by late in the century not just noticeable but downright reprehensible to some. In *Italian Hours* Henry James complains about the "herd of fellow gazers" that he met in Venice. Even as early as 1845, English men and women toured Italy in large enough numbers for Lady Eastlake to snobbishly lament in an essay on women's travel writing that "In times like these the luxury of travel . . . will necessarily be shared by many utterly unfitted to profit by it."[4] Eastlake's comments especially reveal a troubling association between travel and class and a concern that the widening middle class was encroaching on another's territory.

Nearly a century after Charlotte Eaton first visited Italy and almost fifty years after Lady Eastlake expressed her worries, the novelist, E. M. Forster established a career satirizing prim and insular English women who believed themselves to be cultivating taste while abroad. In the second chapter of Forster's *A Room With A View* (1908), the heroine Lucy Honeychurch is led by the aspiring novelist Miss Lavish to visit the Santa Croce in Florence. On their way, the following discussion ensues:

> "I will take you by a dear dirty back way, Miss Honeychurch, and if you bring me luck, we shall have an adventure."
>
> Lucy said that this was most kind, and at once opened the Baedeker, to see where Santa Croce was.
>
> "Tut, tut! Miss Lucy! I hope we shall soon emancipate you from Baedeker. He does but touch the surface of things. As to the true Italy—he does not even dream of it. The true Italy is only to be found by patient observation."[5]

The conversation is noteworthy for its incisive analysis of the kind of experience that the Englishwoman who visited Italy was, by the turn of the century, expected to have, and Forster's satire extends in several directions at once. Miss Lavish hopes that by traveling a "dear dirty way" she and Lucy will experience something more representative of a "true" Italy, the Italy not defined and described within the pages of a guidebook. Lucy, on the other hand, is hopelessly dependent on her Baedeker.

Forster suggests that for both women tourism will be an emancipatory experience, an adventure. For the spinster Miss Lavish, adventure is constituted by contact with the "dirty" side of Florence, a side made "dear" because she believes that by opting for that route she will experience the life of the country inaccessible to the ordinary tourist. As she has already said, "'One doesn't come to Italy for niceness. . . . One comes for life'" (16). Furthermore, by dragging the young, attractive, and as yet sexually inexperienced Lucy Honeychurch with her through this dear, dirty way, Miss Lavish expects to command the attention of Italian men out working in the streets through which they pass and hence to experience vicariously the pleasure of being watched at a distance made safe by virtue of their class and national identity. Lucy's experience getting to the Santa Croce is constituted as adventure as well. Going the back way through Florence and witnessing her companion say "buon giorno" to local wine-cart drivers prompts her to express to Miss Lavish her own solidarity with democratic movements and with the working class. As she explains: "'We are Radicals, too, out and out. My father always voted for Mr. Gladstone, until he was so dreadful about Ireland'" (16). Forster implies that for Lucy talking politics with Miss Lavish is liberating, because she, too, believes she is distancing herself from a certain class of English tourists who would not dare to take a "dirty" way or speak to "dear simple souls" like Italian wine-cart drivers. Lucy's contact with Miss Lavish also—at least temporily—emancipates her from her Baedeker and, hence, enables her to believe she is experiencing the other side of Italy, that which has not already been prescribed for her.[6]

Forster's satire is instructive in its suggestion that Italy offered to middle- and upper-class English women a special kind of adventure, one as rigidly defined by preconceptions and expectations as if they had been the Baedeker-toting tourists they loved to abhor. In his novel, however, the satire of the English tourist that dominates the opening chapters recedes as the narrative progresses, and the story of Lucy Honeychurch, the traveler, evolves. *A Room With A View* explores what happens to a young English woman when she is confronted with the "other" side of Italian culture, the side not made familiar to her through her genteel upbringing or her guidebook to the artistic masterpieces of the country. Instead, Lucy finds in Italy things radically unfamiliar to her—murder, blood, and the passion of men. Although Forster's novel exposes the cultural pretensions of the English tourist abroad, it depicts more suggestively the ways in which the female traveler can be emancipated from her own culture. Other Victorian heroines find relief from the puritanical upbringing associated with England while in Italy. Dorothea Brooke in *Middlemarch* (1871–72), Gwendolen Harleth in *Daniel Deronda* (1876), and Miriam Baske in Gissing's *The Emancipated* (1890) are a few such women.

As these fictional examples suggest, many Victorian women who went to Italy as tourists came home instead as travelers—as women who felt a strong sense of having encountered a place, a history, and a people very unfamiliar, who were changed by the experience, and who capitalized on their encounters by writing about them. The travel accounts of their experiences in Italy were shaped by preconceptions of the order satirized by Forster—those that Paul Fussell would align with the entrepreneurial spirit—but they also documented the intensity of emotion that accompanied the unexpected and unpredictable experiences met en route to and within Italy.

Victorian women who wrote travel accounts of their experiences in Italy were both tourists and travelers. On the one hand, their sense of travel as adventure into a side of culture not prescribed by guidebooks made what they had to write fresh, spirited, and enlightening. On the other hand, their awareness of the interests and demands of the tourist made it possible for them to successfully cater to that branch of the publishing industry. The way in which women combined in their work the activities of the tourist with the insight of the traveler was critical to their appeal to the reading public at home and to their ability to compete in an increasingly overcrowded market. Commenting on this market, Elizabeth Eastlake noted in her review of one woman's account of Italy, "It is fortunate that, at a time when cheap postage has enabled too many people to write badly with the greatest ease, the effusions of returned tourists should be less in vogue than formerly."[7] Although many hundreds of Victorian women documented their experience in Italy in some form— letters, diaries, notebooks, and sketch pads—only a few wrote the kind of travel account that became marketable and that helped to advance their professional status. In other words, only a few travel accounts written by Victorian women were treated as what Bourdieu would term *cultural commodities*—that is, published, reviewed, compared in the periodical presses to male-authored accounts, and hence deemed worthy of serious consideration.

Mary Shelley, Frances Trollope, Frances Elliot, and Vernon Lee— though writing from very different personal positions at different times within the Victorian period—were among this select group: all successfully published accounts of their experiences in Italy at critical points in their professional careers. All of them capitalized on their travel to Italy by representing it as professional work but all, curiously, also thought of it as escape from work. Shelley's first and last published works were travel accounts. *History of Six Weeks' Tour through a Part of France, Switzerland, Germany, and Holland*, issued anonymously in 1817 when Shelley was hoping to launch her career, was based in large part on a journal she kept after having eloped. She established herself as an authority on Italy after having lived there for nearly five years with her husband; after his death, when her career was at a standstill but her need for money was urgent, she returned to England and published several articles based on her experiences there. "Recollections of Italy" was published in *The London Magazine* in 1824 and was soon followed by two *Westminster Review* articles, "The English in Italy" in 1826 and "Modern Italy" in 1829.

Rambles in Germany and Italy, the last of her travel works, was published in 1844, and was based on letters she had written while on two extended trips abroad with her son—one in 1840 and the other in 1842 and 1843.

Shelley had two incentives to write a book-length travel account of her visit to Italy. At the time she needed the money and knew that a written account of her experiences would sell, both because of the widespread appeal of travel books and because her story as widowed mother returning to the place where her husband had died would attract readers. Shelley had promised to help an Italian political exile named Gatteschi, whose poverty had won her sympathies. In her letters, she reveals her plan to "make a volume & make £100 or if possible more by it for him" to repay him for supplying her with some of the political information for her book.[8] But the trip itself was originally undertaken as an antidote to her own depression and professional stagnation. In one of the early letters of the book, she writes:

> You know, also, how grievously my health has been shaken; a nervous illness interrupts my usual occupations, and disturbs the ordinary tenor of my life. Travelling will cure all; my busy brooding thoughts will be scattered abroad; and, to use a figure of speech, my mind will, amidst novel and various scenes, renew the outworn and tattered garments in which it has long been clothed, and array itself in a vesture all gay and fresh and glossy hues, when we are beyond the Alps. (I, 2)

Shelley clearly conceived of travel as an escape that would allow her to regenerate emotionally and to launch a new phase of her career.

Frances Trollope's first travel book, *Domestic Manners of the Americans* (1832), was like Shelley's last undertaken in response to a financial crisis. Travel offered her an opportunity both to escape the impending crisis and to take charge of her own life. In this sense travel writing was, as her biographer Helen Heinemann has written, "the therapeutic discipline that brought her through personal disaster."[9] *A Visit to Italy,* published in 1842, was Trollope's last travel account, and by that time her American study had gone into five editions. Although *A Visit to Italy* was her last travel account, Trollope's career as a novelist continued until 1856. Many of these novels, among them *The Robertses on Their Travels* (1846), *Travels and Travelers* (1846), and *Fashionable Life: or Paris and London* (1856), were noticeably influenced by Trollope's self-fashioned identity as professional tourist-traveler and writer. Much of Trollope's travel writing is sociological in orientation: *Domestic Manners, Vienna and the Austrians*

(1838), and *Paris and the Parisians* (1836) all attempt to delineate foreign character. *A Visit to Italy*, on the other hand, makes little attempt to evoke the Italian character at all. Trollope herself is its central character and her impressions are the focus of interest.

Vernon Lee, too, looked to Italy as a site for work and as a scene of escape. Although publishing *The Spirit of Rome: Leaves from a Diary* (1906) nearly sixty years after Trollope and Shelley, Lee capitalized on the still viable travel vogue to rejuvenate her career. She established her career with the publication in 1880 of *Studies of the Eighteenth Century in Italy* and had already written twenty-five books (art histories, novels, and collected essays on aestheticism) when she published her only travel account in 1906. As Debra Edelstein has written: "Drained by a series of personal and professional crises, she sought solace in travel and in an old literary friend, the travel essay. . . . Lee understood the Victorians' love of travel, and through her essays she invited them to recall old delights and to explore the texture and movement, lines and colors of enchanted places in Italy, Switzerland, Germany, and France."[10] Collecting her past thoughts on Rome enabled Lee to "revisit" places that in the past had brought her confidence, strength, and resilience. For Lee, travel writing was flexible enough to accommodate the personal; it could function as an outlet for the emotional and as a medium through which to express and affirm self-confidence.

For each of these women, travel writing was only one among several forms of writing with which to experiment. They were, after all, aspiring and accomplished novelists and critics as well. Other women made travel writing their speciality, however, and Frances Elliot was one such woman. Although Elliot had at one time harbored hopes of working as a novelist, the success of her travel books apparently convinced her that they were her forte. Playing on the identity Lady Blessington made popular in 1839 with the publication of *The Idler in Italy*, Elliot authored a series of diary-like accounts that documented her experiences in European countries. *Diary of an Idle Woman in Italy* (1871), *Diary of an Idle Woman in Constantinople* (1893), *Diary of an Idle Woman in Sicily* (1871), and *Diary of an Idle Woman in Spain* (1884) all combine Elliot's efforts to adapt herself to other cultures with an attitude that as a representative English woman, she must remain resolutely aloof from them. Despite the fierce defense of her home country that permeates many of her travel works, she throughout these same works reveals an almost obsessive dread of returning home, where her role as a professional was ambiguous at best.

Although these women had very different experiences in Italy, each sought to establish there an identity as a tourist-traveler who synthesized in her work the activities and insights of both. In her introduction to *Hosts and Guests: An Anthropology of Tourism*, Valene Smith provides a useful framework within which to situate Victorian forms of tourism.[11] Smith distinguishes between cultural and historical tourism. Cultural tourists seek out the picturesque and "local color" destinations and value the ordinary and everyday; Forster's Miss Lavish, with her penchant for the "dirty side" of Florence, is a satire of the cultural tourist. The historical tourist, on the other hand, concerns herself not with a country's everyday life, but rather with the extraordinary events that have constituted its past. This tourist characteristically opts for the museum and cathedral route, rather than the local color path.

Nineteenth-century Italy afforded ample room for both types of tourists to flourish, and flourish they did. As early as 1826, Mary Shelley published an essay titled "The English in Italy" for the *Westminster Review* whose sole purpose was to identify the distinguishing features of the "Anglo-Italian," which she described as a perennial tourist. Her description, not surprisingly, draws on many of the same distinctions made by Smith between the cultural and historical tourist:

> Your Anglo-Italian ceases to visit the churches and palaces, guidebook in hand; anxious not to see, but to say that he has seen. Without attempting to adopt the customs of the natives, he attaches himself to some of the most refined among them, and appreciates their native talent and simple manners; he has lost the critical mania in a real taste for the beautiful, acquired by a frequent sight of the best models of ancient and modern art.[12]

Shelley suggests that the best sort of travel is that which combines an appreciation for the local color (albeit the most "refined" color) with an adequate recognition of artistic treasures past and present. One can also sense in her comments the desire to establish an agenda above that of the ordinary tourist. In the same article she lauds the "Anglo-Italian" over the "mere traveller" and writes:

> The Anglo-Italian has many peculiar marks which distinguish him from the mere traveller, or true John Bull. First, he understands Italian, and thus rescues himself from a thousand ludicrous mishaps which occur to those who fancy that a little Anglo-French will suffice to convey intelligence of their wants and wishes to the natives of Italy; the record of his travels is, no longer confined, according to Lord Normanby's vivid

descriptions, to how he had been "starved here, upset there, and robbed everywhere." (327)

This need became increasingly pronounced as the century progressed and tourism increased, and was especially noticeable in the works of women who wanted to establish professional identities as cultural critics. The ideal tourist that Shelley represents acquires from Italy something much more significant than the experience of having been there—she develops "real taste," that all-important component of Arnoldian criticism.

In aspiring beyond the status of mere tourist, however, some Victorian women introduced into their commentaries the problematic discourse so often linked in Victorian literature with the idea of middle-class woman's work. On the one hand, the female tourist could quite easily represent herself as a figure of leisure, Elliot's "idle woman." Tourism was one of the most publicly visible leisure activities enjoyed by middle- and upper-class Victorian women, and it was considered appropriate for these women. Tourism could hardly be considered a liberating public activity, however, especially for the female tourist whose experiences abroad were carefully controlled: she was usually chaperoned and her destinations were predetermined by those who had preceded her.

Furthermore, because middle- and upper-class women were assumed to be accustomed to lives of leisure, they were in some ways "trained" to be capable tourists. Articulating this line of thinking Elizabeth Eastlake claimed "one of [the] greatest charms" of the woman traveler was "that very *purposelessness* resulting from the more desultory nature of her education."[13] Somewhat surprisingly, Eastlake goes on to assert that the female tourist, more likely because of her lack of education to be indiscriminate, would inevitably produce the better travel account, the one less molded according to preconceived ideas. Anna Jameson also explored the capacity of the leisured woman to write about her travel experiences in *Diary of an Ennuyee*, a work that is explored in more detail in chapter 3.

Nonetheless, the woman who chose to write about her experiences as a tourist *and* to publish her account was troublesome to the middle-class English readership precisely because she introduced into the tourist experience an objective that seemed to undermine the very essence of female tourism as Eastlake and others conceived it. In a sense, the tourist-writer actively transformed leisure into labor. That women felt the contradictory status of the female tourist as writer (and by implication worker) can be sensed in many of their travel accounts. Consider, for instance, the reticence with which Hester

Lynch Piozzi opened her account of travels through France, Italy, and Germany:

> That I should make some reflections, or write down some observations, in the course of a long journey is not strange; that I should present them before the Public is I hope not too daring: the presumption grew out of their acknowledged favour, and if too kind culture has encouraged a coarse plant till it runs to feed, a little coldness from the same quarter will soon prove sufficient to kill it.[14]

Piozzi attempts to render her work less problematic by acknowledging her "presumption" in publishing it. She also diminishes its significance by implying that it represents little more than the cumulative product of observations made almost randomly along the way. In this effort Piozzi was not alone; nearly all of the women travelers who followed her in the Victorian period reproduced some variant of this kind of disclaimer in their account. Frances Elliot, for example, wrote in her preface to *Diary of An Idle Woman in Italy*:

> When I call these volumes "The Diary of an Idle Woman," I do so because I went to Italy with a perfectly disengaged mind, with no special objects of inquiry, no definite call or profession. I was idle in that I went where fancy or accident led me; otherwise I hope my readers will not consider me an idle woman. It may be well to mention that some of these chapters (now almost entirely rewritten) have appeared from time to time in some of the leading periodicals.[15]

Elliot's comment both aligns her identity to and distinguishes her activity from that of the original "Idler in Italy," Lady Blessington, who had quite willingly admitted to entire days of "sight-seeing, making excursions, and cultivating pleasant acquaintances."[16] Her preface is relatively guarded in its claims, especially in her insistence that she traveled without ulterior motives. The implication is that woman's travel is justifiable as long as it is conducted without ulterior motive—that is, professional purpose. If perceived as being a means to an end, particularly a published end, then it attains the status of work—and becomes problematic.

Yet Elliot also evidently wants her readers to view her activities as more purposeful than those of Blessington and other women tourists. She labels herself an "idle woman," but asks that they not consider her work the shallow product of a passive personality. Moreover, she makes certain her readers appreciate the fact that her insights into the country have already been judged to be of value (by virtue of having been published in "leading periodicals"). Elliot's defensive posture—and her concern for her public identity and reputation—belies her claim that she traveled without professional motives. The contradictory nature of her comments suggest something of the pressure felt by women who, like her, wanted to write about their experiences abroad. To appreciate why this was particularly so for women who traveled to Italy entails understanding what prospects and promise the country seemed to offer to Victorian women.

Italy was for these women, as for most Victorians, the linchpin of high culture, the place where one went to become more intellectually, spiritually, and aesthetically developed. Years after her travels to Italy, Vernon Lee wrote in the preface to *For Maurice:* "The word culture signified in the earliest 'eighties anything vaguely connected with Italy, art and, let us put it, the works of the late J. S. Symonds."[17] Yet long before Lee, English women celebrated the country's status as king of culture. As Charlotte Eaton had written in her account of Rome: "All that we have read, thought, admired, and worshipped from our earliest years—all that awakened our youthful enthusiasm—all that exalts the mind, fires the imagination, or touches the heart, is concentered on the soil of Italy" (62). Similarly, Frances Elliot paid tribute to Rome in *Diary of an Idle Woman in Italy* with the overwrought declaration: "Oh rare old city! I embrace thee and I love thee as the intellectual home of all mankind . . . the great parent of knowledge and art" (I, 130).

Whereas a trip to Africa for Victorian women was "a step in the darkest dark," a trip to Italy was into the lightest light—a place physically and emotionally warm, colorful, and sensuous. In *The Spirit of Rome,* Vernon Lee wrote: "We must imagine classic antiquity full of this wonderful blond colour of marbles; arrangements of palest lilac, green, rosy yellow and a white shimmer; colours such as we see on water at sunset, ineffable."[18] Italy was, as Lee's embellished description suggests, a place to be enchanted with—to give one's self over to. As Mary Shelley wrote in *Rambles in Germany in Italy:* "I own I like to give myself up to the ideas excited by antique names, and by the associations that have given it vitality."[19] Clearly, Italy and its imagined past were given the power to captivate English visitors, and they correspondingly represented themselves as "captives" of the country. In this, women travelers to Italy differed dramatically from their counterpart travelers to Africa and other regions remote from England and central to imperial interest. The women who ventured to these "hinterlands" aligned their identities to explorers, military men, and other Victorian hero-conquerors. In the outback, an English woman was a bearer of civilization, but in Italy

she was its recipient. The tourist was abroad to acquire—not to impart—taste.

To highlight her status as recipient of culture, women travelers
frequently paid tribute to the educational aspects of their experiences. Charlotte Eaton wrote in her preface that she intended her
letters not for publication but rather as a "register of all I saw and
learnt" (v).[20] Most of the Victorian women who traveled to Italy long
after Eaton had returned home followed her cue and wrote letters
that described in great detail all that they had *learned* abroad. In
Rambles in Germany and Italy, Mary Shelley explained that after arrriv-
ing at her lodgings in Italy, she immediately set herself up with "a
selected nook of the salon," complete with "embroidery frame,
books, and desk" (I, 65). She explained, "I mean to read a great deal
of Italian; as I have even found it pleasant to imbue oneself with the
language and literature of the country in which one is residing" (I,
65). For Trollope, the educational part of the experience was to be
derived not by reading but through rigorous observation. After arriving in Turin, she wrote: "Having contemplated with very vivid admiration and delight the general aspect of the city, we set about the
traveler's hardest work, namely, the examination, in detail, of the
inside and outside of the buildings most remarkable in any and
every way."[21]

With *A Visit to Italy* Trollope sharpened her tourist-student identity.
Studying a collection of Egyptian art work on display in Turin already
made familiar through Wilkinson's work, she was inspired to proclaim: "Few things would be more agreeable than being permitted
at leisure to read his learned, accurate, and most graphic volumes in
these rooms" (27). Trollope was eager to present herself as an enthusi-
astic and serious student, one who would be happy to spend her days
deep in study, and she was not alone. Most of these women sought
to represent themselves as willing, but not opportunistic, students
who wrote to record and preserve what they had learned. Just as
Elliot would take up her pen "in *furore*" at the end of a day's sightsee-
ing to record all that she had learned, so too did other women feel
that their learning experiences had to be preserved in writing.

These travel accounts of Italy thus functioned as a kind of preserva-
tion both of what women had learned and of those endangered
"higher values" they sought to affirm. Such a form of safekeeping
was an inevitable response to the perceived dislocations and vulgarity
of industrial England. The meanings of "culture" changed throughout the period and its semantic variations depended on the discourse
in which it was invoked, but to these women and to many others an
ideal culture was almost always associated with the higher values

propagated by prominent male prophet figures like Arnold. A Victorian woman who sought to establish an identity as a critic—as a spokesperson for higher values—thus had to establish a meaningful relationship to the culture of Italy.

This was not an easy task at a time when so many people were traveling to the country for themselves and keeping their own diaries or writing their own accounts. Furthermore, many of these traveling Victorians were already accomplished writers with professional credentials. Italy was a source of inspiration for well-known artists, academics, and literati. Following an already established tradition, many Victorian writers published travel accounts of their Italian experiences; Dickens, Thackeray, Gissing, and James are among the most prominent. Other Victorians—among them the Brownings, Ouida, Ruskin, and Pater—followed the cue of Byron and Shelley and made more imaginative and extended use of their experiences of Italy.

The predominance of writing about Italy by popular—and seasoned—writers such as these men and women inevitably had important ramifications for the women who were attempting to embark on writing careers through their travel accounts. As the century progressed and travel writing became more common, Victorian reviewers were increasingly more exacting in their expectations. Not many were willing to accept the justification offered by Mrs. R. M. King in a travel account on Italy; according to her *Athenaeum* reviewer, King argued that "any traveler who records his own personal impressions will put things more or less in a new light." Unconvinced, the reviewer scathingly retaliated: "Some things that are new are not of necessity worth recording, and in this category we fear that Mrs. King's impressions of travel must be placed."[22] Although writing their travel accounts at very different times within the Victorian period, Shelley, Trollope, Elliot, and Lee were all very much aware that they would be scrutinized by the sort of reviewer that Mrs. King came up against. Not surprisingly, one of the characteristics distinguishing their works from a host of others was their explicit attempt to represent travel to Italy as a search for authenticity, a quest for what was or would always be "new" about the country.

The Search for Authenticity

Although Shelley, Trollope, Elliot, and Lee established their authority as tourist-writers in very different ways, all sought first to establish the authenticity of their approach. Many travel accounts about Italy written by these women and others reveal an impressive

degree of self-reflexivity, especially as they recognize and call attention to the extent to which their thoughts about Italy were overdeter-
mined by what had already been written. In the "Explanatory and
Apologetic" opening to *The Spirit of Rome: Leaves from a Diary*, Vernon
Lee wrote of the "mixture of familiarity and of astonishment" that
characterized all of her impressions of Rome (9). Similarly, in her
preface to *The World Beyond the Esterelles* (1884), an account of her
travels in the south of France and Italy, Anne Buckland wrote: "I
flatter myself that readers of the following pages will find in them
much that is new in an old subject."[23] Even as early as 1822, when
Charlotte Eaton set to work on *Rome in the Nineteenth Century*, she felt
compelled to offer an explanation for another book on the country.
In the preface to the first edition, she wrote:

> But in describing Rome, which has been already described so often, such
> an explanation seems to be more imperatively called for; yet paradoxical
> as it may appear, it is the want of a good account of Rome that has
> induced the Author of these Letters to attempt, in some degree, to supply
> the deficiency by their publication. For, among all the manifold descrip-
> tions that have appeared, I do not hesitate to say, there is not one that is
> entitled even to the praise of accuracy. (iii)

In the years that followed the call for accuracy that Eaton trumpeted
was met again and again. Aspiring writers had to find innovative
reasons with which to justify the publication of their travel accounts.

Frances Trollope took the most obvious and unconvincing of routes
in claiming that her work was original insofar as every individual
brought abroad his or her own unique perspective—the same strategy
that had failed Mrs. King in *Italian Highways*. Although well aware
of the "rich multitude of descriptive travellers" who had preceded
her in Italy, she argued in *A Visit to Italy:*

> Even as to the outward and visible part of the business, descriptions
> made with all fidelity of spirit may, nevertheless, vary as widely as the
> tastes, temperament, and character of those who furnish them; and as
> great variety of interest, therefore, may arise from this as from any other
> source, deriving its value from individual opinion. (2)

Trollope asks that her work be read as more than descriptive, that
the reader find in the "outward and visible" evidence of an interesting
observer, one whose opinions of another country were of value. Similarly, in *The World Beyond the Esterelles*, most of which focuses on Italy,
Anne Buckland wrote: "My object has been, not to write a guidebook, for that has been admirably done already by Murray, Baedeker,

and others, but rather to record that which I myself had seen with special interest, hoping thereby to interest others" (i). Like Trollope, Buckland implies—almost apologetically—that the interest of her travel account emerges from the insight that she herself brings to the places that she visits. Her apologetic tone in some ways lessens the impact of the message embedded within this seemingly innocuous statement of purpose; in essence Buckland suggests that her perspective engages reader interest in a way that Murray, Baedeker, and others do not. She pays appropriate homage to these superstars of the field, but sets her work apart by acknowledging openly its more subjective status, its grounding in what she calls "special interest." Although she does not explicitly assert that her perspective is valuable because it is a woman's, she foregrounds the authority of her authorial role by writing only about "that which [she] herself had seen." The assurance with which she approached her task can be felt in the early portions of *The World Beyond the Esterelles* where Buckland readdresses her motivations as follows: "Determining to judge for myself of the places so much bepraised by travellers . . . I set out in December, 1879, for a winter in the sunny south" (6–7).

Other women took more explicit approaches to this same issue of authorship and selection of material, arguing, sometimes dramatically, for a woman's ability to find the authentic in the overdone. When Vernon Lee sat down in 1903 to publish her travel account of Rome, she effectively argued that the "outward and visible part of the business" that had so preoccupied earlier travelers like Buckland was uninteresting, uninformative, and ultimately unfaithful to the "real" experience of the country. Explaining why fifteen years had elapsed between her first visit to Rome and her attempt to publish a travel account, Lee wrote in *The Spirit of Rome:*

> One cannot sit down and attempt a faithful portrait of Rome; at least I cannot. And the value of these notes to those who love Rome, or are capable of loving it, is that they express, in however stammering a manner, what I said to myself about Rome; or, perhaps, if the phrase is not presumptuous, what Rome, day after day and year after year, has said to me. (10)

For all of her confidence in her own capacity to "truly" love Rome, Lee turns to an argument for authenticity remarkably akin to that used by Trollope and Buckland. Although she voices her position more creatively—arguing, for instance, that her notes document what the city has "said" to her—she, like her predecessors, relies on the assumption that every individual brings abroad a different mind, a new perspective. The attitude that Lee displays toward the impossibility of representing Rome reflects in part her developing sense that all art was essentially personal, a topic taken up in greater detail in the conclusion of this book. Writing about Rome enabled her to experiment with and develop an aesthetics of the evocative that would play an important role in her later essays and novels.

To a certain extent, then, Lee's work represents an entirely different approach to the travel account than that of Charlotte Eaton, who eighty years earlier had lamented the absence of accuracy in guidebooks to Rome. What is more significant in the context of women's travel writing, though, is that each of these writers felt herself capable of locating and mapping an authentic approach within abundantly overcharted material.

Most spirited and successful in her quest to discover Italy for herself was Mary Shelley, who used her preface to *Rambles in Germany and Italy* as an opportunity to delineate its unique value. Although she had originally "sold" her work to its publisher Edward Moxon on the grounds that it would offer "many facts of expenses" which would "be useful,"[24] Shelley's travel account actually strove to be much more than simply functional. In effect Shelley argued in the preface to *Rambles in Germany and Italy* that because so much had been written on the "outward and visible," she was led, inevitably, to the country's people as the most plentiful source of new and interesting matter:

> When I reached Italy, however, and came south, I found that I could say little of Florence and Rome, as far as regarded the cities themselves, that had not been said so often and so well before, that I was satisfied to select from my letters such portions merely as touched upon subjects that I had not found mentioned elsewhere. (viii)

She goes on in the preface to explain that "it was otherwise as regarded the people, especially in a political point of view; and in treating of them my scope grew more serious" (viii). Although Shelley represents her decision to focus on the Italian people as a by-product of her search for an authentic, original approach, she clearly saw in the subject the promise of more intellectually challenging material as well. She believed that access to another culture was to be found through its people, not through its monuments, a remarkable assertion given the extent to which Italian people and politics were typically written out of the travel account in the interest of representing the country as offering relief from temporal concerns. Her need to justify her focus is nonetheless telling, for it suggests more than the obligatory need to distinguish her work from the ordinary travel guide. By positioning this opinion in a prominent place, Shelley asked that her book be read both as her personal account of the region and as something more—as a manifesto devoted not to Italian landscape, history, or art but rather to the everyday life of its people.

In this effort to exalt within the pages of her travel account the ordinary life of Italian people, Mary Shelley marked herself as one of the most original of all of the period's travel writers. Curiously, a few women traveling to Italy in the early years of the century had focused on the Italian people in ways that, by Shelley's time, were believed to be either unnecessary or inappropriate. In 1800, Mariana Starke devoted several passages of her *Letters from Italy* to evoking and salvaging the character of Neapolitan Italians:

> The character of the Neapolitans has been much mistaken by Travellers, who seem inclined to think the lower classes of People cunning, rapacious, profligate, and cruel. . . . This, however, is not, generally speaking, true; for the common people are good-humoured, open-hearted, and though passionate, so fond of drollery that a Man in the greatest rage will suffer himself to be calmed by a joke.[25]

By the time Mary Shelley wrote *Rambles in Germany and Italy* it had become much the fashion to recreate an Italy almost devoid of reference to the people, even in so generalizing a way as Starke does here.[26] Shelley sought to disrupt that tendency, and not only to arouse interest in the Italian people but also to participate in the formation of public opinion at home. In the preface to *Rambles in Germany and Italy*, she wrote: "In addition, therefore, to being a mere gossiping companion to a traveler, I would fain say something that may incite others to regard [the Italians] favourably, something explanatory of their real character" (viii–ix).

For Mary Shelley, this "real character" was evidenced most in those Italians who fought for political liberation, and although she does not treat this quest in any kind of concrete detail in her work, its spirit nonetheless infuses her appreciation of the country. In her preface she professes an earnest desire for the reading public to sanction revolutionary Italy: "Englishmen, in particular, ought to sympathise in their struggles; for the aspirations for free institutions all over the world had its source in England" (xi). Although her reference to England as a source of free thought was surely meant to temper the hostility with which her comment might be met, she nonetheless unequivocally positions her own politics. Shelley wanted her readers to interpret the agitated political climate of Italy as having been brought on by honorable people seeking decent lives.

Rambles in Germany and Italy is also about the emotional difficulties attached to the quest for liberation, especially to the personal quest. Shelley sought in Italy emotional liberation from the depression of losing not only an important companion, her husband, but also the sense of purpose that Percy Bysshe Shelley had given to her life. Although the specter of Shelley's dead husband on occasion retreats into the background of her travel account, it is never entirely absent. At one point in *Rambles in Germany and Italy*, Shelley appeals to her readers for compassion: "Do not call me a grumbler. A tragedy has darkened my life: I endeavor, in vain, to cast aside the fears that are its offspring; they haunt me perpetually, and make too large and too sad a portion of my daily life" (I, 74).

By situating her personal struggle to escape loneliness and fear within a travel account also devoted to a people's struggle for political liberation, Shelley could not help but represent the common denominator—Italy—as what Sandra Gilbert and others have called a *matria*, or sphere of feminine power and influence. But for Shelley, the creation of an Italian *matria* was less about the exercise of feminine power there than about the struggle to achieve the self control perquisite to that power. In this her chosen title for the work is especially apt, for Shelley's voice in *Rambles in Germany and Italy* is never secure. Instead, her subjects, settings, and moods are in constant flux and the overall effect of the work is to suggest, rather than declare, the region's potential influence. *Rambles in Germany and Italy* divides itself sporadically between the evocation of Shelley's personal struggle and description of the country, but, in the end, its own textual unevenness helps to further Shelley's own sense of the country's emotional and political terrain.

Shelley did not escape censure for this approach. Robert Browning reportedly criticized her failure to realistically depict the Italian people in the ways that her preface seems to promise. In one of his letters to Elizabeth Barrett, Browning hypothetically asked Shelley,

> Why don't you tell us that at Rome they eat roasted chestnuts, and put the shells into their aprons, the women do, and calmly empty the whole on the heads of the passengers in the street below; and that at Padua when a man drives his wagon up to a house and stops, all the mouse-coloured oxen that pull it from a beam against their foreheads sit down in a heap and rest.[27]

One senses the validity of Browning's frustration with Shelley's lack of attention to details of everyday life, but nonetheless, he seems curiously unable to acknowledge the validity of using the emotional to evoke the impressionistic range of the country. For many of the women who traveled to Italy, the region offered itself up in more expansive ways that those suggested by Browning. And it was in establishing and extending an impressionistic mode that they distinguished themselves.

Italy as Intellectual Retreat

The women who traveled to Italy typically represented their experience as emotionally rejuvenating retreats from everyday England. In *Rambles in Germany and Italy*, Mary Shelley gushed:

> Surely on earth there is no pleasure (except that derived from moral good) so great as lingering, during the soft shades of an Italian evening, surrounded by the beauty of an Italian landscape, sheltered by the pure radiance of an Italian sky. (I, 84)

Foregrounding her emotional reaction to landscape and place was, for Shelley and others, a way of avoiding the pressure and limitations of the prefabricated intellectual response. Such gestures might also be seen as a manifestation of the more widespread tendency, noted by Michael Cotsell in his introduction to *Creditable Warriors*, of Victorians to view Italy as "an alternative ideological focus to Empire," one which consequently demanded an alternative approach.[28] As Mary Shelley wrote in the preface to *Rambles in Germany and Italy:*

> When we visit Italy, we become what the Italians were censured for being—enjoyers of the beauties of nature, the elegance of art, the delights of climate, the recollections of the past, and the pleasures of their society, without a thought beyond. (xvi)

Whereas empire seemed to demand of its travelers a certain aggressive posture, Italy exacted just the opposite. As John Pemble has written, Italy "seemed like the realm of Keats's nightingale or Tennyson's lotus-eaters, offering oblivion from weariness, fever, fret, and the consciousness of mortality."[29] Many of the women who traveled to Italy correspondingly adopted liberated postures that highlighted the lightheartedness and receptivity with which they greeted the country.

This receptive posture begins to be conspicuous almost immediately in many travel accounts, especially in passages describing the traveler's literal, physical arrival in the country. Mary Shelley again exemplifies well the tendency, writing near the beginning of *Rambles in Germany and Italy:*

> On the shores of France, I shook the dust of accumulated cares from off me; I forgot disappointments, and banished sorrow: weariness of body replaced beneficially weariness of soul—so much heavier, so much harder to bear. (I, 7)

The rhetoric of wearied traveler arriving ready for rest and recuperation is characteristic of much Victorian travel writing, male and female. Scenes of arrival charcteristically function as occasions for expressing both intense delight and disappointment at recognizing these preoccupations. On arriving in Rome, for example, Dickens wrote: "When, after a mile or two, the Eternal City appeared, at length in the distance—it looked like—I am half afraid to write the word—like London!!!"[30] Many Victorian women tend to be as excessive in their accounts as was Dickens. Well aware of her own exaggerated expectations, Frances Trollope tried to temper her delight on arriving in Italy with the following caveat in *A Visit to Italy:* "In approaching any place that has been during long years the object of hopes, fears, and despair, it is, I suppose, rational to be a little excited" (93–94). For Trollope, the appeal of the Italian landscape was that it elicited a cerebral response. Arriving in Italy after an extended visit in Paris, she wrote:

> It is with a very delightful sort of triumphant feeling that one looks for the first time on the sunny landscape of Italy. . . . There is a positive and a powerful charm, in at once recognizing the form and color of objects which art has made familiar to the mind, as types of all that is most characteristic in the land. (18)

Trollope uses the backdrop of sun and warmth to stage the scene in which she acknowledges her emotional and intellectual familiarity with the archetypes of Italian landscape, art, and culture, a familiarity expected of an upwardly mobile middle class. She offers repeat performances throughout *A Visit to Italy;* on arriving in Florence, for instance, she exclaims: "How much of what has embellished my early years had its origin from thence!" (94).

Although Mary Shelley was, like Trollope, drawn immediately to the country's landscape, she found that landscape to be suggestive of imaginative, rather than intellectual, potential. After arriving in Italy, she wrote in *Rambles in Germany and Italy:*

> All Italian travellers know what it is, after toiling up the bleak, bare, northern, Swiss side of an Alp, to descend towards ever-vernal Italy. The

rhododendron, in thick bushes, in full bloom, first adorned the mountain sides; the pine forests; then, chestnut groves . . . the waterfalls scattered their spray and their gracious melody; flowery and green, and clothed in radiance, and gifted with plenty, Italy opened before us. (I, 60)

Shelley strategically compares the "bleak" and "bare" north to the "ever-vernal" Italy, which functions as an Edenic refuge for travelers. The Italian experience is from the very beginning represented as release from toil. The Italy she depicts is one that willingly unfolds itself to the traveler, and she enters its landscape eager and unimpeded. In this passage, as well as in many other similar passages in *Rambles in Germany and Italy*, Shelley imagines an Italy free from the metaphors of and demand for conquest; in place of conquest, she renders immersion.

In some ways, Trollope and Shelley represent opposite ends of the spectrum of response to the country; whereas Trollope felt compelled to position her response within an intellectual heritage, Shelley was drawn more to the mood of the place. Other women travelers sought to do both. Arriving in Rome after a long train ride through the countryside, Frances Elliot recalled in *Diary of an Idle Woman in Italy:* "It was a glorious scene, and reminded me of a certain landscape I remember by Domenichino, who so well understood the rich Italian tints" (98). Like Trollope, she implies that the landscape is reminiscent of those depicted in the art with which she is familiar, but she also, like Shelley, concerns herself with color and with emotional response.

Like the women who had traveled to Italy before her, Vernon Lee, too, sought to represent her experience of the country as one of recognition and reminiscence. Each essay within *The Spirit of Rome* is structured around Lee's moments of return to the country. Like Frances Elliot and Frances Trollope, Lee was prompted in her travels to compare what she saw to what she had seen depicted. In her second "return to Rome," for instance, she wrote: "The man who has understood Rome best is Piranesi. His edifices, always immensely too big, his vegetation extravagantly too luxurious, are none too much to render Rome" (20). Just as Elliot had aligned her own powers of observation to those of Domenichino, so too Lee implies that she recognizes in Piranesi's work a kindred desire—and ability—to "render Rome." Later in *The Spirit of Rome* she muses: "How Renan, in the *Pretre di Nemi*, has rendered, without descriptions, the charm of that outlook towards Rome from this lower portion of the Latin Hills!" (87).

The direction of all of these comments is toward the unspoken and ineffable—the "charm" of Lee's Latin Hills, the "immensity" of her Rome, the "rich Italian tints" Elliot admired, the "radiance" of the landscape Shelley praised. Even after these women got beyond their moments of arrival and scenes of recognition, Italy failed to yield itself to any kind of concrete description. In *A Visit to Italy* Frances Trollope described Turin as "blessed by an atmosphere of exquisite purity" (19). Even tangible objects became, in Trollope's mind, ethereal. In Pisa, she wrote of the "oranges, lemons, figs, vines, olives, all placed as if in an orchestra, to raise their voices together in a choral hymn in praise of nature" (56). In a similar manner, Frances Elliot in *Diary of an Idle Woman in Italy* depicted the Italian countryside as nearly illusory:

> the whole country is a forest—such a forest! Giant oaks, wild, scathed, and savage-looking . . . spiky cypresses, gathered up like nosegays . . . grey, mystic trees said to have paled into that sad tint out of grief for the Divine One who once wept under their shade; vineyards of yellow-leafed grapes, now laden with ruby fruit. (53)

In Elliot's description the Italian countryside figures in much the same way as it did in Shelley's entrance scene; it tantalizes and awards its ripe bounty freely to the traveler. But Elliot also suggests a certain fear of the place; it is wild, overgrown, even overabundant.

Curiously, Vernon Lee described the Italian countryside with similar language. Remembering a journey to Italy in her essay "On Modern Travelling," Lee wrote:

> We seemed to traverse all countries and climates; lush, stifling valleys with ripening maize and grapes; oak-woods where rows of cypress showed roads long gone, and crosses told of murders; desolate heaths high on hill tops, and stony gorges full of myrtle . . . so that in the evening we felt homesick for that distant, distant morning.[31]

Although the countryside obviously attracts these women on one level, it also frightens and repels. For Elliot it is excessively "savage" and "scathed." For Lee its very bounty stifles. Both women seem to be drawn to that side of Italian nature that seemed most undomesticated. Both represent the landscape in language designed to make it seem unreal, to depict nature as unworldly and ethereal. Similar descriptions appear over and over again in their works, and suggest that they were attracted to the nature and landscape of Italy because it represented an "uncultivated" side the country, one not "developed," "civilized," "learned," one perhaps more authentic and more easily their own.

Another way in which these women developed a strategy to authenticate their experience was, ironically, to choose not to describe the country, to instead evoke its ineffable appeal. Such a technique becomes especially conspicuous in their repeated invocations to the inadequacy of language to represent feelings, impressions, intuitive response. On first seeing the Vatican, Charlotte Eaton wrote in *Rome in the Nineteenth Century:*

> How shall I express the delight, the admiration, the overpowering astonishment which filled my mind! How describe the extent and the splendour of that almost interminable succession of lengthening galleries and marble halls, whose pictured roofs, mosaic pavements, majestic columns, and murmuring fountains far surpass even the gorgeous drams of Eastern magnificence. (91)

Even as she claims not to be able to express her delight and describe the splendor, Eaton manages to do so. Making reference to the inability of language to adequately express impressions did not deter her from describing in great detail what she saw and felt. Similarly, in *Diary of an Idle Woman in Italy* Frances Elliot wrote of St. Peter's Cathedral:

> If it be not irreverent to liken a cathedral to a fairy palace, I would dare to do it. Of form so wonderful, of size so vast, or proportions so exquisite, in colours so indescribably brilliant, as the sun plays a thousand antics with its fantastic sculptures and glowing mosaics, until they glitter like a kaleidoscope. Who can describe it? (33)

Elliot, like Eaton, rhetorically argues that something cannot be described after she has done much to evoke it. "How easy to give the details; how impossible to paint the varied tint and magic changes of light and shade on this blue horizon," she later lamented (54). Both women implicitly distinguished in their commentary between the descriptive and the evocative, and seemed to value the latter for its suggestive, impressionistic emphasis. With this distinction in mind, Mary Shelley wrote in *Rambles in Germany and Italy*, "But words are in vain, and in description there must ever be at once a vagueness and a sameness that conveys no distinct ideas, unless it should awaken the imagination" (I, 23).

Frances Trollope also sought to escape from facts into feelings in her evocation of the Italian landscape. Describing her view of Genoa from the sea in *A Visit to Italy*, she wrote:

> I really think it is impossible to speak of the beauty of this scene hyperbolically. I know of no words expressing beauty, splendour, and majesty

that are strong enough to do it justice. . . . Most surely I find them not in my vocabulary, and yet, did I push such verbal power to its utmost, I doubt not but you would think the picture overcharged, the lights too brilliant, and the shades too exquisitely transparent. (45)

Trollope finds simple description to be too narrow of an approach, one that fails to capture the intensity of what she sees and feels; she opts instead for the enhancing, enlarging, and deepening effects of hyperbole. She blames language for not providing the vocabulary with which to fully represent the beauty of Italian landscape, and insinuates that, even were language to fulfill its mission, a reader who had not physically experienced the place would not be able to believe that which was described.

Of all of the women who wrote tourist accounts of Italy, none was more apt or better able than Vernon Lee to represent its ethereal appeal. Throughout all of the essays that make up *The Spirit of Rome*, Lee privileges what might be called imaginative traveling. As she explained in her essay "On Modern Travelling": "The reality, so far as my own experience goes, never once tallies with the fancy" (307). And it was for her ability to evoke, rather than describe, that Lee was praised. A critic for *The Atlantic* wrote that Lee's *The Spirit of Rome* "contains some of her subtlest and most suggestive word painting, the short-hand notes of things felt rather than seen in Rome."[32]

The subtext of all of these references to the inability of language to represent Italy is the same: Italy demanded a different kind of language, one less rooted in ordinary human experience. One of the many consequences of this perceived demand was that women writers dehistoricized the country, represented it as in some way cut off from the march of time that was presumably overtaking the rest of the world. Just as Rome was lauded as the "Eternal City," so too was all of Italy endowed with a sense of perpetual, unchanging essence. Lady Blessington had greeted the museums of Florence with the celebratory proclamation: "Beautiful art! that snatches loveliness from the rude grasp of all-devouring time."[33] Some of her Victorian counterparts highlighted the country's atemporality by endowing their descriptions of even the most mundane features of life with otherworldly appeal. "How Rome seems to have been isolated from all life save the life eternal and unchangeable of grass and water, and cattle and larks. . . . [It seems] to have been suspended in a sort of void!" Vernon Lee wrote in *The Spirit of Rome* (85).

Representing Italy as eternal and unchangeable relieved Lee from addressing the very real changes that affected Italy during the period, changes made all the more dramatic by the rise of Italian nationalism in the early part of the century and the ensuing series of wars through which the country became politically unified. In her personal life, Lee seems to have been at least moderately active politically. She collected money from her friends to help advance various local causes, among them a drive among English expatriates to prevent efforts at modernizing Florence. But it was important to her to preserve *in writing* as well an Italy "free" from the kinds of strife that might disrupt the restorative sphere that she and others imagined it to be.

Other women found different means to the same end. Some rendered the otherworldliness of Italy in spatial terms, recreating in their works a place seemingly uncircumscribed, even boundless—endowed with what Gaston Bachelard in *The Poetics of Space* calls "intimate immensity."[34] With little sense of her overstatement, Frances Elliot wrote in *Diary of an Idle Woman in Italy* that the country's "lofty cavernous streets engulf[ed] her" (16). Frances Trollope wrote in *A Visit to Italy* that "vast, vast, vast, was certainly the epithet that recurred the oftenest" during her visit to the Santa Maria del Fiore (96–97). Their comments point suggestively to a basic discomfort with the place that relieved itself by conceptualizing it as more different than it actually was. Such a fear seems to be operative in Mary Shelley's description of part of the Italian countryside she toured with her son:

> The scene is inconceivably wild. Earth looks rent, convulsed, shattered—isolated, disjointed mountains, rising abruptly from the plain, their sides clothed by firs, are spread around. The majestic arch forms an object of great beauty in the midst. (*Rambles in Germany and Italy* I, 273)

In keeping with Shelley's tendency to "ramble" through her memories of her stays in Italy, however, such moments—although vividly rendered—are short-lived.

The fears, anxieties, and apprehensions that appear throughout Victorian women's writings about Italy in some ways expose a reluctance to give themselves over to the country, to relinquish what strength they seemed to feel their national identity had given them. Shelley, Trollope, Elliot, and Lee all fall back at some point in their travel accounts on what they left behind in England. Such reminiscences at times simply reveal homesickness, as for instance when Shelley observes "There are some superb magnolias and other flowering trees, but one longs for English gardening here" (*Rambles in Germany and Italy* I, 83) or when Trollope concludes that Italian "mulberry and olive trees cannot compete with our oaks and elms" (*A

Visit to Italy, 33). But, as often, comparisons between the two countries were made to affirm in some way pride in the national identity that they took with them abroad. Most were not as vociferous as Charlotte Eaton, who proclaimed in *Rome in the Nineteenth Century:*

> Nor is it only in domestic life that our superiority consists: at the hazard of being accused of national partiality, I will maintain, that not only is the society abroad generally inferior to our own, but that in Italy there is scarcely anything worthy of the name of society at all. (vii)

Although Eaton fails to establish the grounds with which she condemns Italian society, it is worth noting the confidence with which she, at the age of twenty-two, renders her opinion. And Trollope claimed that her trip to Italy in the end taught her

> that the Constitution of England, when guarded with common prudence from the democratic innovations which have late years buzzed about it . . . is the only one which appears to be formed in reasonable, honest, and holy conformity to the freedom of man as a human being, and to the necessary restraint inevitable upon his becoming one of a civilized social compact. (*A Visit to Italy*, 167)

Affirmation of national identity was very much a part of what many Victorian women felt had to be done in Italy, and such an affirmation did not go unnoticed at home in the reviews that travel accounts written by women received. Although Lady Eastlake covers the works of women who traveled to all parts of the wider world in her review-essay "Lady Travellers," she chose to feature for special commendation Catherine Taylor's *Letters from Italy*. This account was worth calling attention to, Eastlake argued, because its author so well represented "the national type of female character—minds of the highest intellectual culture, and manners of the most domestic simplicity" (105). Eastlake's comment reveals the extent to which English women travelers were representatives of both their gender and their nation. Gender and nationality worked mutually to constitute the public identity of the woman who toured Italy and wrote about her experiences.

To suggest that ideologies of gender and of nationality helped to shape a woman's experience and representation of another country is not, however, to condemn the women who accommodated these assumptions. The lived experience of Italy corroborated many of the beliefs that Victorian women brought to it; it was warm and colorful, and it offered a social climate amenable to an alternative life-style, one that many women felt to be more relaxed than the one they had left behind. It is this sense of the *lived* appeal of Italy that Frances Power Cobbe, another Victorian woman who traveled to Italy, seemed to have in mind when she wrote toward the end of *Italics:*

> If I were asked which was the greatest pleasure incident to a residence in Italy, I should not say it was either beholding classic memorials, and treading historic soil, nor yet admiring the glories of Italian art. . . . To my thinking, the Social life of Italy offers greater enjoyment than any of these. I am not speaking of the society of Italians themselves. Into actual native circles a foreigner rarely enters, and, when he does, seems to find few topics of common interest. There are in Italy, more than anywhere else in the world, a multitude of men and women, more or less gifted, who lead *real* lives. . . . who find themselves enabled in Italy to enjoy nearly all the pleasure and *quite* all the honour and independence conveyed by wealth in England.[35]

Cobbe's comment is intriguing from several standpoints, not least of which is her apt reminder that to expect a traveler to be able to readily immerse herself in foreign society would be unrealistic. Although not explicitly saying so, she also suggests that part of Italy's unique appeal to a Victorian woman traveler was the sense of liberation and independence that it offered. Such independence—especially for women— was hard to come by in England, where people's lives to Cobbe seemed to be more rigidly confined by class distinctions. In Italy, she argued, the liberties of independence were freely given and readily available to men and women of all classes. Although overly idealistic on this point, Cobbe in essence points to the enlarged horizon of opportunity that Italy offered, and she alludes to this opportunity as both intellectually and psychologically rewarding. And in seeming to offer to women a more expansive horizon of opportunity, broader interest and appeal, Italy served women like her as a *matria*, a place of feminine empowerment.

Unlike most of the women discussed in this chapter, however, Cobbe involved herself in a network of intellectual English women who lived for varying periods of time in Italy. For example, she stayed in close contact with Mary Somerville, who also lived for periods of time in Italy. Cobbe also regularly called on Elizabeth Barrett Browning and Anna Jameson while in Italy. With the exception of Vernon Lee and Alice Meynell, who are discussed in the concluding chapter, the women who wrote *tourist accounts* of Italy visited the country but never made it their home. Even Mary Shelley, whose tour documented in *Rambles in Germany and Italy* included a lengthy stay in Italy, never seriously considered living there after her husband had died. Part of what attracted Victorian women tourists to travel in Italy was its impermanent and transitory nature. As temporary visitors, these tourists could feel unencumbered by the realities of everyday life; they could preserve the kind of country they chose to find, create the kind of experience they wanted to have. It was the imaginative power of the tourist that Vernon Lee wanted to capture when she wrote in "Modern Travelling": "Honour the tourist; he walks in a halo of romance" (311).

Victorian women tourists flourished throughout the period for just this reason; in their works they recreated for their readers an imaginative Italy, one perhaps more fanciful and, in a sense, more exotic than those of their male counterparts. These travel writers searched for an authentic approach and in doing so discovered an uncultivated Italy, one offering more potential for vision, if less potential for learning. In doing so they "relieved" the country of its ties to history; they focused instead on its multifaceted landscapes, exuberant nature, ineffable appeal. These dimensions of Italy, they implicitly argued, were as much a part of taste as were its churches, museums, galleries. Much of what Victorian women tourists wrote about Italy cannot help but strike the modern reader as unrelated to the material conditions of the country's history; although writing in very different parts of the nineteenth century, for example, much of what Eaton, Shelley, Trollope, Elliot, and Lee had to say about the country cannot be distinguished by time—that is, by specific economic, social, or political circumstance. Yet, as Nancy Armstrong has argued in her work on feminine authority, many women writers in the nineteenth century perfected tropes to distinguish their work from historically bound writing. Each of the women travelers studied in this chapter in her own way created and refined ways to translate historical circumstance into something else, something more uniquely her own.

3

The Professionalization of Taste: Art Historians Abroad

In 1858, Elizabeth Rigby Eastlake, already a prominent art historian and critic, wrote to her friend Jane Harrison to report on the activities of another friend and art historian, Anna Jameson. Jameson was at the time planning a trip to Italy to begin research for a book on the history of Christian art, and Eastlake wrote:

> It is only a few days since I heard from Mrs. Jameson; she said she was going to Rome as soon as the weather became milder. She is a woman of very determined mind, who has worked beyond her strength; this is the side I admire in her. Her great acquirements and most conscientious works I need not allude to, though no one admires them more. She is a friend of art, and has just been taking great interest in the acquisition of the Lombardi pictures at Florence for the National Gallery.[1]

In openly admiring one particular "side" of Jameson, Eastlake also alluded to the side she could not sympathize with, Jameson's avowed feminism. Eastlake's comments are noteworthy for their solicitous tone, however. Despite very different life situations and political beliefs, Elizabeth Eastlake and Anna Jameson—arguably the mid-Victorian period's two most influential women art historians—felt great concern and respect for one another. Although they did not socialize together, they corresponded and monitored each other's activities abroad and at home. Their friendship was developed and maintained through recognition of the value of each other's work. Indeed, as if to publicly ratify this friendship, Lady Eastlake agreed to finish Anna Jameson's last book for her, when she died before its completion.[2]

The sense of solidarity implicit in Eastlake's remarks about Jameson points to an important and distinguishing feature of their work. Although both women were recognized during their lifetime as travel writers and art historians, it was their joint interest in the latter that facilitated their collegial friendship. Although scholars have long rec-

71

ognized the significance of female solidarity in creating a "tradition" of domestic women novelists and poets, little has been made of other female communities of authorship—probably because so few existed. The Victorian women celebrated as adventuresses, for example, were notoriously standoffish with one another and often highly critical of one another's accomplishments.[3] Victorian women who used their travels for more explicitly professional purpose were equally disinclined to seek out a community of women with similar ideas. Beatrice Webb seemed willfully to have disregarded the achievements of two significant sociologists who had traveled to America before her—Emily Faithfull and Harriet Martineau. Although Frances Power Cobbe made passing reference in *Cities of the Past* to Harriet Martineau's eastern study, she in no way attempted to build on a tradition. Finally, the drive for authenticity—so critical to the tourist's accounts of Italy—demanded an independence of experience in many ways incompatible with the ideal of professional community.

Eastlake, Jameson, and other women art historians stand apart from these groups of women in several distinctive ways. They used their experiences abroad to cultivate professional identities that eventually subsumed their role as travelers, and as Eastlake's remarks on Jameson suggest, they shared a sense of common purpose through their professional work as interpreters of art. Their shared sense of community both at home and abroad had a significant influence on their written work as well as on their sense of themselves as professionals. Louisa Twining's *Symbols of Early and Mediaeval Christian Art*, published in 1852, was indebted to *Sacred and Legendary Art*, Jameson's pioneering study of iconography published four years earlier. That she explicitly drew for both subject matter and style on Jameson suggests that by midcentury Victorian women already recognized their own contributions to a specific field of scholarship. Indeed, in her preface to *Symbols of Early and Mediaeval Christian Art* Twining lists Jameson as one of her "principal authorities."[4]

Open acknowledgement of indebtedness between women art historians permeates their personal correspondence and diaries as well. References to Vernon Lee's work, for instance, are liberally scattered throughout Julia Cartwright's diaries and correspondence.[5] Another measure of their strength as a community is the fact that many other women explicitly positioned their own work in relation to either Jameson or Eastlake. In her 1896 essay "The New Art Criticism," Julia Ady wrote: "In Lady Eastlake's oft-quoted words, the best connoisseur in the end will always be 'he who compares on the largest scale and with the narrowest nicety.'"[6] And Mary Heaton opened her study of Flemish art by quoting Anna Jameson: "'After looking at a grand work of art,' says Mrs. Jameson, 'we naturally turn to look into the mind that conceived and created it.'"[7] Emilia Pattison Dilke, Lucy Baxter ("Leader Scott"), and Vernon Lee are just a few of the other women who worked to interpret the arts and who, like Ady, were significantly influenced by Jameson and Eastlake.

Another distinguishing feature of this group of women is the unique way in which travel, art history and criticism, and social criticism were interwoven in works that implicitly challenged the conventions and boundaries of genre. Anna Jameson's work in art history and criticism first took the form of a fictionalized travel biography; later she published several collections of "visits and sketches," handbooks to public and private galleries, and a catalogue of sacred art. Most of Eastlake's work took the form of wide-ranging review articles for prominent periodicals, but she also dabbled in translation. Women art historians of the latter part of the century continued like their predecessors to experiment with hybrid forms—Julia Ady with art historical biography and Vernon Lee with psychological aesthetics.

Although all of these women traveled extensively to garner the knowledge and experience necessary to their professional careers, only a few published what might be thought of as "traditional" travel accounts, chronologically rendered records both impressionistic and documentary in nature like those that tourists wrote. More often than not, those art historians who did publish straightforward travel accounts recorded experiences not directly related to their work as art historians. Despite Eastlake's many trips in pursuit of central and southern European art, her only direct record of travel was her first book, *Letters from the Shores of the Baltic; Described in a Series of Letters* (1841), which described a brief period in her life (before she married Charles Eastlake and became involved in the art world) when she lived in the Soviet Union with her married sister. Jameson's only travel account, *Winter Studies and Summer Rambles in Canada* (1838), described the time she lived in North America with her husband. Finally, while Julia Ady kept extensive diaries of her visits to Italy, she never attempted to publish any of her personal reflections. That these women did not publish travel accounts of their experiences in the places deemed central to their professional work is telling. Elizabeth Eastlake evidently disapproved of traveling for the sake of writing, noting in her journals that "It always becomes apparent" (*Journals and Correspondence* I, 166), a comment that reveals her sense that the increasing opportunities for middle-class Victorians to go abroad was creating an unfortunate glut in the market for travel writing. She seemed to believe that her professional work—and image—needed to be preserved from the taint of this overcrowded middle-class market.

All of the women who worked as art historians believed their experiences abroad to be central to their professional success, however. Many limited their professional work to the art of an individual country or to particular regions within a country. Not surprisingly, Italy was a favored choice, and many women chose to restrict themselves to particular periods of Italian history. Julia Cartwright Ady and Maud Cruttwell focused on the Italian Renaissance, though they exhibited a range of interest within this period.[8] Other women chose to study particular regions in Italy, rather than specific periods. Lucy Baxter's *Tuscan Studies and Sketches* (1887) is one example of this kind of approach.

Italy was not, however, the only country to attract the sustained interest of the art historian. Mary Heaton focused on the Netherlands in *Masterpieces of Flemish Art* in 1869. And Emilia Dilke, following her first husband's (Mark Pattison) advice to make herself "*the* authority on some one subject" limited herself primarily to French art and made her professional name in 1879 with *The Renaissance of Art in France*.[9] Several years later, she published *Claude Lorrain, Sa Vie Et Ses Oeuvres* (1884) and became a frequent contributor to *Gazette des Beaux-Arts*. By the end of her life, she had published separate studies of French painters, architects and sculptors, and engravers and draughtsmen, as well as work on French architecture and decoration.

Although they shared many of the same destinations, these women differed substantially from the tourists in their assumption that foreign countries offered better opportunity for work, rather than retreat and rest. This was especially true for Julia Cartwright, who was first ordered to Italy as a young woman by her doctor after he determined that her "nervous disorder" had issued from her interest in a writing career.[10] Ironically, his advice to travel proved fortuitous; she discovered in Italy not the refinements that would make her more marriageable and less career-oriented, but rather the incentive for her "life's work" as an author of Italian histories and biographies.

Julia Cartwright was not the first to go abroad to find the inspiration and materials for a professional career. Most of the art history and criticism published by Eastlake and Jameson was based on their experiences in Germany, France, and Italy, and these countries were featured in their facilitating capacities—that is, as scenes for research. In their journals and personal correspondence, the rhetoric of work permeates discussion of travel. From Munich, Eastlake wrote to her family: "I have been working very hard in the Gallery here: I am so constantly taking notes now for my particular object, that I see no chance of getting any sketches unless I could have time to draw for my own purposes" (*Journals and Correspondence*, I, 141). Like East-lake, Jameson sent frequent and lengthy letters home to her family that read like progress reports. In a letter written to her mother and sister from Rome in 1849, she reported: "On the whole I am living very economically and going on with my work; the facilities here, both for study and society, are far superior to anything I can command in England on the same terms, and, on the whole, I do not feel inclined to return yet."[11] One can sense in Jameson's defensive tone a need to justify staying abroad. By stressing the frugality of her lifestyle and the diligence of her pursuits, she absolves herself of any implication of idle pursuit or escapism. Jameson was also simply being realistic. To gain both the breadth and depth of knowledge required of art historians she had to study abroad—to visit museums, galleries, and churches throughout Europe and to document and assimilate what she found. Travel, as she recognized, had by the middle of the century become a prerequisite for art historical study.

Nineteenth-century England—as well as Europe and America—witnessed the flowering of art history as a discipline. Giorgio Vasari's *Lives of the Most Eminent Italian Painters, Sculptors, and Architects* (1568) and Johann Winckelmann's *History of Ancient Art* (1764) introduced to nineteenth-century art historians several modes of analysis, including the identification of artists and works of art within definable historical matrices. Not until the nineteenth century, though, did art historians attempt to adopt rigorously objective research standards, and this ideal in part accounts for the extent to which personal impressions of abroad were largely absent from women's art history. Like other historiographers and social scientists of the period—including some of the women historians and social scientists discussed in chapters 5 and 6—they looked to scientific method to validate their claims and to authorize their professional identities.[12] First and foremost, this meant direct observation of both the art itself and of its local context. The primary goals of art historical analysis—dating, localization, and attribution—all required firsthand examination of works of art. Travel to foreign collections hence became indispensable to one's competency as an art critic and historian. Not only did it offer the opportunity for direct observation of a variety of art work, but also it enabled the art history student to master a foreign language, another talent considered requisite to authoritative scholarship.

Those middle- and upper-class women who could afford to travel were thus given—if informally—the training and opportunities demanded of a professional career. That art history was by midcentury becoming increasingly professionalized is evidenced by its growing institutional support in the form of exhibitions, universities, and museums. Universities began during the period to include art history in their curriculum, but they had far less of an impact on the evolution of art history as a valid profession than did the museums. The National Gallery (1824), the National Portrait Gallery (1856), and the South Kensington Museum (1857) were all founded in the Victorian period and spawned many regional offshoots. By the time she wrote about the status of art history for the Jubilee year, Julia Ady was able to proclaim:

> There are picture-galleries and schools of art not only in the metropolis itself, but in all our large provincial cities; Edinburgh, Glasgow, Birmingham, Manchester, Liverpool, Oldham, are themselves important centres of art, the home of flourishing schools, each of them marked with a character of its own.[13]

The abundance and accessibility of these museums and schools had important implications for the professional development of women working in the arts. Whereas they were essentially excluded from choosing the university as an avenue for professional achievement, they could and did use the museums to advantage.

Museums functioned as the sites at which women art historians worked abroad and at home. Unlike other travelers whose professional identities were entirely dependent on what they did abroad, women art historians had in the museum a tangible place to work professionally once they had returned home. Eastlake, Jameson, and Ady all spent days at a time viewing home collections, typically taking detailed notes and making sketches. Many museums included library facilities as well, and these proved equally indispensable to their work. In her diary Julia Ady wrote of "constant trips" to the Art Reference Library in South Kensington where she "studied plates" for her book on Mantegna and "walked[ed] through the galleries and corridors without end" (125). Museums provided women literally and metaphorically with an art historical home away from home, and one can sense just such a sentiment in Elizabeth Eastlake's description of the British Museum as "a building to be lived and studied in" (*Journals and Correspondence* I, 124).

A significant part of the appeal of the museum rested with its status as the preeminent place in which the culture of abroad was brought home for safekeeping. As Eastlake's letter to Jane Harrison noted at the beginning of this chapter implied, it was just as important for the woman art historian to appreciate Roman and Florentine art while she traveled as it was to see the necessity of acquiring that art for the British Museum. In essence, Eastlake recognized the connection between art historians and connoisseurs; both, she implied, were "friends" of art—patrons, as it were, of high culture.[14]

The museum served as standard fare for the upwardly mobile segments of Victorian society. Middle- and upper-class women could make "idle" time culturally profitable by visiting museums, because contact with high art was felt to be morally uplifting and intellectually edifying. Furthermore, many nineteenth-century museums were intended to help "civilize" the working class, an assumption evident in Julia Ady's proclamation that "Our galleries and libraries are open to all. Books and pictures have been brought within the reach of all classes."[15] Nonetheless, as Francis Sheppard ironically notes in *London 1808–1870: The Infernal Wen,* most of these museums were closed on Sundays, thus effectively keeping them off-limits to the working class.[16] As Sheppard notes, "their use was therefore restricted 'to persons of leisure, or (to quote the regulations of the British Museum in 1810) to persons of decent appearance.'"[17] An implicit analogy between the museum and the middle-class household suggests some of the ideological complexities helping to determine and shape the representation of the Victorian woman art historian's work. Most obviously, middle- and upper-class Victorian women shared symbolically the status of the historical relics "housed" in museums; ideologically detached from their economic origins, they inhabited a domestic sphere "protected" from the public world of commerce and labor. Although public space, a museum was safe as it, too, was protected from this world; by visiting a museum, or even working within it, as the Victorian women art historians did, they essentially substituted one protected sphere for another.

Although the art historians did not consciously represent the museum as a home, they often paid tribute to its comforts and implied that it served as a substitute abroad, a place to go for culture while one was stuck in England. By referring to the British Museum as "a building to be lived and studied in," for instance, Eastlake suggested that she felt accepted and at ease there.[18] The enormous amount of time Jameson had to have spent in museums and galleries is evidenced by the fact that she published handbooks to their collections, complete with meticulous catalogues of the paintings and critical, historical, and biographical indexes. Julia Ady took her infant daughter Cecily with her on her frequent afternoon excursions to the London galleries. Although limited, these instances suggest that these middle- and upper-class women found it natural to *work* in museums and that their status as workers did not demand any of the apologetic tone, maidenly demurral, or overt justification prominent in the work of other women writers struggling to accommodate their professional goals and working habits to their identities as proper Victorian ladies.

The cultural assumptions that legitimized a Victorian woman's presence in the museum (as opposed to, say, the laboratory, the classroom, or the public galleries of Parliament) were of course more complicated than a simple museum/household analogy would suggest. That museum work could seem "natural" is also explained by the fact that many middle- and upper-class women were educated to be "accomplished" practitioners of such arts as sketching, painting, needlework, and musical performance. The significance of this kind of feminine education is in several ways borne out in the lives of the women who became art historians. Lady Eastlake and Lady Dilke expressed their desire for a vocation in the arts as a natural outcome of what they had mastered as young women. Elizabeth Rigby's first "studies" of abroad were sketches, and it was to these that she referred when she wrote to John Lockhart, her editor: "my pen has never been a favorite implement with me; the pencil is the child of my heart" (*Journals and Correspondence*, I, 10). Upwardly mobile middle-class families encouraged their daughters to develop many of the same talents, but their purpose in doing so was practical: unmarried middle-class women in "reduced circumstances" could be required to demonstrate such abilities to land jobs as governesses. Anna Jameson profited from her work as a governess accompanying a family to Italy in 1826 by writing *Diary of an Ennuyee*, a travel account that masquerades as a diary replete with detailed descriptions of Italian art.

All of these women forged their professional careers abroad, and in the process of becoming professionals dealt with the related issues of gender and class. For each woman, travel functioned in a different way and to a different degree to facilitate this process. And nowhere are the implications of such differences made more evident than in the lives of Anna Jameson and Elizabeth Eastlake.

Anna Murphy Jameson and Elizabeth Rigby Eastlake stand out as the two most prominent figures whose work was central to a tradition of women art historians. Their work is distinctive in several ways. Unlike most of the other women art historians made reference to in this chapter, neither woman restricted herself to one particular region, time period, or genre. Instead, Jameson and Eastlake based their authority as art historians on the extent and breadth of their travels abroad and tried to translate that experience abroad into work at home. Through their travels, both women sought to create a base of knowledge about several places, periods, and genres and both wrote authoritatively in many areas of art history.

Jameson and Eastlake invite comparison on several other grounds as well. Although they constructed public identities as art historians, their professional reputations enabled both to write authoritatively on other issues as well. Eastlake wrote an influential piece on the education of English women for the *Quarterly Review* as well as on a variety of social issues, including the problem of widespread alcoholism and pauperism. What ties Eastlake's social criticism to her work as an art historian is her insistence—sometimes overt, sometimes implicit—that one's perspective on any topic take into account the issue of class. Because class differences seemed to her to be so immutable, the idea of class itself was in all of her work endowed with ultimate explanatory power. It could be invoked to justify any one of her positions. Thus she saw the question of suffrage as "a property—not a sex qualification" and wrote that "if women can hold property, then *that* should give the vote" (*Journals and Correspondence*, II, 283).

Jameson, too, consistently moved from her work in art history to other areas of interest. She had from the beginning of her professional career evinced a concern with the position of women in contemporary society and throughout history. *Memoirs of Celebrated Female Sovereigns* (1831) and *Characteristics of Women* (1832), a study of Shakespearian heroines, were two of her earliest scholarly works. *Winter Studies and Summer Rambles in Canada* (1838) brazenly compared the predicament of Indian women to those European-born women who lived ostensibly civilized lives. A few years later, Jameson issued a pamphlet titled *On the Relative Social Position of Mothers and Governesses* (1846). Jameson, who began her career as a governess, continued to work for a living throughout her life and for a time supported both her father and her husband.

Despite these similarities, Jameson and Eastlake lived very different lives, Eastlake's one of relative ease and Jameson's one of almost constant economic and emotional pressure. One might generalize that Eastlake found through her professional career a way to affirm the class position that protected her and that doing so enabled her to overcome the institutional barriers that restricted many nineteenth-century English women from full participation in some of these institutions. By comparison, one might argue that Jameson used her professional career to overcome the disadvantages of her class position and that to do so she necessarily made strategic use of the "powers" ideologically associated with her gender. But such a comparison would gloss over the more complicated and provocative ways that both women recognized and responded to the interplay of class and gender as mutually constitutive influences on individual lives and social relations. Both women were directed in their work by what they believed appropriate in terms of class and gender. That they took very different directions testifies to the power of both women to shape their own careers.

Anna Jameson

Anna Jameson's career as an art historian really begins with what on the surface looks like a fictionalized travel account. Like much of the work written by women art historians, *Diary of an Ennuyee*, first published in 1826 as *A Lady's Diary*, defies the conventions of genre. In her discussion of travel in *Literary Women*, Ellen Moers calls it "a hybrid work, part novel, part guidebook."[19] Clara Thomas, one of Jameson's biographers, labels it "a fictionalized travel-biography,"[20] but notes its "guide-book quality" and "preoccupation with art."[21] In both form and content *Diary of an Ennuyee* mimics Madame de Stael's *Corinne, or Italy,* and both Thomas and Moers acknowledge its indebtedness to this work. In *Literary Women*, Moers argues that Jameson "suppressed the governess and presented herself as the highly improbable English Corinne, that is, as a husbandless, parentless, spinster who most respectably but in an independent grandeur tours the sights of Italy and feasts upon its art."[22]

Diary of an Ennuyee was a product of Jameson's experience as a governess traveling with a wealthy family on a Grand Tour of France and Italy. But the fictional experience of the diary keeper more closely approximates that of an upper-class young woman, not of a governess. The heroine of Jameson's diary travels alone to Italy, a self-proclaimed "idle" woman with no more specific itinerary than "to be amused and to forget."[23] Because the trip to Italy occurred just after Anna Murphy had broken off her engagement to Robert Jameson, the temptation is to read such lines as these as the author's recreation of her self as heroine. A strictly biographical interpretation over-emphasizes the heroine's emotional struggle at the expense of her intellectual development, however. Recognizing this progress allows one to read *Diary of an Ennuyee* as Jameson's reflections on the complex relationship between travel abroad, the study of art, and the position of women.

The rhetorical question with which *Diary of an Ennuyee* begins ("What young lady, travelling for the first time on the continent, does not write a Diary?") suggests that Jameson wants her heroine's record to be read initially as the document of an untutored mind, one particularly susceptible to the charms of Europe. In the beginning of her travels, she doubts her ability to see in works of art what her guidebooks have told her she should see:

> The unobtrusive grace and simplicity of Raffaelle do not immediately strike an eye so unpracticed and a taste so unformed as mine still is: for though I have seen the best pictures in England, we have there no opportunity of becoming acquainted with the divinest masters of Italian art, Raffaelle and Correggio. (102–3)

The passage is exemplary in its explicit criticism of the opportunities afforded to the art scholar in England. Yet even after she has had more time to study in Italy, Jameson's heroine continues to doubt her own powers of judgement. At times she simply disassociates herself from an intellectual sphere: "I would rather not think, nor speak, nor write upon matters which are too high for me" (234). On other occasions she devalues her critical acumen by arguing that her experience is more pleasurable because it is unburdened by intellectual thought:

> I am no connoisseur; and I should have lamented as a misfortune the want of some fixed principles of taste and criticism to guide my judgment. . . . Had I visited Italy in the character of a ready-made connoisseur, I should have lost many pleasures; for as the eye becomes more practiced, the taste becomes more discriminative and fastidious; and the more extensive our acquaintance with the works of art, the more limited is our sphere of admiration. (104)

On the one hand, she seems to suggest that her travels in Italy have been especially valuable because they have enabled her to develop (not simply to practice) an ability to appreciate art. Yet at the same time her comments lack the force of conviction. At this point in the narrative she has already proven herself a capable connoisseur and has begun to accept that such competency necessarily limits the range of works she will value. Indeed, as the narrative of the diary progresses, the heroine feels her taste "become more and more fastidious every day" (156). She dutifully records what she sees at various galleries, museums, and churches. Claiming that she doesn't want her journal to be "a mere catalogue of objects," she makes "a few notes of admiration and commemoration" for her "peculiar use" (213). Despite these disclaimers, the observations that permeate the diary could hardly be called "a few notes." In both their range of knowledge and depth of insight, they reveal the heroine's growing capacity to judge works of art.

Diary of an Ennuyee charts not only the heroine's increasing ability to appreciate the country's art but also her corresponding growth of confidence in her own judgement. As if to lend credibility to her heroine's increasing taste, Jameson includes concrete examples of her formation of judgement:

> I stood today for some time between those two great masterpieces—the Transfiguration of Raffaelle and Domenichino's Communion of St. Jerome. I studied them, I examined them, figure by figure, and then in the ensemble, and mused upon the different effect they produce, and were designed to produce, until I thought I could decide to my own satisfaction on their respective merits. (173)

Jameson represents her heroine as more than a tourist casually traipsing through the museums to say that she had seen two great masterpieces. She approaches the works of art as objects for study and proceeds as if trained as a critic, looking both for distinctive detail and broad effect. More important, she relies on her own opinion:

> I am not ignorant that the Transfiguration is pronounced the 'grandest picture in the world,' not so insensible to excellence as to regard this glorious composition without all the admiration due to it. I am dazzled by the flood of light which bursts from the opening heavens above, and affected by the dramatic interest of the group below. What splendour of colour! What variety of expression! What masterly grouping of the heads! I see all this, but to me Raffaelle's picture wants unity of interest; it is two pictures in one. (173)

The comparative analysis of Raffaelle and Domenichino continues well beyond the aforementioned passages, but they illustrate well Jameson's method and purpose in *Diary of an Ennuyee*. Whereas some claim that Jameson's heroine turns to art for consolation, it seems as reasonable to conclude that she finds in it intellectual sustenance. In finding in Italian art both emotional consolation and intellectual sustenance, Jameson's heroine cannot help but remind one of *Middlemarch* heroine Dorothea Brooke in Italy on her honeymoon.

Jameson wanted to depict her heroine in the process of finding an identity abroad. Such scenes also clearly afforded Jameson the opportunity to display her own growing professional interest in Renaissance and baroque art. Using a similar passage in which the heroine goes to the Pitti to compare the styles of the different masters, Adele Holcomb has argued that part of Jameson's achievement was to delineate for other art historians a working definition of style.[25] Deprived of its explicitly subjective bias, much of the diary would seem equally at home in a primer for beginning art historians, and in this context it is interesting to consider that *Diary of an Ennuyee* masquerades as a travel journal. Far from being an unwary tourist dictated by the judgements of others, Jameson's heroine by the end of the narrative stands, studies, compares, and, most important, decides on her own. The judgement she ultimately renders (against Raphael and in favor of the then less popular Domenichino) suggests her confidence in her own competence to render judgement.

Diary of an Ennuyee tells the story of two women, one a hesitant amateur, content to rely on the judgements of others, and the other a critic, increasingly confident in her own analysis and evaluation. The seeming contradictions of the diary writer's self-assessment can in part be explained by Jameson's own sense of how much a woman might properly know, or at least admit to knowing. At one point toward the end of the work, her heroine writes: "Nothing can be more animating and improving than the conversation of intelligent and clever men" and that "lady society is in general very *fade* and tiresome" (268). These are sentiments Jameson as governess imagines her upper-class heroine to have, and it is significant that it is shortly after these sentiments are expressed that the narrative closes abruptly with a report of the heroine's death. Most critics, in keeping with a biographical reading of the diary that privileges the romance plot, view the death as resulting from the heroine's broken heart; Holcomb labels it a suicide. These critics forget that the diary also closes with the intimation that the tour is coming to an end. Given the emphasis throughout the diary on the heroine's intellectual development, it seems more reasonable to read the death as Jameson's sense that her heroine's opportunities for intellectual exercise would end with the tour.

Diary of an Ennuyee was enough of a success to enable Jameson to make some money and continue to publish travel pieces. That the diary had been a testing ground for Jameson's emerging identity as an art critic and historian is evident in much of the work she did subsequently. Of the eighteen books that were to follow, eleven were studies of the fine arts in which Jameson related her work as an interpreter of the arts to her travels. In fact, the diary was reissued in 1834 with a collection of short essays as *Visits and Sketches at Home and Abroad*.

The years between *Diary of an Ennuyee* and *Visits and Sketches at Home and Abroad* were important ones for Jameson. She returned from Italy to marry Robert Jameson, but almost immediately afterward left without him to stay for several years in Germany. There she virtually memorized the collections in the Munich, Nuremburg, and Dresden galleries and there the confidence she had cultivated as an interpreter of Italian and German art was matched by a growing concern that women and their achievements be publicly recognized. For Jameson this concern took overt shape in the form of two books, *Memoirs of Celebrated Female Sovereigns* (1831) and *Characteristics of Women, Moral, Poetical, and Historical* (1832). Addressed specifically to a female audience, these works focused on extraordinary women (both real and fictional) who Jameson believed had effected great change in the world around them. In her own life, female friendship began to become increasingly significant. Most influential was Ottilie von Goethe, who nearly every afternoon assembled a group of literary women together for talk. Here Jameson met and befriended the sisters Johanna and Adele Schopenhauer, the archaeologist Sybille Mertens, and the painter Julie von Egloffstein, all successful women with highly visible public roles. Through participation in these gatherings she found support, solidarity, and role models. She began to correspond regularly with Lady Byron and Elizabeth Barrett Browning, who also attended the gatherings. The frequent and extended visits to Germany to stay with Ottilie von Goethe were also to provide her with a wealth of material for the essays in *Visits and Sketches at Home and Abroad*.[25]

Although its title suggests a random collection of travel pieces, most of the essays included in *Visits and Sketches at Home and Abroad* focus exclusively on the art work Jameson encountered abroad. It marks her adoption of what Holcomb calls an "ambassadorial role for women,"[26] a role she defined as growing out of her appreciation for the art of other cultures and periods. Jameson refers to her successful acclimation into a foreign culture by writing in *Visits and Sketches*, "I begin at length to feel my way among the pictures here" (130). She catalogues German artists, compares German and English art, discusses the revival of fresco painting, and describes the frescoes in the Royal Chapel. Most evident throughout the work is the impact that she felt the works of the Flemish Masters to have had on her development as an art critic and historian. In her essay on the "Munich Gallery," she wrote:

> My devoted worship to the Italian school of art rendered me long—I will not say *blind*—to the merits of the Flemish painters—for that were to be "sans eyes, sans taste, sans everything!" but in truth without that full feeling of their power which I have since acquired. (131)

Whereas she had once "worshipped" at the altar of Italian art, Jameson came to see herself less as a convert than as a critic. Although she praised Rubens's "St. Theresa Kneeling before Christ," she found his representation of "The Slaughter of the Innocents" reprehensible: "It has absolutely polluted my imagination. Surely this is not the vocation of high art" (134). The ability to discriminate became to her the mark of the professional, what separated the critic from the connoisseur. She would later explain in her *Companion to the Most Celebrated Private Galleries of Art in and Near London:*

> There is an immeasurable difference between the mere liking for pretty pictures, the love of novelty and variety, and the feeling and comprehension of the fine arts, their true aim and high significance; still, the *capacity* to discriminate as well as to feel is given to many, and I would raise such from love up to knowledge.[27]

To interpret art professionally, she argued, one must aspire to more than a sympathetic response.

As Jameson grew increasingly confident in her own proficiency, she came also to measure the proficiency of those around her. "I see the uneducated eye is caught by subjects in which the individual mind sympathizes, and the educated taste seeks abstract excellence," she wrote after observing other people at the Munich Gallery (133). That Jameson clearly positioned herself with the "educated" is evident not only in her own comments but also in those of others. After having been guided through Rome by Jameson, Nathaniel Hawthorne reportedly wrote: "It was impossible not to perceive that she gave her companion no credit for knowing one single simplest thing about art."[28]

Although Jameson cultivated a sense of assuredness in her own professional prowess, it would do her a disservice to suggest as Hawthorne did that she assumed more judgement than she had. In many of the essays of *Visits and Sketches at Home and Abroad* Jameson sought explicitly to recognize their subjective bias. More important, she strove throughout this and much of her later work to argue that her perspective was unique because she was a woman. "I can see only with a woman's eyes, and think and feel as I believe every woman *must*, whatever be her love for the arts," she wrote in *Visits and Sketches*. Moreover, she believed that her womanhood made her peculiarly sensitive to the subject matter of art. After decrying the "endless multiplication" of "revolting and sanguinary images" encountered in the art work from Milan to Naples, she wrote:

> I do not know how *men* think and feel, though I believe many a man, who with every other feeling absorbed in overpowering interest, could

look unshrinking upon a real scenery of cruelty and blood, would shrink away disgusted and sickened from the cold, obtrusive, *painted* representation of the same object; for the truth of this I appeal to men. (247)

Jameson came increasingly to believe that the perspective she offered as a woman art historian was unique—that the sympathetic heart "intrinsic" to woman's nature enabled her to interpret art in a way not accessible to male critics. In an essay on "Female Criticism," she reinterprets Goethe's claim that women look only for devotion and love in works of art:

That female critics look for something in a production of art beyond the mere handiwork, and that "our sympathetic veneration for a creation of human intellect," is often dependent on our moral associations is not a reproach to us. Nor, if I may presume to say so, does it lessen the value of our criticism, when it can be referred to in principles. Women have a sort of unconscious logic in these matters.[29]

Jameson's sense of woman's unique and "natural" capacity to interpret art influenced much of her choice of subject matter as critic and historian.

Artistic renderings of the virgin and child was one subject she felt uniquely qualified to deal with.[30] It was "a subject which comes home to our own bosoms and dearest feelings," she observed in *Visits and Sketches* (248). After having itemized "maternal tenderness," "virgin meekness," and "childish innocence" as themes of which she never tired, Jameson embarked on a comparative analysis of various attempts to represent these high ideas. Both Raphael and Correggio fare well in her estimation, principally because both impart what she calls "devotional feeling." Titian's virgins, on the other hand, seem to her "far too like his Venuses and his mistresses" (251). Rubens finishes nearly last on Jameson's list: "Rubens painted Virgins— would he had let them alone! fat, comfortable farmers' wives, nursing their chubby children" (253). In other work Jameson objects to anything bordering on the anthropomorphic, a tendency that underscores her concern to keep art in a realm above the everyday. The casual yet authoritative tone of Jameson's remarks is also typical. She presents them as haphazard reflections on all that she has seen in her travels and ends her ruminations on the virgin and child theme by writing in *Visits and Sketches*, "I might pursue this subject further, but my memory fails, my head aches, and my pen is tired for to-night" (254). With *Visits and Sketches*, then, Jameson experimented with a new public persona, one markedly less reluctant and hesitant than that of the "ennuyee."

Encouraged by the success of *Visits and Sketches at Home and Abroad,* Jameson took a chance and moved to join her husband in a remote area of Canada. After a brief stay together, she left his home and traveled through the countryside on her own, an experience that proved to be a psychological turning point. Afterward Jameson wrote to her mother:

> I am just returned from the wildest and most extraordinary tour you can imagine, and am moreover the first Englishwoman—the first European female who ever accomplished this journey. I have had such adventures and seen such strange things as never yet were rehearsed in prose or verse, and . . . thinking it a shame to keep these wonders only to make my hair stand on end, I am going to make a book and print it forthwith.[31]

The kind of woman Jameson projects in comments such as these stands in sharp contrast to the languid woman who stood at the center of *Diary of an Ennuyee.* One can sense in her spirited comments the enthusiasm for woman's potential that she had encountered in Germany and a greater sense of her own ability to live independently. Shortly after writing this letter to her mother, she left her husband for good. From this point onward she would unabashedly embrace an independence won through her own work and travel.

Jameson's most active years as a feminist followed the experience in Canada. In 1846 she published the pamphlet *On the Relative Position of Mothers and Governesses.* She also protested the conditions of women's social existence in an article published in *The Athenaeum,* "Report of the Commissioners on the Employment of Children, &c: Condition of the Women and the Female Children." This work offers a striking contrast to her scholarship in art history and criticism. Perhaps because her concern was with everyday conditions of working women, Jameson adopts a male voice in the article, which exposes the brutal conditions in which London milliners worked.[32] That she chose to position her authority as male suggests an assumption on her part that doing so would ensure that her argument be read as rational—not as an overly emotional woman's response. It also suggests that while she felt it legitimate to write as a woman art historian, her authority as a social critic was still uncertain.

An important dimension of Jameson's social critique involved a look at the work opportunities apportioned to women of particular classes. She noted in an *Athenaeum* article that while two-thirds of lower middle-class women worked, their choices of employment were strikingly more limited than those of men.[33] Only a few of these women could make a career in literature or art successful, she argued.

The overwhelming majority were forced to become governesses or milliners.[34] Exposing the unfair impact of a woman's class on her chances for professional satisfaction was an explicit objective of Jameson's social criticism.

Given Jameson's social awareness, it is surprising that class issues figure relatively indirectly in her work as an art historian. During the time that she was writing some of her most engaging and powerful social criticism, she was also redirecting her work as an art historian. But the two strands of her career as a professional remained separate from one another for much of the time. She wrote a lengthy introduction to G. F. Waagen's study of Peter Paul Rubens in 1840 and in the same year began what was to be one of her largest projects—a guide to the public galleries of art in London. At the same time she began work on a related project that would culminate in *The Poetry of Sacred and Legendary Art* (1848). Rather than guide her readers through specific collections, it aimed to provide them with the tools to understand iconography.

Nonetheless, Jameson was able to unite her social goals with her art historical interests in some discernible ways. Between 1843 and 1845 she published in forty-five installments a series of "Essays on the Lives of Remarkable Painters" for *The Penny Magazine,* an affiliate of the Society for the Diffusion of Useful Knowledge. This work represented itself as fundamentally educational and appealed to a body of readers largely unfamiliar with the tools of the art-historical trade. That Jameson's work was written for a less educated body of readers illustrates her concern for the very class that seemed to be left out of the high art enterprise, and her views on this matter position her in opposition to those of Elizabeth Eastlake. Her role as proponent of art-for-the-masses took other forms as well. She published her views on "primitive" art in *The Penny Magazine,* whose editor, Charles Knight, later claimed that her contributions were evidence of the magazine's work to educate the masses.

It was as a guidebook writer and popularizer that Jameson was able to assimilate the sense of her self that she had cultivated abroad with her sense of who she should be at home. *A Handbook to the Public Galleries of Art in and Near London* (1842) and its sequel, *Companion to the Most Celebrated Private Galleries of Art in London* (1844), were both addressed to the beginner. Explaining that she wanted to produce a book both "portable and pleasant in the hand," she asks in her preface to the handbook that "nothing be expected from it" except as "a compendious register of the works of art existing in our public and private galleries."[35] The primary appeal of the reference work was that it would be "useful." Jameson came increasingly to believe that women had to justify their professional work in terms of utility for it to be accepted, a belief similar to those held by other intellectual Victorian women, most notably Harriet Martineau. Another part of its appeal was that it demanded a deliberate exclusion of personal bias. She explained:

> It was necessary to repress the inclination for critical gossip—to coil up the thread of my discourse now and then, and leave the reader to unravel it in his own fancy; for if in a diary, or a book of travels, it be very pretty and pleasant to launch out into discussions, and enlarge on individual impressions and predilection, it appeared to me that everything of the kind was *here* out of place, and mere gratuitous impertinence.[36]

Jameson felt that she had mapped out a new direction for herself. Diaries and travel books were of course two areas in which she had already published; her reference to their necessarily subjective bias as "pretty and pleasant" suggests that she believed them to be considered too feminine to be read as serious scholarship. She seems to have felt the need to distinguish herself in a more directed, ostensibly rational mode.

The handbook to collections offered the perfect solution. Not only did its comprehensiveness allow her ample room to demonstrate breadth of experience, but also it afforded many an opportunity to instruct. She prefaces the whole work with introductory material designed to give "popular and concise explanations of the terms of art, and many things relative to painting and pictures."[37] She distinguishes between historical painting, portrait painting, landscape, genre, and still life and provides a glossary of such terms as *manner, chiaroscuro, impasto,* and *handling.* She also includes "Thoughts on Painting, Pictures, and Painters, from various Authors," a collection of extracts in which she includes her own observations (and witticisms) along with those of Coleridge, Hazlitt, Jonathan Richardson, and Sir Joshua Reynolds. In many ways, her work was an exercise in authority.

In the central portions of the handbook, Jameson depicts herself as an experienced critic and tour guide. She takes her readers with her on a walk through the galleries, stopping to elaborate at some length on the more noteworthy paintings. Here Jameson is by no means the undiscriminating enthusiast she presented in the beginning of *Diary of an Ennuyee.* Instead, she comes across as crusty and on occasion garrulous—not in the least reluctant to attack even the most revered works of the masters. On Reynolds's "The Holy Family," she writes: "This picture is pleasing as a scene of domestic life, but utterly deficient in the elevated historic feeling which ought to belong to the sacredness of the subject; call it an aged peasant and his family, and it may pass."[38] And on Caravaggio's "Christ and his Disciples at Emmaus" she writes:

> The incident is treated here with great dramatic power, great energy of execution and depth of tone, but the conception is vulgar. The eatables are painted with a sort of obtrusive reality, which, while it evinces the skill of the artist, displays also his bad taste. What more can be said of a picture in which a roast chicken disputes our attention with the head of the Saviour?[39]

The verse conveyed in both passages represents well the tone of Jameson's handbook as a whole. Although she offers it up as an objective compendium, it was as much an opportunity to project her self as urbane authority. In this sense she sought implicitly to rival some of her own culture's most commanding representatives of urbane authority, all of them male.

It is no coincidence that at the same time she was working on these handbooks she was attacking Dr. Johnson in an essay titled "On the Female Character" and Goethe in an essay titled "Goethe's Ideas on the Position of Women."[40] In her essay on Goethe, Jameson attacks his physician's claim that women turn to writing because they are disappointed in love. In this piece one senses how much her feminism was related to her work as an art historian. She laments the "false position" her society imposes on women and describes the correlative "void of existence" felt by women. Curiously, Jameson uses her claim that society is becoming increasingly artificial to create a professional role for women: "We have gone away from nature, and we must—if we can, substitute another nature. Art, literature, and science, remain to us."[41] Representing work in art scholarship as "another nature" enables Jameson to posit it as legitimate woman's work. She then validates this claim by arguing its religious basis:

> Religion . . . teaches us another lesson, that only in utility, such as is left to us, only in the assiduous employment of such faculties as we are permitted to exercise, can we find health and peace, and compensation for the wasted or repressed impulses and energies more proper to our sex—more natural—perhaps more pleasing to God; but trusting in his mercy, and using the means he has given, we do the best we can for ourselves and for our sisterhood.[42]

In this important comment, Jameson reveals how much she believes and accommodates the ideology that represents marriage and motherhood as "natural" parts of womanhood. But she also argues that professional work is a "God-given" means of compensating for unused maternal energy. In a formal "statement of belief" Jameson wrote, "By maternity I do not mean the actual state of motherhood, which is not necessary nor universal, but the maternal organization common to all women."[43] By using utility as a primary standard for women, Jameson substantially widened the boundaries of what could be considered appropriate, proper, and within a woman's sphere, although her beliefs clearly accommodated traditional patriarchal divisions of work by according to women "auxiliary" kinds of tasks, much along the lines of those described by Deirdre David in *Intellectual Women and Victorian Patriarchy*. She implies, further, that doing useful work is both personally beneficial and beneficial to women as a group. The "sisterhood" Jameson envisions is one based on a conception of gender and work as mutually constitutive.

The feminist argument proposed by Jameson in her essay on "Goethe's Ideas on the Position of Women" only indirectly affects interpretation of her work as an art historian. There overt feminist commentary is for the most part absent, except insofar as one assumes that the work is useful and hence represents potentially "proper" work for a single woman. Other kinds of social criticism emerge in her work as an art historian and critic as well. In her discussion of the National Gallery, for instance, she argues that more government support should be given to the arts:

> The public spirit of England, so magnificently displayed in the building of hospitals and bridges, and fighting, at her own cost, the battles of all Europe, has not till lately been directed to the fine arts: not till lately has a feeling been awakened in the public mind, that, in the endeavor to humanise and educate the heart of a nation for all noble and all gentle purposes, art, if not the most important, is no despicable means toward that great end.[44]

It was with comments like these that Jameson ingratiated herself to the Eastlake set, those more directly responsible for the national art collection. That Jameson wanted her work to be recognized by these people is evident in other ways. She dedicated her *Companion to the Private Galleries* to Sir Robert Peel, then Prime Minister. By publicly appealing to art as a force with which to "humanise and educate," Jameson aligns herself with culturally elite arbiters of national taste. Such people could take a "noblesse oblige" attitude toward the national art collection, which functioned as a means to display their moral obligation and charitable conduct toward the public-at-large.

Jameson seems to have recognized that becoming a vocal part of the support for the national art collection could help secure her a place within the professional establishment.

Anna Jameson's bid to establish a lasting public role for herself in the arts in England was so successful that Lady Eastlake continued to champion her work long after Jameson died. Jameson's willingness to take on the work of a "popularizer" also pleased intellectual women like Harriet Martineau. In one of her *Biographical Sketches*, "Mrs. Jameson," Martineau wrote:

> Her early readiness to assume the function of Art-critic gave way in time . . . to the more fitting pretention of making Handbooks of Art Collections, and some valuable keys to Art-types, supplied in an historical form. . . . She studied long, and familiarized herself with so extensive a range of Art, that her metaphysical tendencies were to a considerable extent corrected, and she popularized a great deal of knowledge which would not otherwise have been brought within reach of a very large class of readers of her later works.[45]

Praising Jameson's handbooks and guides as "works of real utility," Martineau's comments reveal much of her own predisposition to endorse the ancillary status of the intellectual woman living in a patriarchal society.[46] But there is ample evidence in Jameson's own work to suggest that she, too, accommodated, if not openly endorsed, the ideologies that represented women's work as auxilliary. In her preface to *Sacred and Legendary Art*, she claimed, "It has been written for those who are, like myself, unlearned."[47] A year later she published in *The Art Journal* a short piece entitled "Some Thoughts on Art Addressed to the Uninitiated." Much of the work published in the last decade of her life continued to aim to popularize or familiarize rather than to originate. In 1854 she published another handbook, this one to the sculpture in the Crystal Palace. Her last work, *The History of Our Lord as Exemplified in Works of Art* was like *Sacred and Legendary Art* conceived as a "primer" designed to introduce to an unlearned audience the general characteristics of a certain genre of art.

In authorizing her work as "useful," Jameson made a very powerful statement about her identity. As she herself had written, "only in utility" was a "sisterhood" of working women possible. For Anna Jameson, working as an art historian and critic was also a concrete way of translating her experience abroad into professional identity. Indeed, it was in her ability to bridge the gap between her identities at home and abroad that she most influenced other women writers. In his study of the mid-Victorian artistic community, *Consort of Taste:*

1830–1870, John Steegman writes that Jameson's *Visits and Sketches* "was beyond doubt one of Elizabeth Eastlake's main early sources of inspiration, and must have impelled her to her own first studies of German art published in the *Quarterly*."[48] Indeed, Jameson continued to inspire Eastlake long after this point. Immediately after she heard Jameson had died, Eastlake wrote: "I shall miss her sorely. She was ever kind to me—excellent in judgment and advice, a very *strong* woman, though never approaching the man—profound and conscientious in all she did, and devoted to such good works as the world knew nothing of" (*Journals and Correspondence*, II, 137).

With comments like these, Eastlake protected Jameson by praising her professional reputation (as worker) without compromising her character (as woman). Her comments suggest something of how much the two seemingly contradictory ideologies worked together in mutually constitutive ways to construct identity. And as a professional woman herself, Eastlake recognized in her friend's career some of the same difficulties she had in very different ways struggled to overcome.

Elizabeth Rigby Eastlake

Eastlake's career took hold on 14 February 1843 when she received a letter from John Lockhart, the editor of the *Quarterly Review*, praising her submission to his magazine and encouraging her to continue writing for him. Lockhart had received from her a manuscript review of an evangelical novel by Mrs. Sherwood. The review criticizes the novel on several grounds and ends by lamenting the lady author's excessive display of "the extent of her travels and the range of her learning."[49] The comment proved to be ironic, given the extent of travel and range of learning that Elizabeth Rigby later enjoyed (and displayed) as Lady Eastlake. Nevertheless, her opinions and style evidently pleased Lockhart, who wrote:

> You seem to have it in your power to render the 'Quarterly Review' an instrument of great improvement among classes of readers that have hitherto probably given no attention to its contents. You are the only lady, except Mrs. Somerville, who once gave us a short scientific article; and I had long felt and regretted the want of that knowledge of women and their concerns which men can never attain, for the handling of numberless questions most interesting and most important to society. (*Journals and Correspondence* I, 51)

Rigby's admittance into the ranks of *Quarterly Review* "regulars" was no small accomplishment. The *Quarterly Review* and the *Edinburgh Review* were the early Victorian period's most prominent "voices of culture" and were designed both to articulate and to shape public opinion. The *Quarterly Review* in particular had enormous influence in shaping public attitudes toward literature, art, and political economy. With John Lockhart's encouragement, Elizabeth Rigby continued to write regularly for the *Quarterly Review* for the remainder of her life, and her articles appeared alongside those of Francis Palgrave, J. W. Croker, H. H. Milman, and William Gladstone.

Lockhart's early words of encouragement are interesting from several standpoints. In one sense, he appeals to Rigby's ostensible fund of womanly knowledge and concerns and suggests that he values her contributions because the journal had hitherto lacked appeal to female readers. Yet as a contributor to a periodical with a firmly established policy of authorial anonymity, she would have been expected to invoke the magisterial "We" in all of her commentary. Her authority, in this sense, was a function not of her womanhood and still less of her identity as an individual, but rather of her ability to espouse the views of the ruling class. A related dimension of Lockhart's appeal to Rigby, then, is his suggestion that the value of her work would derive from its didactic effect—not only its ability to educate but also to improve an unspecified class of readers. The readership he had in mind certainly included women, but it also probably included the upwardly mobile middle- and lower-middle classes who Lockhart believed were within reach of the *Quarterly Review* elite.[50]

Given these assumptions of the *Quarterly Review*, it is instructive to consider the kinds of contributions that Elizabeth Rigby made as one of its first regular female writers. Her initial selection as a potential contributor came on the heels (and probably as a consequence of) her success as a travel writer. After an extended visit with a married sister, she published the letters she had written to her mother. *A Residence on the Shores of the Baltic; Described in a Series of Letters* (1841) was tremendously popular, a second edition being published just months after the first. (Rigby's first travel-related piece was actually an article on Goethe for the *Foreign Quarterly Review* in 1835, written after taking a trip to Germany with her father). Although the book was published anonymously, the influential publisher John Murray openly voiced his approval of her literary talent and introduced her to Lockhart.

In the early years of writing for the *Quarterly Review*, Rigby was asked to contribute essays on topics for which her travels—and womanhood—qualified her. She initiated her identity as an art historian and critic with the limited experience of German art and architecture that several trips to Heidelberg had given her. But nearly all of her essays are also explicitly directed to topics within the purview of a woman writer. Among her early contributions were "Biographies of German Ladies," "Lady Travellers," "The Cologne Cathedral," and the now infamous review of *Jane Eyre* and *Vanity Fair*.

Although many of these early essays had topics that Lockhart deemed suitable for a woman critic, Rigby seems to have felt that her gender was something to overcome. While working on her review of women's travel writing, for example, she wrote in her journal: "To keep down the redundancy of mere words, and keep up the succession of real thought is a task beyond the usual strength of women" (*Journals and Correspondence* I, 156). Later during the same year she complained, "I am sure there is no more difficult writing than for the 'Quarterly'" (*Journals and Correspondence* I, 169), a comment that may allude to her sense that the authoritative voice of the *Quarterly* was male. Despite her hesitation, the essays Rigby wrote during these early years garnered widespread approval, and although they did not mark her as an authority in any specific area of expertise, they helped her accrue what Bourdieu would call her "symbolic capital."

She did not become an accepted authority as an art critic until she married Charles Eastlake, who as an artist and art scholar had close ties to London's established art institutions. Eastlake probably read her early work in the *Quarterly*, and she in turn probably met him in one of her frequent visits to art exhibitions, which helped her begin to assimilate her views on contemporary art. In May of 1846 she wrote: "To the Exhibition. A mighty world: some painters all self, but that self splendid, as with Landseer and Ettly. Others have crucified the flesh with the lusts thereof, and have merged themselves in a higher life. Eastlake all that natural man can do, Turner living by the grace of Art" (*Journals and Correspondence* I, 211–12).

Her marriage to Eastlake allowed her to inhabit this "mighty world." Soon after the marriage, he was elected President of the Royal Academy and in 1854 was appointed director of the National Gallery. A busy social calendar kept Elizabeth Eastlake in almost constant contact with others working in the arts. She helped her husband to fulfill his Royal Academy and National Gallery duties; she helped to build home museum collections and to increase public awareness of the service that such collections did for wider public interest.

More important, the marriage enabled her to continue to travel; she went abroad for extended periods for nearly every year of her married life. The Eastlakes made annual trips to Europe, typically stopping for weeks in Germany, France, Belgium, Holland, and

Spain, as well as Italy. Her husband's need to secure art for the home collection necessitated the rigorous schedule. "All the charms of travel were enhanced by a purpose, honourable and responsible," she wrote in her memoir of her husband (*Journals and Correspondence* II, 279).

That Eastlake was able to conceive of these trips as "tours of duty" is in part owing to her tendency to enjoy a country almost exclusively through its art, and her journal entries from abroad are remarkable in their near total exclusion of all other interest. In Spain she wondered, "What can induce people, who don't dote on pictures, to come to Spain?" (*Journals and Correspondence* II, 126). What little reference she makes to people encountered along the way indicates that she rarely interacted with others at all, and on those few occasions that she did it was with high society. She half-heartedly complains of being "taken to one palace after another" (*Journals and Correspondence* II, 61) and bemoans contact with the "lower orders" of foreign societies. When describing foreigners Eastlake is at her worst—her most snobby, her least sensitive. Italians she found to be uniformly deceitful: "They lie in Italy before they think" (*Journal and Correspondence* II, 13), and her critique of the Venetians was equally scathing: "The people in their indolence, their dirt, and their quickness would make excellent Irish" (*Journals and Correspondence* I, 293). Physical surroundings—the climate, the landscape, the countryside—were equally unappealing to her. After a jaunt into the countryside in the south of France, she wrote: "The scenery was all of this awful nature, and I was not sorry to be out of it" (*Journals and Correspondence* II, 56–57). Eastlake translated her discomfort into sweeping generalizations; Hanover was "a frightful place" (*Journals and Correspondence* II, 93), Rome "odious" (*Journals and Correspondence* II, 106), and Spain "a strange, barren, hungry country" (*Journals and Correspondence* II, 126).

Eastlake's uninformative and insular generalizations can be partially attributed to the single-mindedness with which she traveled. In her letters and diaries the features of foreign countries that characteristically interested the tourist were marginalized; she wanted only to render those aspects of a country that contributed to her *work*. One of her strategies was to see only that which seemed to have a artistic referent:

> We live in the past—the pictorial past—as we walk about Bruges, Ghent, and Antwerp. Here are the same houses and canals, the same stiff trees so true to life; for one's eye is so full of pictures, that originals and copies change places, and we feel trees and colours to be true in nature, because

they are identical with what is true in art. (*Journals and Correspondence* I, 281)

Scenes in which Eastlake tours the streets are relatively rare, however. The majority of her time was instead spent indoors, taking detailed notes and sketches of museum collections and studying individual pieces for hours or even days, always with the goal of broadening her base of knowledge and sometimes with the ulterior motive of acquiring something for England's national collection.

References to time spent indoors studying art reveal Eastlake at her most comfortable. In a letter written to her friend Henry Austin Layard from Venice she reported: "I have been studying, always with increasing interest—learning to appreciate the great Assunta better" (*Journals and Correspondence* II, 245). And from Arles, France, she breathlessly wrote "On to the Museum, in which all the richest sculptured sarcophagi have been placed. . . . The celebrated Venus of Arles was found there. This was most interesting to me, who am trying to clear up the history and dates of the Catacombs" (*Journals and Correspondence* I, 199).

It was through Eastlake's museum visits that she developed the confidence not only to develop her own sense of art history but also to contradict the histories that had been constructed by others. In 1871, she spent a great deal of time at the Holbein Exhibit in Dresden to compare two Madonnas, one of which had been declared by several prominent critics to be an inferior copy. In another lengthy letter to Layard she proclaimed:

No one, without closer and longer and minuter inspection than was possible to a traveller, could thoroughly interpret the relation in which the two rivals stand to each other. But I did examine them with considerable care, and came to a very different solution from that which you report to be Morelli's. There is no question that the Darmstadt picture is the earlier, and in that sense, and in a genuine sense, the original; but there are circumstances evident in the Dresden one, which entirely remove it from the category of the copy. (*Journals and Correspondence* II, 221–22)

She goes on to substantiate her conclusion with considerable detail of personal observation and speculation on Morelli's possible motives for having come to his conclusion.

The broadened base of knowledge and confidence that Eastlake garnered through these and other museum visits abroad were put to good use at home, where she was actively involved with other professionals. She regularly attended lectures at the Royal Institute where she heard prominent critics such as Tyndall, Huxley, and Lubbock speak. She was also asked to write several essays for the *Quarterly Review* and *Edinburgh Review,* among them reviews of John Harford's work on Michelangelo and Ruskin's *Modern Painters.* These lengthy review-essays enabled Eastlake to more thoroughly develop her own theories of art and its relation to class.

Eastlake found in almost every essay—no matter what the topic— an opportunity to position her opinions in relation to issues of class. Her review of Harford's biography of Michelangelo, for instance, makes much of the author's "station."[51] A lawyer by trade, Harford and his work seemed to Eastlake "no slight testimony to the enlightened attention now devoted to the subject of art by the class most at liberty to choose their own studies and recreations" (436). "Mr Harford," she continues, "expresses not only his own feelings, but that of an important and highly cultivated class" (437). Although she disagrees with some of his focus, she concludes: "Whatever reason, indeed, leads the educated and the excellent to take an interest in art is a good reason, though it may not be one of sound philosophy" (438).

One senses that Eastlake protests too much in favor (or defense) of Harford's education and excellency. His study had taken note of the extent to which Michelangelo's work had been commissioned, and it was this that perturbed Eastlake. What was at issue for her was the necessity of preserving art and the study of art from contact with a working class, and by featuring the artist's economic motives Harford had come dangerously close to tainting his subject. She preferred to see the artist as occupying a "godlike vocation" and his art, by implication, as above contract. "We must descend to a low class of society both as regards art and manners to find those would either give or take a commission in this spirit," she wrote (443).

Eastlake's review of Ruskin's *Modern Painters* reveals a similar way of thinking. She critiques his work on several levels, contending, for instance, that his language is too imprecise: "It is no easy task to ascertain what he really means by 'thought,' 'ideas,' 'subject of intellect,' &c., as applied to painting."[52] She is also bothered by his blatant disregard for already valued art. "None (except Mr. Ruskin) can question the beauty of the Sistine Chapel" (393), she notes. But the thrust of her review focuses on his problematic moral aesthetic: "We boldly meet the accusation of the religious and moral shortcomings of landscape art, or any art, by the utter denial and denunciation not of those shortcomings, which we gladly confess, but of those doctrines which so mischievously misrepresent the real mission of art" (404). All of her criticism seeks ultimately to expose Ruskin's "false reasoning," which to her is not only intentional but also evidenced by the sheer bulk of his work: "Only on the wrong road could so much have been said at all" (432). And it is in her emphasis on truth and falsehood that Eastlake validates her critique in terms of class. His falsehood is dangerous, she implies, because it is effective. What in the end bothers her most about Ruskin is his evident persuasion of "a large class of the educated English public" (384), an unspecified group of followers who she later describes as "this common herd whom his misleads" (401).

Eastlake's concern to protect art as the property of a select group surfaces in other ways as well. In 1857 she wrote an influential essay on photography in which she charts its progress as an art form.[53] One consequence of the advancement of photography was that its products—photographs—were increasingly accessible to the general public: "Who can number the legion of petty dabblers, who display their trays of specimens along the great thoroughfares in London, executing for our lowest servants, for one shilling, that which no money could have commanded for the Rothschild bride of twenty years ago?" (443). To her mind, photographers who peddled their wares to servants were no better than "petty dabblers." Evidently she felt threatened by the idea that art could be overtaken by people ill-equipped to appreciate it but able to afford it.

That Eastlake should choose to foreground class as an ideological truth in much of her work is hardly surprising, given the social, intellectual, and financial support that she had secured through her marriage. Such a strategy ultimately enabled her to diminish at least some of the more restrictive aspects of being a woman writer. By making class the ultimate determinant of authority, she went some way toward easing the ideological tension between conceptions of the proper lady and the woman writer.

That she was sensitive of this tension is evident in many of her journal entries and personal letters. When she was angry at her government's handling of the Lord Cavendish murder, she wrote to a male friend, "You see I am chafing under the trammels of my sex, and should like for once to possess your prerogative of redressing injuries" (*Journals and Correspondence* II, 276). Although Eastlake tended to publicly espouse conservative opinions on women's issues, her reasoning was by no means uncomplicated. In a *Quarterly Review* essay devoted to women and education, she not only argued forcefully that places for unmarried women must be found within English society, but also claimed that education for women be subordinate to duty.[54] Despite this "liberal" thinking, she ends the essay with the following remark:

We trust that the ladies will forgive us if, in consideration of our having, as we hope, treated the question of the education of women with impartiality and courtesy, we deliver our souls of a slight parting thrust, to the effect that, while the example set by the sex they have undervalued will do some men much good, it will also do some women no harm to realize more gratefully the toil incurred by most fathers and husbands to secure them homes of softness and ease.[55]

Eastlake clearly adopts a male point of view here, not only in the authorial "We" who addresses "the ladies," but also in her condescending "parting thrust" directed to women presumably relaxing in their "homes of softness and east." At this point, Eastlake had reached a very comfortable position in her own career as art historian and social critic; her work was well known and influential. Despite the solidity of her professional status, she still seemed to believe that her public voice was rendered more authoritative if masked as male.

Elizabeth Eastlake was evidently on some occasions troubled by and on other occasions comfortable with the marginalized position that women occupied in her society. Despite all of the personal freedoms that her privileged class position conferred on her, she struggled with a public identity that was complicated—perhaps inevitably—by the contradictory status of the woman writer. That these contradictions helped to create her public identity can be felt in a reminiscence of Eastlake written by her friend Mrs. Boyle shortly after she died: "Her intellect, her learning, never crushed—they did but stimulate. That intellect, which was like a man's for breadth and capacity, seemed to adapt itself in some wonderful way to all who came within its influence" (*Journals and Correspondence* II, 311). Although Boyle praises Eastlake's intellectual achievements, she legitimizes them in much the same way that Eastlake had legitimized Jameson after her death. She points to the capacity to think like a man, but suggests that as a woman, Eastlake's impact derived from her "influence," that strangely unempowered Victorian concept applied almost exclusively to women.

In Boyle's eulogy, Eastlake got the kind of public recognition that she had imagined and desired. As a young woman beginning her career she lamented: "How little the female writers of the present day seem aware of their great responsibility! Eager to show what they do like men, they disregard the fact that they are capable of much more as women" (*Journals and Correspondence* I, 39). Her comments are ironic, coming as they do from a woman who just a few years later would willingly—even eagerly—assume the male voice of the *Quarterly Review*. Although seemingly confident, her comments reveal also a subtle fear of participation in the male world of public activity and a corresponding retreat to the private apolitical world of influence where the middle-class Victorian woman was allegedly more capable, more powerful. Eastlake of course contradicted herself over and over again, as the ostensibly male-authored passages already cited attest. Such contradictions also evidence what Mary Poovey called "ideological work" in its unevenly developing process. One typically thinks of ideology as working to shape a person's belief according to socially constructed standards. Jameson and Eastlake were both conscious of the ideologies that informed their identities and exercised a degree of control over them, and they responded in different ways in their careers as art historians, drawing from each what seemed to make the most sense.

Jameson and Eastlake were of course not the only women to work as art historians and critics during the period. They were by far the most influential, however, and in this sense their work and lives are representative of the larger tradition that would later include Julia Ady, Vernon Lee, Emilia Dilke, and Lucy Baxter. Tastes in art and artists inevitably changed as the period progressed, as did the subject matter and methods of art historical scholarship. Nonetheless, these women were confronted with many of the same complicated career choices as had faced Jameson and Eastlake. They, too, were affected by what they thought they should *do* as professionals and these beliefs were in turn shaped profoundly by what they thought they should *be* as women. "Why should my days be all duty and those of others all demand?," asked Emilia Pattison after having begun her career as a scholar of French art.[56] Most of these women developed their own strategies to solve—or at least respond to—the dilemma implicit in Pattison's lament. After her husband died, Pattison found intellectual support for her work and social status in her marriage to Sir Charles Dilke. Julia Ady absorbed herself in work and in motherhood, saving the money she made from her historical biographies to pay for her daughter's education. Writing that "no one reads a woman's writing on art, history, or aesthetics with anything but unmitigated contempt," Vernon Lee took another route altogether toward resolving the woman writer "problem," choosing to publish under a male pen name.[57]

Although this second generation of art historians built on the tradition established by Jameson and Eastlake, they—like their predecessors—traveled abroad to find their own particular niche. Travel authorized their public, professional identities in much the same way as it had for Anna Jameson and Elizabeth Eastlake. It did not, however, ultimately empower any of them as women. If Jameson found the inspiration for her feminism in a circle of intellectual women abroad, she found her subject matter at home, in the conditions of the homebound governess. Eastlake's sense of professional identity was nurtured through marriage and the social circle into which her marriage had introduced her. Later in the century Julia Ady satisfied her feminist inclinations by joining the Women Writer's Club in London and maintaining close friendships with other intellectual women, including Mary Augusta Ward, Mary Kingsley, Alice Meynell, and Vernon Lee. Lee's series of relationships with other women—Mary Robinson, Annie Meyer, and Clementina "Kit" Anstruther-Thomson—were surely both professional and personally empowering. All of these women found opportunity—a place to root their professional identities—at home in England. Although travel was a necessary part of their professional careers, much of the *making* of the woman art historian happened, in the end, in England—in the museums, the galleries, the libraries, and homes in which these women lived, wrote, and interacted.

4

Fair Amazons Abroad: The Social
Construction of the Victorian Adventuress

I$_N$ 1880, Sir Algernon Borthwick, editor of the *Morning Post*, made Lady Florence Dixie his newspaper's war correspondent and assigned her to cover the war in South Africa. The editors of the society paper *London Figaro*—offended at the news—smugly wrote in retaliation, "We think that our feminine patricians should not lightly follow the example of the fair Amazon who will soon be in the Transvaal.[1] By identifying the outward-bound "fair Amazon" both in opposition and as a threat to the homebound "feminine patrician," these editors implicitly call attention to the susceptibility of the Victorian conception of woman to other ideological constructions. Although the editors of the *London Figaro* foreground gender in their paternalistic condemnation of the woman traveler, they implicate class and race as factors affecting their judgment as well. The woman who travels is "fair" both by virtue of her gender and as opposed to the "dark" inhabitants she is likely to encounter in another culture. By entering this other culture she positions herself against the patrician class of whom she is a member and to whom she is an affront.

Although Florence Dixie was at the center of the *Morning Post/ London Figaro* controversy, it could have been any number of Victorian women whose activities in the wider world engendered widespread discussion and debate. As Mary Poovey demonstrates in *Uneven Developments: The Ideological Work of Gender in Mid-Victorian England*, representations of women throughout the period functioned as the sites at which middle-class ideologies of sex, race, class, and national identity were constructed and contested. During the Victorian period the idea of a woman traveler was particularly troublesome because the qualities that identified her as an adventurer seemed also to compromise those ostensibly "natural" qualities that made her a woman.

The celebrated Victorian travelers Isabella Bird Bishop, Florence Dixie, Amelia Edwards, Constance Gordon Cumming, and Mary

Kingsley all traveled to exotic places—places removed or distanced from what the English public considered "civilized" and appropriate spheres for woman's work—and wrote to capitalize on reputations as adventure-seekers. These women comprise only a small portion of Victorian women explorers. Unlike many of these women, though, they were both travelers and travel writers: they used their travel experiences to write and to garner public recognition for their findings. Most published more than one account of their experiences abroad and some came home to active careers on public lecture circuits. A further distinguishing feature of this group is that they thought of themselves primarily as travelers; none intended to live permanently abroad and none—with the exception of Isabella Bird Bishop—used travel to missionary purpose.

Typically cast in the form of either letters written home or diaries kept while abroad, their works often assume the form of autobiography and by implication introduce the relationship of identity to the experience of travel. Their travel accounts were less studies of place (as one might expect travel guides to be and as the works of the tourists were) than studies of woman's position in the foreign place. In his study of travel books as literary phenomena, Paul Fussell writes: "A travel book, at its purest, is addressed to those who do not plan to follow the traveler at all, but who require the exotic or comic anomalies, wonders, and scandals of the literary form romance which their own place and time cannot entirely supply.[2] What their own place and time did supply to middle-class Victorian women was a model of personal development predicated on domesticated, feminized morality that, while indirectly helping to justify British economic expansion abroad, nonetheless positioned them firmly at home. The success with which the travel accounts of Victorian adventuresses were received in England suggests how much the readers at home desired the kind of unusual story they supplied.

Part of what constituted the identity of an adventuress was her association with terra incognita, places about which little was known and that had yet to be explored by Western Man. The 1883 study *Celebrated Women Travellers of the Nineteenth Century* by W. H. Davenport Adams is representative in that it applauds those female explorers who, he claimed, had "penetrate[d] into regions hitherto untrodden by civilized man and add[ed] new lands to the maps of the geographer.[3] Victorian adventuresses capitalized on such overstated representations of their activities. Among the most popular of Isabella Bird Bishop's travel accounts was *Unbeaten Tracks in Japan: An Account of Travels on Horseback in the Interior* (1880); Amelia Edwards related her experiences in the mountains of southeastern Tyrol in *Untrodden*

Peaks and Unfrequented Valleys (1873); and Florence Dixie subtitled her first travel account, *Across Patagonia* (1880), with "Descriptive of Six Months' Wanderings over Unexplored and Untrodden Ground." An adventuress typically went "into," "up," "beyond," or "across" these ostensibly unbeaten, unfrequented, unexplored, and untrodden places. Edwards' most successful travel account was *A Thousand Miles Up the Nile* (1889); Constance Gordon Cumming charted one of her journeys in *From the Hebrides to the Himalayas* (1876); and Bird Bishop recorded her travels through China in *The Yangtze Valley and Beyond* (1899). By highlighting her movement across great physical distances in the title of her account, an adventuress underscored her spatial and psychological separation from England.

Many women used the titles of their works to highlight social status as well. Isabella Bird launched her career as an adventuress with *A Lady's Life in the Rocky Mountains*, and Constance Gordon Cumming authored *A Lady's Cruise in a French Man-of-War*. Class position was not surprisingly a crucial factor in the ability to finance travel—especially for a single woman, which many of these women were. But women also wanted to highlight their gender in a captivating title because it helped to constitute her experiences abroad as unusual: Mary Seacole's *The Wonderful Adventures of Mrs. Seacole in Many Lands* (1857) and Lucy Broad's *A Woman's Wanderings the World Over* (1909) are just two of many such titles.

Victorian adventuresses frequently corroborated the implications of their titles early in their accounts, often using a preface to explain their reasons for choosing the remote place. Florence Dixie was lured to Patagonia because it was "outlandish and far away," a land of "vast wilds, virgin as yet to the foot of man."[4] Edwards chose as one her many destinations the Dolomites, a "district scarcely known even by name to any but scientific travellers."[5] And Bird Bishop found in the "grand beyond" of the Yangtze Valley a landscape "unprofaned by the foot of man."[6] Victorian women mythologized the places to which they ventured, preferring to see them not only as untrodden but also as repositories of the primitive. In the beginning of *At Home in Fiji* (1882), Gordon Cumming explained:

A cruise in the South Pacific has been one of the dreams of my life; and the idea of going actually to live for an indefinite period on isles where there are still a number of ferocious cannibals, has a savour of romance which you can imagine does not lack charm.[7]

Like many other adventuresses, she depicts her corner of the wider world as one of the last bastions of the primitive and suggests a fascination with its sinister qualities. Similarly, Kingsley described the west coast of Africa as being like a "belle dame sans merci" that drew her inexplicably and inextricably back (11).

Victorian adventuresses hence willingly chose as their destinations not only the least visited but also the presumably least civilized places, the places about which most new knowledge could be garnered. The "dark continent" of Africa was one such place in which Victorian women could represent their experience as adventure, but so also were parts of South America (where Florence Dixie traveled), the western states of America and Hawaii (where Isabella Bird Bishop traveled), the South Seas ("home" to Constance Gordon Cumming) and war zones such as the Crimea (where Mary Seacole worked). Curiously, though, most of these regions were throughout the century ceasing to be places of the unknown to the Victorians. During the century, Africa especially was transformed from a "dark continent," a mythical place about which few Victorians knew anything substantive, into a land central to the British imperial mission and lurking very large in the public sphere. Its "depths" were explored by popular heroes like Stanley, Livingstone, and Burton. Africa and other regions of the world associated with imperial interest were populated during the century by missionaries, soldiers, merchants, and explorers, and Victorian adventuresses were associated with this activity. That many of these women continued, despite the widespread activity in these regions, to represent them as if they had hitherto been "unknown" suggests the extent to which they wanted to marshall evidence of their own contributions to geographic knowledge.

Not surprisingly, Victorian adventuresses sought to establish public identities that were in some ways comparable to the military man and the intrepid explorer, two Victorian heroes familiar to the reading public. Jamaican-born Mary Seacole, while anxiously awaiting news of a descent on the Crimea, wrote that she "long[ed] to join the British army before Sebastopol."[8] Alone in the Sandwich Islands in 1876, Isabella Bird wrote: "I have just encamped under a lauhala tree, with my saddle inverted for a pillow, my horse tied by a long lariat to a guava bush, my gear, saddle-bags, and rations for two days laying about."[9] And Mary Kingsley claimed in *Travels in West Africa* that "stalking the wild West African idea . . . has a high sporting interest; for its pursuit is as beset with difficulty and danger as grizzly bear hunting" (430). In the same book, Kingsley had earlier warned fellow female travelers: "Always have your revolver ready loaded in good order, and have your hand on it when things are getting warm, and in addition have an exceedingly good bowie knife" (330). In varied voices each of these women aligned her identity to that of a male adventurer, someone whose boldness, fortitude, and enterprise make him capable of undertaking dangerous experiences.

Familiar figures of empire, the military hero and intrepid explorer whose identities appealed to women travelers were characteristically resolute, fearless, and strong-willed; their stories satisfied a public eager to see examples of English imperial superiority and control abroad. Travel accounts of adventure were related to empire in several ways.[10] Many of the countries about which women wrote were directly although in different ways associated with Victorian England's imperial interest—for example, India, northern Africa, and the Crimea. In a less concrete sense, though, adventure narratives that challenged central characters by positioning them in settings remote from the domestic served as what Martin Green in *Dreams of Adventure and Deeds of Empire* has called the "energizing myth" of empire.[11] In Green's sense, adventure is by definition anterior to the domestic and hence ideologically weighted; women, by "nature" domestic, are marginalized from the experience of adventure.

These ideas are articulated in several important Victorian works of fiction, among them George Eliot's *Daniel Deronda* (1876) and Joseph Conrad's *Heart of Darkness* (1902). In *Daniel Deronda*, the high-spirited heroine Gwendolen Harleth laments: "We women can't go in search of adventures—to find out the North-West Passage or the source of the Nile, or to hunt tigers in the East. We must stay where we grow, or where the gardeners like to transplant us. We are brought up to look as pretty as we can, and be dull without complaining."[12] Adventure, as Gwendolen suggests, is ideologically male and happens far away from English homes. *Daniel Deronda* is only part a novel of adventure though; a more typical adventure novel, that of and about male experience, is *Heart of Darkness*. In Conrad's novel, the narrator Marlow exclaims: "Girl! What? Did I mention a girl? Oh, she is out of it—completely. They—the women I mean—are out of it—should be out of it. We must help them to stay in that beautiful world of their own, lest ours gets worse."[13] Adventure narratives like Conrad's in some ways become a literary equivalent of imperial gender politics; women are marginalized from the central story under the auspices of protection. As *Heart of Darkness* in particular makes clear, middle class white women were "protected" from the economic and political aggression that underwrote imperial expansion. Instead, they relied on ostensibly inherent maternal instinct to administer morality at home, where they were, at most, indirect recipients of imperial exploits.[14]

Travel accounts of adventure written by Victorian women hence challenged assumptions about the female need for protection that were underwritten by their culture's binary organization of sexual difference. They served as a medium through which Victorian women could inscribe their lives into the aggressive side of their national identity. An adventuress most overtly countered the ideology that positioned her at home and defined her in need of protection by depicting herself in the places where she was ostensibly most in its need. In *Across Patagonia* Florence Dixie describes the "extremely exciting" ostrich hunt she participated in as follows:

> The class of fall above alluded to is the most frequent and by no means the least perilous part of the hunt and generally knocks the breath nigh clean out of one's body! I know that several which I got in this manner did so, and I am quite certain that had I not been riding on the cross saddle I should have been killed. (248–49)

"The moral of this," Dixie concludes, "is that all ladies who go to Patagonia should abjure the use of the side saddle!" (249). Like Dixie, Isabella Bird in *A Lady's Life in the Rocky Mountains* describes a series of encounters taxing her physical fortitude. Of her successful attempt to scale Long's Peak in Colorado, Isabella Bird writes:

> It took one hour to accomplish 500 feet, pausing for breath every minute or two. The only foothold was in narrow cracks or on minute projections on the granite. To get a toe in these cracks, or here and there on a scarcely obvious projection, while crawling on hands and knees, all the while tortured with thirst and gasping and struggling for breath, this was the climb; but at last the Peak was won.[15]

Isabella Bird—who had left home an invalid—was clearly eager to convey not only the danger of the situation but also her physical fortitude and success. "Winning" the Peak, she represents herself as a conqueror of nature.

Like Florence Dixie and Isabella Bird, other Victorian adventuresses recorded at length their successful encounters with danger. After describing the "collar of leeches" she emerged with after traipsing through a swamp, Mary Kingsley wrote in *Travels in West Africa*: "Of course the bleeding did not stop at once, and it attracted flies and—but I am going into details, so I forbear" (303). Similarly, Constance Gordon Cumming in *At Home in Fiji* reported with glee her "never-to-be-forgotten week on the very brink of [a] great active crater" in Hawaii (290). Later, in *In the Himalayas* (1884) she directly addressed the reasons she found thrill in danger:

> I believe that in our innermost hearts we were both very much delighted at the novelty of finding ourselves thus literally "unprotected females"

in this wild place, so on the morrow we pitched our tiny tent (we had brought but one) on an open space in the heart of the great forest.[16]

By counterposing the "tiny tent" that she and a friend occupied to the "great forest" which enveloped them, Gordon Cumming heightens the appeal of her story. A related strategy sometimes invoked by women travelers was to recount those episodes in which they were called on to fend for themselves. Recalling her struggles in the waters of West Africa Mary Kingsley wrote: "I wiped a perspiring brow, and searched in my mind for a piece of information regarding navigation that would be applicable to the management of long-tailed Adooma canoes" (*Travels in West Africa* 198). In *Across Patagonia* Florence Dixie remembered "many a discomfort—the earthquakes, the drenching rains, the scorching sun, the pitiless mosquitoes, and the terrible blasting winds" (250). Adventure enabled all of these women to act out and recreate their own "survival of the fittest" stories. Because they undertook traditionally male activities without male protection, their "survival" in remote regions of the world was thought to illustrate their ability to keep pace with their male counterparts.

Those women who documented their experiences in remote corners of the world could be relatively sure their accomplishments would be duly noted at home in England, and representations of these adventuresses that appeared throughout the Victorian period reproduced many of their own rhetorical strategies. Many periodicals capitalized on the representation of the woman traveler as conqueror of unknown lands; the *Scottish Geographical Magazine*, for example, hailed Isabella Bird Bishop as "the first European woman to find her way into the heart of Japan."[17] And Mary Kingsley's reviewer in *The Athenaeum* wrote that "she [was] undoubtedly the first of her sex who has dared to face the manifold dangers of the pestilential regions of the French Congo and other parts of barbarous Western Equatorial Africa."[18] The unprotected status of the woman traveler was often highlighted by overstating the extent to which her presence was dwarfed by her physical surroundings. In his discussion of Isabella Bird, for example, W. H. Davenport Adams wrote: "Hour after hour our heroine—for a lady who crosses the Rocky Mountains alone may surely claim the title!—rode onward in the darkness and solitude, the prairie sweeping all around her, and a firmament of frosty stars glittering overhead" (434). The qualities of endurance and fortitude that Adams sought to convey become more attenuated in the context of the darkness and solitude he creates. With a prairie "sweeping all around her," Isabella Bird's experience carries with it the weight of a one-woman pilgrimage.

Physical accomplishment was perhaps the most defining trait of an adventuress—the characteristic most often remarked on in newspapers and the periodical press. The *Scottish Geographical Magazine* monitored the activities of Mary Kingsley while she was in Africa and gave its readers detailed updates of her physical accomplishments: "She ascended the Ogowe, and crossed the Sierra de Cristal, mountains ranging from 7000 to 8000 feet in height. Subsequently she ascended Cameroons Peak, 13,700 feet high."[19] Such bald statements of Kingsley's accomplishments are in part 'a reflection of the magazine's style, but at the same time they suggest how much evidence of physical accomplishment helped to identify Kingsley as an exceptional traveler *and* woman. Similarly, after Isabella Bird climbed the "American Matterhorn," 14,700 feet high Long's Peak in Colorado, W. H. Davenport Adams praised her as "the first woman who has had the courage and resolution to reach its summit" (423). Adams also honored Florence Dixie for having

> hunted pumas, ostriches, guanacos; witnessed the wild and wayward movements of the wild horses on the plains . . . suffered from the burden of the heat, and the attacks of the gnats; explored the recesses of the Cordilleras. (443)

Clearly part of the identity of an adventuress was her ability to withstand physical hardship. Reviewers for *The Athenaeum* singled out as "the most thrilling" those portions of *Travels in West Africa* where Kingsley showed "her indifference to danger, hardships, and privations."[20] Even before Kingsley documented her explorations of West Africa, W. H Davenport Adams had already been prompted to proclaim in *Celebrated Women Travellers of the Nineteenth Century* that "a female traveller has ceased to become a rara avis; delicately-nurtured women now climb Mont Blanc or penetrate into the Norwegian forests, or cross the Pacific, or traverse sandy deserts, or visit remote isles, in company with their husbands and brothers, or 'unprotected'" (383–84). Adams implies that all women are at least to a degree "delicately-nurtured," and this disadvantage makes their physical accomplishments all the more remarkable. Writing for *Blackwood's Magazine*, W. G. Blaikie lauded the achievements of those traveling women whose adventurous spirit defied

> hurricanes, shipwreck, artic cold and darkness, and all other dangers and discomforts of the sea: and by land, fatigue, hunger, and sickness, robbers and extortioners, wild beasts, scorpions, mosquitoes, heat and cold, filth and fever.[21]

Although overstated, his comments suggest the importance of both real and imaginary danger lurking in the landscape of Victorian adventuresses. "In such an age as this," Blaikie concluded, "we need wonder at nothing that women will dare."[22]

Despite Blaikie's unwavering admiration, many Victorians *did* wonder at what women would dare. When a few women—led by Isabella Bird Bishop—began to agitate for admittance as fellows into the Royal Geographic Society, the debate took a nasty turn. In a letter to the editor of *The Times*, the influential MP George Curzon wrote:

> We contest *in toto* the capability of women to contribute to scientific geographic knowledge. Their sex and training render them equally unfitted for exploration, and the genus of professional female globe-trotter is one of the horrors of the later end of the nineteenth century.[23]

Curzon's letter touched off a series of responses in the paper, and these were soon after followed by an appeal in *Punch*: "Let them stay and mind the babies, or hem our ragged shirts; but they mustn't, can't, and shan't be geographic."[24]

The geographical knowledge to which Victorian adventuresses had access threatened the public at home on some level, and this threat was articulated by translating geographic experience into sexual knowledge. Although these women found a measure of ideological support for their activities by aligning them with imperial endeavor, they nonetheless left home branded as sexual anomalies—they became, like Dixie, "fair amazons." W. H. Davenport Adams wrote that Isabella Bird "carried in her bosom a man's heart" (433), and Mary Kingsley was described in *The Gentlewoman* as exhibiting "manly strength" abroad.[25] Many Victorian critics were more direct in their condemnation of the anomalous sexuality of the female traveler. Returning to England in 1895 after her West African travels, Mary Kingsley wrote: "I discovered, to my alarm, that I was, by freak of fate, the sea-serpent of the season" (xv).[26]

Kingsley's ability to find in her representations in the press an analogy between the woman adventuress and the sea-serpent is telling. In *Woman and the Demon: The Life of a Victorian Myth*, Nina Auerbach studies the images of lamias, serpent-women, and hybrid mermaids that permeate Victorian depictions of woman and concludes that in their "inexhaustible vitality" they represented a power to possess that found its greatest triumph in "displacing male authorities."[27] In likening herself to the serpent figure popularized in the Victorian imagination by women like Thackeray's Becky Sharp, Kingsley picks up on the tendency of the press to represent the woman adventuress both as a figure of vitality and as one whose vitality and willfulness were threatening.

In some ways, Victorian adventuresses helped to perpetuate such representations by emphasizing in their works the energy and stamina they exerted—and wanted to exert. Mary Seacole remembered of her stint in the Crimea: "I have never felt since that time the strong and hearty woman that I was when I braved with impunity the pestilence of Navy Bay and Cruces. It would kill me easily now" (146). Seacole implies that the presence of disease in her surroundings amplified her own sense of livelihood and well-being. Other adventuresses found sources of strength and energy in places associated with pestilence and impunity as well, suggesting that for some women the "energy" that underwrote imperialistic expansion was part of what appealed about adventure. The expenditure of energy demanded of adventurous women was conceptualized by many as an antidote to suffering, stagnation, and ill-health endured in England. In *Across Patagonia* Florence Dixie explained her decision to "escape" to South America as the result of a weariness with life that left her without energy and yearning "to taste a more vigorous emotion" (2). Mary Gaunt echoed Dixie's remark in suggesting that the dangers of Africa were actually incentives to travel: "There is something in the thought of danger that . . . quickens the blood and gives an added zest to life."[28] And in the first chapter of *At Home in Fiji*, Constance Gordon Cumming explained to a friend: "I had not time to write you before my hurried departure from England, but you see my locomotive demon has allowed me a very short spell of rest" (9). Each of these women represents travel as an empowering vitalizing experience.

That they do so is especially interesting given the almost incapacitated state some were in when they made the decision to venture abroad. Although Victorian adventuresses were often represented in the popular press as women with exceptional physical strength and resilience, many were far from healthy while in England and some explicitly undertook travel for recuperative purposes. Mary Kingsley left home to spirit herself out of the lethargy and despair she felt after both of her parents died. Suffering from depression and insomnia, Isabella Bird decided to travel to America after an arduous recovery from a spinal operation. As Mary Tinling suggests, "Perhaps her doctor had enough insight to realize that her problems stemmed from a strong personality at odds with an enfeebling environment; at any rate, he prescribed travel."[29] She would later travel to Hawaii, China, Japan, and—at the age of eighty-six—Morocco. That a woman who suffered from physical ailments that left her all but completely debilitated at home could make such enormous use of strength and fortitude abroad suggests much about the energizing function of travel for Victorian women.

Complicating such representations was the notion that all women—not just those who like Isabella Bird were physically debilitated—were delicate and, if not lethargic, at very least passive. Women who flaunted their physical fortitude and vitality abroad thus seemed to challenge their own "natural" limitations and to invite the classification they received. They became "manly women," "fair amazons," and "sea serpents." The representation of adventurous women as aggressively sexualized is just one manifestation of what Mary Poovey has shown to be the instability of Victorian conceptions of woman. Because the domestic ideal was constituted, she argues, by the antinomies of the moral and the immoral, the woman who did not align her identity to that of the moral angel was by implication ideologically positioned into the role of sexually aggressive misfit. Adventuresses were disturbing because their travels signified a decision to opt for and embrace this "other" side of the domestic.

Given the implications of such a decision, it is not surprising that many Victorian women who chose to travel expressed their decision with ambivalence. In the beginning of her autobiographical travel account, *The Wonderful Adventures of Mrs. Seacole in Many Lands*, Mary Seacole wrote: "As I grew into womanhood, I began to indulge that longing to travel which will never leave me while I have health and vigor" (4). Although Seacole evidently found in her travels vigor, energy, and endurance, these were feelings in which she "indulged." To choose to travel was to gratify desires that might better be resisted. In *A Woman's Wanderings the World Over* (1909), Lucy Broad wrote: "I had been fighting a burning desire in my own heart that craved for the whole world."[30] Still another woman traveler, Mary Gaunt, remembered in *Alone in West Africa* (1911) her "vague longings after savage lands" (4). Florence Dixie wrote in *Across Patagonia* of the "yearning gaze" she fixed as a child on "bright fields of activity" (16). This language of restlessness, longing, and desire is common among accounts of leaving home written by adventuresses; its cumulative effect is to link travel with the acting out of an irrepressible physical and, by implication, sexual drive. The discourse of these adventuresses could thus be readily appropriated by people like those who labeled Kingsley the "sea-serpent of the season."

More than any other adventuress, Kingsley bristled at such implications of anomalous sexuality and aberrant womanhood. She publicly retaliated against being labeled a "new woman," and in a reply to a *Daily Telegraph* report identifying her as such claimed she could not have accomplished anything without help from "the superior sex." As Dea Birkett suggests, Kingsley publicly denied "the very independence she had in private so desperately and determinedly sought.[31] Although perplexing, her attitude helps to elucidate the inconsistencies embedded in the identities of Victorian adventuresses.

Not all women were as willing as Kingsley to acquiesce to the implied demands of the English public, however. Others counteracted the threatening components of their identities by reconceptualizing them in ways that would be deemed socially acceptable. One of the most characteristic strategies invoked by adventuresses to domesticate their activities abroad was to conceptualize them as health-related. Although many of these women aligned their identities to imperial (and hence male) heroes, they capitalized on those components of the domestic ideal that assigned them special abilities that served imperial interest. Most often, they featured their "natural" competence as supervisors of their family's moral and physical health. But they moved the sphere for this activity from the English hearth to places where people—for example, the natives—were ostensibly more in need of their care, places where morality was assumed to be absent.

The Domestication of Adventure

Some women who traveled simply transferred their duties as English housewives and mothers overseas, a tactic evident in Lady M. A. Barker's travel account, *A Year's Housekeeping in South Africa* (1877). But the women who constructed identities as adventuresses used the domestic in less overt and more strategic ways. Some women recorded the means with which they were cured of illnesses abroad, often suggesting in their letters home remedies to interest—or placate—the sick at home. Lucie Duff Gordon, for instance, traveled to Egypt to recuperate from consumption, and claimed in one letter that "the Arab specific, camel's milk, has done me great good."[32] And from the Rocky Mountains Isabella Bird wrote with glee: "The curative effect of the climate of Colorado can hardly be exaggerated" (47). More often, however, adventuresses found in travel abroad opportunities to administer health.

The facilitation of health abroad became the primary way in which some Victorian women travelers introduced the domestic into their adventure narratives. Like Florence Nightingale, they could "work" abroad by bringing moral and physical health to the peoples of nations lacking those presumably English advantages. This work, in turn, could be conceived as "natural" to women, as simply extending their instinctive capabilities. As many historians have shown, Victorian women were assumed to be by nature the helpmates of men, and in addition to doling out large measures of cheerfulness, sympathy, and love, they were morally responsible for the physical well-being of those in their homes. The Victorian doctor T. S. Clouston argued in *Female Education from a Medical Point of View* (1882) that the innate helpfulness of woman in fact made her most capable "not only of bearing her own share of ills, but helping to bear those of others."[33]

By finding ills abroad and by helping to attend to and cure those ills, women who constructed identities as Victorian adventuresses went some way toward justifying their status as women working outside of the home. On arriving in Egypt in the early 1860s, Lucie Duff Gordon was quick to ascribe to herself a role as ministering angel from England, frequently writing home to have medicines sent so that she could distribute them to "her people." In one letter home, she half-heartedly complains, "I don't know what to do with my sick: they come from forty miles off, and sometimes twenty or thirty sleep outside the house" (41). Duff Gordon was clearly eager to represent herself as foreign caretaker. By casting the Egyptians as sick people surrounding her house, she could both transfer her own illness onto others and transform her recuperative sphere into a female workplace. By turning foreigners into sickly or unwieldy children in need of care or—at very least—discipline, an adventuress could represent England's imperial efforts as womanly self-regulation.

Similar rhetorical strategies are evident in other adventuress accounts. To justify her trip to South Africa during the Boer War, Florence Dixie wrote in the beginning of *In the Land of Misfortune* (1884): "In many cases the mortally stricken soldier is left to his last agony on the spot whereon he fell . . . and the one who might bring relief and tenderness to soothe his last moments is not always by. It was in this capacity that I decided to proceed at once to South Africa."[34] By strategically placing her appeal after a description of the soldier's "last agony," Dixie resolves the problem implicit in her ostensibly selfish decision to leave home. Escaping the confines of the English home could be rewritten as self-effacement and linked at the same time to patriotism and England's imperial mission. Other adventuresses appropriated roles similar to that of Dixie. In Fiji during a period of native rebellion, Constance Gordon Cumming wrote:

> I am preparing for emergencies by attending the infirmary several days a week, to pick up a few ideas about simple nursing. It is under the care of Miss Osborne, a cousin of Florence Nightingale. Evidently her whole

heart is in her work; and kindness and order reign supreme. (*At Home in Fiji*, 17)

In Gordon Cumming's remarks, the infirmary metonymically appropriates the role of England in Fiji; she glosses over the conditions that have given rise to a state of emergency by focusing instead on the state of "kindness and order" that she finds in the local infirmary.

Significantly, Gordon Cumming uses Nightingale's name as a strategic device to legitimize her own presence as a nursing student in the foreign infirmary and, by implication, the general presence of Britain in Fiji. More than any other person, Florence Nightingale symbolized for many Victorians the selfless bringer of cleanliness, health, and order to the wider world. One popular ballad that memorialized Nightingale depicted her as savior on the imperial battlefield: "She'd lay down her life for the poor soldier's sake; She prays for the dying, she gives peace to the brave; She feels that a soldier has a soul to be saved."[35] In her work on Nightingale in *Uneven Developments*, Mary Poovey argues that such discourse was often appropriated by apologists for empire who invoked altruistic language to mask the economic motivations behind territorial expansion. Not surprisingly, Nightingale's identity was appropriated by many women seeking to establish a legitimate role for themselves abroad. The idealization of the working woman abroad as humble nurse tending to the health of England's sick soldiers—always figures of sympathy—helped the public to see their presence in foreign countries as fundamentally beneficent. By invoking Nightingale's name in her discussion of the situation in Fiji, Gordon Cumming introduces into a situation of instability one of her country's most powerful figures of order and control.

Constance Gordon Cumming was not the only adventuress to explicitly associate her activities abroad with those of Florence Nightingale. Mary Seacole literally followed Nightingale's footsteps into the Crimea. *The Wonderful Adventures of Mrs. Seacole in Many Lands* documents the discrimination she came up against as a black woman seeking to find work routinely associated with upper-middle class, white English women. Although not allowed to take the position she desired as an assistant nurse in the hospital administered by Nightingale, Seacole established her own domesticated command post. While Nightingale set up shop as head nurse abroad, Seacole started a trading post designed to bring English goodness to men at war in the form of plum-puddings and mince-pies. There she wrote: "I am not ashamed to confess . . . that I love to be of service to those who need a woman's help. And wherever the need arises—on whatever distant shore—I ask no greater privilege than to minister to it" (26).

Masking an opportunity to travel in the language of womanly privilege, Seacole lessens the possibility of being perceived as incongruous. When she was not doling out pastries, however, she was monitoring activity at the local hospital, helping out to the extent that the official employees would let her. There Seacole could even more effectively construct the kind of domesticated public identity that appealed to her English readers. Lamenting the conditions of the hospital she wrote: "If it be so here, what must it not be at the scene of war—on the spot where the poor fellows are stricken down by pestilence or Russian bullets, and days and nights of agony must be passed before a woman's hands can dress their wounds" (89). Seacole's goal—like that of Dixie in South Africa and Gordon Cumming in Fiji—was to make her presence on the imperial battlefield seem a necessity. On the hardships of supervising health on the battlefield at Christmas time, Seacole wrote:

> I have seen many a bold fellow's eyes moisten at such a season, when a woman's voice and a woman's care have brought to their minds recollections of those happy English homes which some of them never saw again; but many did, who will remember their woman-comrade upon the bleak and barren heights before Sebastopol. (126)

Like Dixie and Gordon Cumming, Seacole transforms the politics of British presence abroad into the exigency of woman's presence in the war zone. As "woman-comrade," she legitimizes the imperial by making her presence on the battlefield seem indispensable to the health and well-being of the English men in need of home healing.

By recreating in their travel accounts battlefields on which to serve as facilitators of order and healing, Florence Dixie, Constance Gordon Cumming, and Mary Seacole all found a way to transform adventure into domestic activity. The experiences of these women were exceptional, however, in that they traveled to places of war, or, at very least, rebellion and upheaval. The English men stationed in these places as protectors of Britain's imperial interests could naturally serve as objects of their care and support. As often, though, an adventuress traveled to places where English presence and purpose was not as overt or commanding; there she was forced to find in her surroundings not English men but natives to serve as the recipients of her womanly concern. Much of her authority derived her ability to represent these people as in need of her care, education, and supervision.

One of the most characteristic ways adventuresses invoked this authority was to position themselves as mother figures in relation to the natives. One obvious manifestation of this strategy can be seen in those travel accounts with passages devoted to critique of the treatment of native children. Commenting on the condition of children, an adventuress could write on a womanly province of knowledge, one which could be justified as an extension of her "natural" maternal instinct. From Colorado, for instance, Isabella Bird observed: "One of the most painful things in the Western States and Territories is the extinction of childhood. I have never seen any children, only debased imitations of men and women, cankered by greed and selfishness, and asserting and gaining complete independence of their parents at ten years old" (*A Lady's Life in the Rocky Mountains*, 77). Similarly suggestive of the mock sympathy and barely masked superiority characteristic of imperial rhetoric, Amelia Edwards wrote in *A Thousand Miles Up the Nile*:

> Nothing in provincial Egypt is so painful to witness as the neglected condition of very young children. Those belonging to even the better class are for the most part shabbily clothed and of more than doubtful cleanliness; while the offspring of the very poor are simply encrusted with dirt and sores, and swarming with vermin. (85)

By highlighting the pain they felt at having to witness the suffering of native children, both Isabella Bird and Amelia Edwards suggest that their concern is founded on maternal-like compassion. But both introduce into their commentary a tinge of contempt. Bird overstates her case by depicting the United States version of childhood as "cankered," and suggesting that, like the rotten element from a sore, children are erupting in widespread rebellion from their parents.

Edwards was more explicit in *A Thousand Miles Up the Nile*. After noting that even the "better" class of Egyptian children were shabbily clad and dubiously cleansed, she wryly concludes that the overall "condition of the inhabitants is not worse, perhaps, in an Egyptian Beled than in many an Irish village" (86). Her critique derives its authority as much from her ostensible maternal concern for the welfare of the children as from a complex of beliefs about the interconnections between race and class. She implies that the "very poor" are sadly in need of the sanitizing vision that only different class and a different race can offer, and by representing the vermin-ridden Egyptian children as analogous to those likely to be observed in an Irish village, she rhetorically argues for English supremacy and control in both places.

Adventuresses characteristically justified these attitudes by conceptualizing the native population as morally threatening. To combat the threat allegedly posed by the native population, an adventuress could represent adults as moral children and thereby gain maternal authority to discipline, supervise, and instruct. Describing her adult Arab servant, for example, Amelia Edwards condescendingly wrote: "Like a child, too, he loves noise and movement for the mere sake of noise and movement, and looks upon swings and fireworks as the height of human felicity" (*A Thousand Miles Up the Nile*, 24). By turning the native into the tractable child, this adventuress cast herself in the role of social and psychological superior. Harriet Martineau says as much in *Eastern Life, Present and Past* (1848), invoking as she does that prototypical Victorian sage voice, the anonymous "We":

> We do not agree with travelers who declare it necessary to treat these people with coldness and severity—to repel and beat them. We treated them as children; and this answered perfectly well. . . . They were always manageable by kindness and mirth.[36]

Martineau's unabashed remark captures the confidence with which many Victorian women travelers operated as self-proclaimed international disciplinarians in places of English colonization.

These women sought to manage the people they came into contact with by means consistent with English domestic ideology and repeatedly represent in their travel accounts solutions to the behavioral problems encountered. Martineau brought with her a handful of thimbles to present to the unruly natives as useful incentives to good behavior. Amelia Edwards, too, delighted to find effective strategies of submission. She solved one disciplinary crisis by offering gifts of tobacco and sugar to her sailors responsible for steering her boat. Finding this tactic successful, she gleefully concluded: "More docile, active, good-tempered, friendly fellows never pulled an oar. Simple and trustful as children, frugal as anchorites, they worked cheerfully from sunrise to sunset, sometimes towing the dahabeeyah on a rope all day long, like barge-horses" (*A Thousand Miles Up the Nile*, 41–42). By transforming the natives into tractable children, Edwards aligns the success of England's presence in the wider world with that of the mother's presence in the home—both derived their authority from an ability to discipline.

Unfortunately, Edwards's disturbing analogy is representative of many Victorian travel accounts that mask the desire to dominate the natives by characterizing them as animals. Writing of poverty-stricken Egyptians, for instance, Edwards ostentatiously wrote: "Hungry? well, yes—no doubt they are hungry. But what of that? They are Arabs, and Arabs bear hunger as camels bear thirst. It is nothing new to them" (*A Thousand Miles Up the Nile*, 380). Similarly, Harriet Martineau in *Eastern Life, Present and Past* compared the "screaming Arabs" who greeted her boat to "a frog concert in a Carolina camp" (18). It would be convenient to conclude, as Catherine Stevenson does in her study of women travelers to Africa, that these women developed "strategies of accommodation that starkly contrasted the force and domination implicit in the discourse of the male traveler to Africa," but such was not always the case, as the disturbing rhetoric of Edwards and Martineau suggests. Like their male counterparts, some Victorian women adopted with apparently little hesitation disciplinary and domineering behavior and language, much of which sought to depict foreign culture as both "primitive" and tractable. Despite a few feeble attempts to recognize a common humanity, for example, Amelia Edwards finally concludes in *A Thousand Miles Up the Nile*: "The natives, in truth, are still mere savages au fond— the old war-paint being but half disguised under a thin veneer of Mohammedanism" (255).

Victorian Adventuresses as Ethnographers

Whereas Amelia Edwards willingly adopted the role of moral disciplinarian, other adventuresses sought to establish their authority in less offensive ways. Many sought to identify themselves not as taskmasters but rather as detached and objective observers of foreign cultures. During the latter half of the century especially, the observation of foreign culture was increasingly seen as necessary to the progress of several emerging sciences, among them anthropology, ethnology, and natural history. The traveling Victorians competed with other Europeans to "claim" the bodies of knowledge that hitherto unknown worlds and their peoples offered. Frazer's *The Golden Bough* (1890), Tylor's *Primitive Culture* (1889), Westermark's *Human Marriage* (1891), and Waitz's *Anthropologie* (1863) were all read as authoritative and scientific studies of the development of culture that depended to varying degrees on the accounts of "savage" life provided by explorers from civilized nations. The Victorian women who traveled to remote regions of the wider world capitalized on the need to provide their nation's social scientists with data.[37]

Of all Victorian adventuresses, Mary Kingsley was most explicit in aligning her identity as a traveler to that of an ethnologist. In a letter published in *The Athenaeum* after *Travels in West Africa* had been reviewed, Kingsley wrote: "I make no pretensions to being a traveler; I am an ethnologist who believes that the best way of studying one's subject is to go and work at the material of it in a native state, instead of relying entirely on information from untrained observers."[38] Her comment is noteworthy for several reasons, not least of which is her confidence in her own authority as a trained observer, reporter of customs, and interpreter of culture. Despite her disclaimer, Kingsley uses her identity as an ethnologist to raise herself above the ordinary traveler. In *Travels in West Africa* for instance, she advises her readers to "read, until you know it by heart, *Primitive Culture*, by Dr. E. B. Tylor, regarding which book I may say that I have never found a fact that flew in face of the carefully made, broad-minded deductions of this greatest of Ethnologists" (435). Kingsley strategically uses her praise of Tylor's authority as an opportunity to remind her readers of her own credentials. She was not, however, reluctant to criticize the findings of Tylor and other authoritative figures. Throughout *Travels in West Africa* Kingsley takes advantage of opportunities to take issue with the findings of some of the most influential men of her day. In the same passage that corroborates the findings of Tylor, for instance, she diminishes the significance of Frazer's *The Golden Bough*: "His idea is a true key to a certain quantity of facts, but in West Africa only to a limited quantity" (435).

As Kingsley's comments suggest, some adventuresses garnered for themselves a measure of authority that derived from their presence "in the field." Many of the women who traveled to remote regions of the world and documented their findings in essence worked as fieldworkers, establishing what James Clifford and Marc Manganaro, among others, have described as anthropological authority. Using Clifford's work on the discourse of the ethnographer, Manganaro writes:

> the "presence" of the writer in the field creates in the reader a strong sense of the anthropologist-author's "ethnographic authority," the rhetorical command that field-based anthropologists construct for themselves in the creation of ethnographic discourse. Primarily through the claim "I was there" (on the cultural spot), the modern ethnographer becomes the voice of culture.[39]

By participating in the creation and dissemination of field-based discourse, these adventuresses established for themselves just this sort of ethnographic authority.

Isabella Bird Bishop, Mary Kingsley, Florence Dixie, and Constance Gordon Cumming all found in their travels the opportunity to "scientifically" assess the character of the native and often recorded the physical traits they observed in inordinate detail. In *The Yangtze Valley and Beyond*, for example, Isabella Bird Bishop wrote:

From an ethnological point of view the Man-tze deserve some attention,
as they differ considerably from the Sifan to the north and the Lolos to
the south. . . . Their handsome, oval faces; richly-coloured complexions;
thick straight eyebrows; large, level eyes, sometimes dark grey; broad
upright foreheads; moderate cheekbones; definite, though rather broad,
noses; thin lips, somewhat pointed chins, and white regular teeth are far
removed from any Mongolian characteristics, and it is impossible not to
believe that these tribes are an offshoot of the Aryan race. (227–28)

Like Isabella Bird Bishop, Mary Kingsley filled all three of her travel
accounts with lengthy descriptions of the variations of species she
encountered. The Fans in West Africa particularly caught her attention:

They are on the whole a fine race, particularly those in the mountain
districts of the Sierra del Cristal, where one continually sees magnificent
specimens of human beings, both male and female. Their colour is light
bronze, many of the men have beards, and albinos are rare among them.
The average height in the mountain districts is five feet six to five feet
eight, the difference in stature between men and women not being great.
(*Travels in West Africa*, 328–29)

Both Bird Bishop and Kingsley thought of the native populations
as scientific samples—specimens—for their scrutiny. Although they
represent themselves as detached observers who merely "measure"
the people they observe, their descriptions also appeal in their emphasis on the exotic. Bird Bishop's subjects are, after all, "handsome," "richly coloured," "broad," and "upright." Kingsley, too, is
evidently attracted to her subjects; they are "magnificent" and
"bronze[d]" beings.

Bird Bishop and Kingsley were only two of many women to appeal
to their readers on this level. In *Letters from Egypt* (1876), Lucie Duff
Gordon describes the "stupendous physical perfection" of a woman
she encountered: "Her jet-black face was like the Sphinx, with the
same mysterious smile; her shape and walk were goddess-like, and
the lustre of her skin, teeth, and eyes showed the fullness of
health;—Caffre of course" (214). After describing the woman in more
detail, Duff Gordon writes: "I walked after her as far as her swift
pace would let me, in envy and admiration of such stately humanity"
(214). Similarly, Amelia Edwards describes two natives of Khartoum
as follows:

Their small proud heads and delicate aristocratic features were modelled
on the purest Florentine type; their eyes were long and liquid; their

complexions, free from any taint of Abyssinian blue or Nubian bronze, were intensely, lustrously, magnificently black. (*A Thousand Miles Up the Nile*, 185)

She then concludes: "They were like young and beautiful Dantes carved in ebony" (185). Edwards represents these men as appealing because their dark skin encloses something essentially white—"aristocratic," "pure," and "Florentine." But she, too, represents for her readers their exotic—and sexual—appeal; they are "intensely, lustrously, magnificently black."[40]

Despite these evocations of the exotic appeal of their subjects, as often an adventuress represented the native as physically repulsive. Amelia Edwards did not find the natives encountered along the way up the Nile uniformly appealing; traveling through Egypt, for example, she wrote; "Here were Abyssinians like slender-legged baboons; wild-looking Bishariyah and Ababden Arabs with flashing eyes and flowing hair" (184). Florence Dixie found in her travels many an opportunity to assess and condemn the physical characteristics of the natives she confronted. Throughout *Across Patagonia*, she focused on those physical features of the "primitive inhabitants" that she saw as evidence of their possibilities for survival. Her description of the "pure-bred" Tehuelches, for example, is part of an extended discussion designed to prove that "lesser" types will naturally be weeded from the species. Of those natives who had in them "a mixture of Aracuanian or Fuegian blood," she predicted demise: "The flat noses, oblique eyes, and badly proportioned figures of the latter make them most repulsive objects. . . . The Tehuelches are a race that is fast approaching extinction" (*Across Patagonia*, 66–67). Similarly, Mary Kingsley explained her attraction to the Fans of West Africa on the basis of their promise for survival as a species: "Their countenances are very bright and expressive, and if once you have been among them, you can never mistake a Fan. But it is in their mental characteristics that their difference from the lethargic, dying-out coast tribes is most marked" (328–29):

Constance Gordon Cumming also represented herself as an ethnographer concerned with studying species survival and used her travels to Fiji to observe and compare several groups of natives in meticulous detail. Of the aborigines she encountered in Fiji she wrote: "Hideous indeed they are, far beyond any race I have yet met with; and of so low a type that it is impossible in their case, to regret that strange law of nature which seems to ordain the dying out of dark skinned races before the advance of civilisation" (17). In part such comments are representative of a kind of imperial discourse that sought to justify the domination of one group over others as the natural progress of civilization. But Victorian adventuresses repeatedly returned in their accounts to observations designed to corroborate a "survival of the fittest" paradigm.

This was by no means their only strategy for dealing with native encounters, however. The adventuress often recreated in her account situations in which she was physically distanced from the possibility of contact with, sympathy for, and attraction to the native population. In *A Thousand Miles Up the Nile* Edwards wrote that she would "willingly go any number of miles out of the way rather than witness [native] suffering" and that she "had not been many weeks on the Nile before [she] began systematically to avoid going about the native towns whenever it was practicable to do so" (86). That Edwards would so unabashedly admit to such a strategy suggests that distance was an accepted and necessary ingredient of travel writing because it enabled the author/ethnographer to preserve a sense of difference. As John Pemble has written, "Difference was the traveler's joy and the writer's inspiration; and difference existed only so long as ordinary humanity, the common denominator, was held at bay."[41] A Victorian adventuress could justify her detached attitude toward the native population along these lines, and Amelia Edwards said as much in her comments on the landscape of Nubia: "It is all so picturesque, indeed, so biblical, so poetical, that one is almost in danger of forgetting that the places are something more than beautiful backgrounds, and that the people are not merely appropriate figures placed there for the delight of sketchers" (201). Representing the peoples she encountered as either radically different—or, worse, entirely absent—allowed some women travelers to preserve the contrasts that made traveling new, exciting, strange, and appealing. It allowed her to attach more credence to the wildness of her sphere for activity.

The Landscape of Victorian Adventuresses

Distancing herself from the native population, the women who constructed identities as Victorian adventuresses turned their attentions elsewhere. For many, the focus of interest was the landscape, and they used their depictions of scenery to highlight their unique position. More often than not, an adventuress chose to recreate for her readers not the cities or villages she visited, but rather the wildernesses—landscapes seemingly void of population. Florence Dixie celebrated the "vastness" of Patagonia's "lonely and, save by the red man, uninhabited prairies" (247). And in *The Yangtze Valley and Beyond*

Isabella Bird Bishop praises the snow-peaked mountains she climbed because they kept her "separate . . . from all other earthly things" (159). By emphasizing the vastness of the landscapes in which she roamed, she magnified the significance of her own position there.

As Bird Bishop's description suggests, many adventuresses positioned themselves in wildernesses evocative of power and change, in spaces that could not be mapped or charted. Mary Kingsley described the Cameroon Mountains as

> wreathed with indigo-black tornado clouds, sometimes crested with snow, sometimes softly gorgeous with gold green, and rose-coloured vapours tinted by the setting sun, sometimes completely swathed in dense cloud so that you cannot see it at all; but when you once know it is there it is all the same, and you bow down and worship. (550)

Kingsley here focuses on the mutability of landscape—its capacity to adopt protean forms and to unsettle those who attempt to capture it in one form. Many other adventuresses like Kingsley sought in nature objects for their interest and sympathy and endowed the landscapes with the capacity for powerful feeling and expression that they wouldn't let themselves see in the natives. Describing the scenery of Rio De Janeiro, Florence Dixie wrote:

> Nowhere else is there such audacity, such fierceness even of outline, coupled with such multiform splendour of colour, such fairy-like delicacy of detail. As a precious jewel is encrusted by the coarse rock, the smiling bay lies encircled by frowning mountains of colossal proportions and the most capricious shapes. (*Across Patagonia*, 27–28)

Dixie here empowers the landscape with the same qualities she wants her readers to associate with herself; she represents it as bold and aggressive yet at the same time ethereal and inviting. Throughout *Across Patagonia* she sought to harmonize opposites through her evocation of landscape: "Nowhere have the rugged and the tender, the wild and the soft, been blended into such exquisite union as at Rio; and it is this quality of unrivalled contrasts that, to my mind, gives to that scenery its charm of unsurpassed loveliness" (27). Here again, Dixie empowers the landscape with qualities she identifies with her self, and she uses language often associated in Victorian discourse with sexual difference. By suggesting that the opposite effects of the landscape conjoin in "exquisite union," Dixie suggests the appeal of contrasts that do not rival but rather complement one another.

Isabella Bird Bishop, too, positioned herself in places whose stark contrasts evoked images of power with which she sought to identify.

In *A Lady's Life in the Rocky Mountains* she described Long's Peak in Colorado as "one of the noblest of mountains" and explained: "In one's imagination it grows to be much more than a mountain. It becomes invested with a personality. In its caverns and abysses one comes to fancy that it generates and chains the strong winds, to let them loose in its fury" (98). The language she uses to describe the mountain is revealing: she focuses on that part of the landscape—caverns and abysses—from which hidden power arises and sees in those places of hidden power the capacity for control. Having identified the mountain's hidden sources of power, she designates it as her own:

> Such as it is, Estes Park is mine. It is unsurveyed, "no man's land," and mine by right of love, appropriation, and appreciation; by the seizure of its peerless sunrises and sunsets, its glorious afterglow, its blazing noons, its hurricanes sharp and furious, its wild auroras, its glories of mountain and forest. (120)

Part of her attraction to no-man's-land is that it is unmapped; it is a place not yet demarcated and controlled by men. It also challenges and has physical appeal—with a "sharp," "wild," and "furious" climate and landscape. In no-man's-land, the task of an adventuress is two-fold: she must nurture it and at the same time must appropriate and conquer it as her own.

Victorian adventuresses thus represented themselves both as traditional agents of morality and as unconventional—even aberrant—women. In "Feminist Criticism in the Wilderness," Elaine Showalter argues that women writers have tended to seek out experimental and experiential "wild zones" outside of, unknown to, and uncontrolled by men.[42] Showalter identifies the wild zone as a no-man's-land, but for the Victorian adventuress it was as much a he-man's-land. It was a place to align one's identity to the Victorian hero—the spirited, willful, and successful conqueror of foreign place. At the same time, however, it was a place to construct identity without the institutional and psychological barriers imposed on that identity in England. Summarizing the work of some feminist critics, Showalter claims that "through voluntary entry into the wild zone . . . a woman can write her way out of the 'cramped confines of patriarchal space.'"[43] Although many adventuresses did indeed find in the wild zones of the wider world a way out of cramped, patriarchal England, they used it also, by dint of the widespread attraction to their stories, as a way back in. They used their stories of adventure abroad to critique their position at home.

The Adventuress at Home

Most adventuresses on returning home took advantage of the reputations their travels had brought them. After her journeys abroad, Florence Dixie became an active public advocate for a variety of causes, most notably the rights of women and the humanitarian treatment of animals. Her article "Woman's Mission," written for *Vanity Fair* in 1884, branded her as a "new woman," a reputation solidified several years later with the publication in 1904 of a pamphlet on woman's political rights, *Towards Freedom: An Appeal to Thoughtful Men and Women.* She also published several novels linking travel with a woman's yearning for political freedom; both *The Two Castaways* (1890) and *Aniwee, or, The Warrior Queen* (1890) have adventurous heroines whose power is launched abroad. Dixie's travels enabled her to acquire a measure of political power as well. She published *A Defence of Zululand and Its King* in 1882 and afterward was widely regarded as the figure most instrumental in the deposed king's release and return to power. The editors of the *St. James Gazette* depicted has as "the lady in command of the happy transformation—Zulu, into Dixie's land."[44]

Florence Dixie was not the only adventuress to use her experience of power abroad to effect change at home. Isabella Bird Bishop's worldwide travels were over by the end of the 1890s, and her status as "globe-trotteress" was well known. She was made an Honorary Fellow of the Royal Scottish Geographical Society in 1890 and was the most instrumental figure in the highly publicized and successful war women waged in the early 1890s to be admitted to the Royal Geographical Society. These were notable achievements, and suggest the pivotal role that women travelers played in changing public attitudes toward the physical and intellectual competence of women. Amelia Edwards, too, positioned herself firmly in the public sphere after returning home from abroad. The success of *A Thousand Miles Up the Nile* enabled her to found the Egypt Explorer's Fund, whose purpose was to prevent the destruction of antiquities and to sponsor annual excavations to Egypt.[45] Edwards wrote about Egypt for *Academy, The Times,* and *Harper's Magazine,* and soon after returning to England began a lecture circuit abroad. She was invited to lecture on Egyptian antiquity in America in 1889 and in 1891 published these essays as *Pharaohs, Fellahs and Explorers.*

The status of Victorian adventuresses at home is more complicated than such success stories suggest, however, and the example of Mary Kingsley is instructive in this respect. She, too, returned from her journeys to be lionized by society. Her activities abroad had been closely monitored in the newspapers and geographic periodicals, and her travel books—*Travels in West Africa, West African Studies* (1899), and *The Story of West Africa* (1900)—all were reviewed favorably. *Travels in West Africa* was so successful, in fact, that it was reissued in 1900 in a popular edition, *The Story of West Africa*. Kingsley published letters, essays, and articles in widely read and influential periodicals such as *The Spectator, National Review, Cornhill Magazine,* and *British Empire Review* and gave lectures to a variety of learned societies, often drawing huge crowds. *The Spectator* reported her death in 1900 as "a loss suffered by the nation and the Empire."[46]

However, Kingsley did not whole-heartedly embrace her success as a public figure. In a letter written to the editors of *The Athenaeum* in 1897, Kingsley criticized an article that had praised the bravery of her activities abroad at the expense of other British women living in Africa:

> I assure you that the wives of the officials and missionaries and traders who are resident there, not for their own pleasure of instruction, but from the noble motive of duty to their husbands, do not lead either an easier or a safer life than I do in the bush.[47]

She likewise sought in other prominent places to disparage her own achievements and to refute the accolades that had been given her in the periodical presses. In the preface to *West African Studies,* for example, she wrote of her first book, *Travels in West Africa*:

> It has led to my being referred to as "an intrepid explorer," a thing there is not the making of in me, who am ever the prey of frights, worries and alarms; and its main effect, as far as I am personally concerned, has been to plunge me further still in debt for kindness from my fellow creatures, who, though capable of doing all I have done and more capable of writing about it in really good English, have tolerated that book.[48]

This kind of self-effacement clearly does not mesh with the kind of person Kingsley projected in the pages of her books on Africa. The woman who kept her revolver "ready loaded" and who "stalked the wild West African idea" is hardly one we would expect to be "ever the prey of frights, worries and alarms."

Such contradictions, though, are to be expected from an adventurous woman living and writing in a period dominated like no other by a domestic ideal. Part of Kingsley's concern is evidently to work out an identity that includes the concept of work but that privileges the concept of woman. In the same letter to the editor of *The Athenaeum* she admits: "The present is a very unpleasant time, owing to the morbid state of opinion regarding women's work, for any student who happens to be a woman to come before the public."[49] Although she represents herself as a student who "happens to be a woman," it is clear that in her mind the public served as a jury that would judge her work *and* her womanhood.

Kingsley's intuition was correct, for critics at home did plumb the works of these women for evidence of their "essential" womanhood. Sensitive to such expectations, most adventuresses attempted to write accounts that would satisfy the demands of a public simultaneously attracted to adventure but expecting and exacting the domestic. Their success in doing so can be measured by the extent to which they were memorialized for the way that their travels evidenced a womanly spirit. William Andrews recognized these dual objectives in his introduction to Mary Seacole's travel account: "This work . . . beside being an adventure narrative, is a special kind of success story in which a woman tries to reconcile her desire for economic independence and worldly recognition with a more socially acceptable role of being properly selfless and useful to men" (xxix). Again and again tributes to Victorian adventuresses attempt to gloss the inconsistency embedded in their identities as people of accomplishment by focusing instead on their value as women. In the preface to Mary Seacole's book, W. H. Russell cautioned: "I trust that England will not forget one who nursed her sick, who sought out her wounded to aid and succour them, and who performed the last offices for some of her illustrious dead" (viii).

Isabella Bird Bishop was memorialized in much the same way. W. H. Davenport Adams reported in his work that Isabella Bird Bishop's gender "appears to have ensured her an uniform courtesy of treatment and cordiality of reception in the most remote places and among the wildest and most reckless men" (437). And in a review of *A Lady's Life in the Rocky Mountains*, a critic for *The Spectator* wrote: "her whole experience is a singular combination of the natural and the dramatic, as well as a most encouraging record of feminine confidence and masculine chivalrousness."[50] Writing about all women explorers in his article "Lady Travellers," W. G. Blaikie explained:

> It goes without saying that our story reflects high credit on the courage, the perseverance, and the benevolence of the gentler sex; it is a record of which women may well be proud. And there is this further to be said—

that in no case has their travelling enthusiasm involved the sacrifice of obvious domestic duty; nor has it brought out any qualities inconsistent with the modesty and the gentleness that must always be regarded as the fitting ornaments of the sex.[53]

Although all are praiseworthy in intent, comments like these—based as they were on conventional ideas about woman's essence—diminish the real achievement of Victorian adventuresses, which was to introduce to the public at home new ways of thinking about a woman's potential. That this was her sincere interest can be sensed in the words of Lucie Duff Gordon, whose life—unlike that of Isabella Bird Bishop, Florence Dixie, Mary Seacole, and Mary Kingsley—never became a public commodity. In the last of many letters written to her husband from Cairo, Lucie Duff Gordon wrote: "Now that I am too ill to write I feel sorry that I did not persist and write on the beliefs of Egypt in spite of your fear that the learned would cut me up, for I honestly believe that knowledge will die out with me which few others possess. You must recollect that the learned know books, and I know men, and what is more difficult, women" (179–80).

Travel enabled many Victorian women to compete with the "learned" in a market shaped—as Duff Gordon rightly suggests—both by beliefs about what should be written and about who could write. As Lucie Duff Gordon seemed to sense, the work of Victorian adventuresses was most significant insofar as it helped to redefine this market. By writing about her travels—and by using the authority she had gained from her travel experiences to write about other things—the celebrated Victorian adventuresses could not help but have an influence on public opinion at home, and their involvement in the public sphere undercut the very domestic ideology that their writing seemed in some ways to accommodate and support. Victorian adventuresses did not ultimately change beliefs about what a woman was, but they did enlarge expectations about what women could do.

5

Spots of Time: Victorian Women in the Middle East

In the second of three appendices included in *Eastern Life, Present and Past*, Harriet Martineau offers several pages worth of directions for future lady travelers to the east. Most of Martineau's remarks are precautionary; she warns her fellow countrywomen not to expect health, comfort, ease of sleep. She advises them to carry with them gimlets, waterproof cloth, and washable clothing, and she encourages them to "try the virtues of the chibouque" (522). She then ends the section with the following exhortation:

> Her chief care should be to look to the health of her mind—to see that she keeps her faculties awake and free, whether she is ill or well; that in the future time she may hope to be at once in possession of her English health, and the stores of knowledge and imagery she is laying up by her Eastern travel. (522)

Martineau's comments suggest that for Victorian women travel to the Middle East was an exercise of the mind. While abroad, the woman traveler needed to take extra care to remain alert, not because the experience would deaden her senses but because it would be too stimulating. What is most interesting about Martineau's remarks, however, is her assumption that she will have to wait until she is back in England to retrieve and make sense of her experience. The conscientious woman traveler she envisions hordes her eastern knowledge and imagery for later use. Martineau suggests that her essential work will be one of recovery—that with the rational mind which life on English soil ensures she will be able to reclaim and put to proper use the ideas she has had on eastern sands.

That Martineau chose to position her directions in the appendix and not within the body of her text reflects her fundamental assumption that *Eastern Life, Present and Past* was different from the typical kind of travel account in which advice to future travelers was a regular feature. Although she filled her works on America with recommendations and warnings for future travelers to the country, such guidance would acquire only marginal status in her work on the Middle East. Instead, Martineau would focus her study—much of which was written retrospectively—on the region's past and on the extent to which its past continued to color and shape its present. To Martineau, the Middle East—with its barren landscapes but fertile history—offered a different kind of travel experience, one replete with opportunities for more imaginative self-fashioning. Although she sought—as in all her work—to render her account with objectivity, *Eastern Life, Present and Past* was in many ways her most personal travel account because the act of recovering the region's past became for her a way to see herself and her relation to history in new, regenerating ways.

Martineau, like many of her contemporaries, was influenced well before she traveled abroad by the different readings of the meaning of history championed by various early- and middle-Victorian sage figures, most especially Carlyle. In his essay "On History," written in 1830, Carlyle set forth a view of the function of history that many people—including Martineau—embraced as a basic intellectual paradigm for their thought and writing.[1] At the same time that he declared history to be at the root of all science, Carlyle characterized it as the first clear product of man's spiritual desire. He argued that the historical spirit had epistemological and imaginative dimensions, both of which contributed to its essence and shaped its prophetic effect. "Stern Accuracy in inquiring, bold Imagination in expounding and filling-up. These are the two pinions on which History soars," he wrote in another piece."[2] Carlyle ended "On History," published initially in *Fraser's Magazine*, with the following directive:

> Let us search more and more into the Past; let all men explore it, as the true fountain of knowledge; by whose light alone consciously or unconsciously employed, can the Present and the Future be interpreted or guessed at.[3]

Many Victorian women, with or without Carlyle's prompting, found in the past "fountains of knowledge" from which they could drink. And whereas a few incorporated their thirst for history into works of fiction (one thinks of novels of the recent past like Charlotte Brontë's *Shirley* as well as of those of the distant past like George Eliot's *Romola*), others used nonfictional genres to pursue their interest in history. Peter Allan Dale uses the term *historical-mindedness* to encompass the widespread manifestations of Victorian historical thinking.[4]

Of the many kinds of history writing undertaken by Victorian women, several were informed by travel experiences. Many historical biographies written by Victorian women, for example, were prompted by interest in the wider world, among them Julia Ady's *Isabella d'Este* (1903) and *Beatrice d'Este* (1905), Anna Jameson's *Memoirs of Celebrated Female Sovereigns* (1831), and Margaret Oliphant's *The Makers of Florence: Dante, Giotto, Savonarola* (1876). Certain regions of the wider world—for example, the Levant, or Middle East— seemed to many Victorians to be particularly amenable to a historical approach. Margaret Oliphant began *Jerusalem, The Holy City* (1891) by emphasizing its status as history: "The writer scarcely needs to say that this book is no record of Eastern travel: her experiences in the Holy Land having no special importance, save as making more vivid to herself the scenes to which the following history is devoted."[5] Curiously Oliphant denies her work the very kind of personal value that some travelers—especially the tourists who wrote about Italy and other places associated with high culture—sought to attach to their works. The difference in approach can be attributed both to assumptions about region and what it offered and to assumptions about travel writing as history.

Margaret Oliphant sought explicitly to draw the boundaries between travel writing and history, but others found such demarcation impossible. These women sought instead to cultivate the affinities between the two modes, to demonstrate the ease with which travel writing shaded into history. Frances Power Cobbe, for instance, affirmed the connections between travel and history writing in her autobiography, praising those eastern travelers who quested after what she termed *historical faith*. And in *Eastern Life, Present and Past*, Harriet Martineau referred to the region's travelers as "historical inquirers." She later wrote in her autobiography that eastern travel had reshaped her way of conceiving history: "All the historical hints I had gained from my school days onwards now rose up amidst a wholly new light."[6]

Harriet Martineau's *Eastern Life, Present and Past* and Frances Power Cobbe's *Cities of the Past* stand out as two of the period's most engaging historical travel accounts. As their titles indicate, both women represented their experience as explorations of a region's past, as immersions into its history. What makes their work most distinctive, however, is the extraordinary emphasis both placed on the capacity of the eastern past to facilitate a personal process of recovery. Both women endowed the pasts they recreated with the power for personal replenishment. Martineau and Cobbe invoked this theme of recovery for a variety of reasons. In addition to its obvious therapeutic connotations, recovery offered a compelling way to represent travel as historical work. The essential work of the historian was, after all, recovery.

That Martineau and Cobbe chose to represent themselves as hybrid historians is in part a reflection of the widespread cultural interest in history as a discipline and emerging profession throughout the Victorian period. But their choices also reflect their thinking about why the historical approach offered the most potential for recovering out of the region a sense of personal identity.

Most recent studies of the Victorian conception(s) of history are akin in their assumption of the intellectual hegemony that it enjoyed throughout most of the period. Rosemary Jann describes the historical as "the common coin of the nineteenth century,"[7] Philippa Levine in *The Amateur and the Professional* credits history as one of "the dominant intellectual resources which shaped Victorian culture,"[8] and Peter Allan Dale proclaims at the outset of his study: "That the nineteenth century was dominated as no period before or since has been by the 'historical sense' is a truth of intellectual history sufficiently well established to need no extended reiteration here."[9]

Although correct in their estimation of the powerful hold of history on the Victorian imagination, such assured testimony implies somewhat erroneously a degree of comfort and confidence with the abundant meanings of history. The "historical sense" on which Dale in particular focuses was one challenged and transformed throughout the period by scientific and technological innovations that inaugurated new conceptions of time. The emergence of geology, archaeology, and natural history as legitimate fields of scientific inquiry all depended on a fundamental reconceptualization about the relationship between past and present, as J. H. Buckley in *The Triumph of Time: A Study of the Victorian Concepts of Time, History, Progress, and Decadence* has well shown.[10] Although many Victorians continued like their predecessors to embrace a providential notion of history, they did so with increasingly less confidence as the century progressed. Indeed, the consistency with which Victorians turned to the past for explanatory or prophetic purposes suggests something of the extent to which this loss of confidence was felt.

The Victorians did not simply debate the meanings and function of history. They reassessed who could write it. In *The Amateur and the Professional*, Philippa Levine documents the process whereby the institutionalization of history as a discipline redefined the intellectual boundaries on which the amateur and professional status of its practitioners—antiquarians, historians, and archaeologists—depended. Levine charts the institutional development of history in three Victorian communities of study—antiquarianism, history, and archaeology. As the century progressed, archaeology won academic recognition and antiquarianism was pushed to the peripheries of what was considered serious inquiry. She points out that the few women who actively participated in such communities of study (e.g., Amelia Edwards and the Egyptian Exploration Fund) were exceptions. For the most part they "suffered an inferior status" and "were rarely permitted a vote on the society's council."[11]

Although the boundaries of history as a profession were redrawn, the identity of the historian remained throughout the century at least implicitly tied to the "man of letters" tradition with which it began, a tradition associated in Victorian discourse with the sage voice. The leading figures were men, essayists like Macaulay, Carlyle, Thomas Arnold, and James Anthony Froude. This *belles lettres* tradition was challenged by philosophers such as Ranke, who strove to establish the scientific basis of the discipline. Although its parameters were clearly open to change and challenge, history was throughout the century generally regarded as a learned man's profession, the province of the sage.

Although the transformation of history as profession and mode of inquiry influenced their work, it would be misleading to suggest that either Martineau or Cobbe pitched their travel accounts as histories solely to forge professional identities as historians. Instead, both women seemed to have found that the language of the historian accommodated their desire to render their observations "objectively" while allowing them room for imaginative recreations, the "expounding" and "filling-up" to which Carlyle paid tribute. More important, the discourse of history appealed because it allowed them to embrace recovery as a mode of inquiry. Carlyle had suggested that one could recover from history the "spiritual desire" that had produced and directed it, and this is exactly what Martineau and Cobbe both seemed to have set out to do in their Middle Eastern journeys.

The Middle East was in many ways the ideal realm for this kind of historical work, for it inspired in many of its visitors throughout the period a unique amalgam of secular curiosity and sacred hope. Some Victorians traveled with the explicit aim of proving biblical stories to have been literally true to landscape. William Holman Hunt's famous painting of 1845 "The Scapegoat" is one prominent and frequently cited example of the urge to confirm biblical prophecy. But the desire to look for the realization of prophecy was felt by nearly all who traveled there. Traipsing through Jerusalem, for example, Augusta Klein ruminated: "It is strange to wander about the site of the Temple, and to realise how literally has been fulfulled that prophecy about there not remaining so much as one stone upon another."[12]

Whereas some Victorians sought to affirm what they had been taught they would find, others traveled with a bitter sense that their religious upbringing had betrayed them. Early in an essay titled "City of the Sun," first published in *Fraser's Magazine* and later collected with other travel essays in *The Cities of the Past*, Frances Power Cobbe lamented, "The teaching of the miserable theology of the last century infects us still, though there are signs on every hand that we are outgrowing it."[13] Yet even doubting Victorians like Cobbe endowed the east with a unique spiritual content, one that was visually represented by the landscape and that revealed to travelers the relationship between past and present.

To many of the Victorians who traveled there, Middle East regions represented not only a segment of history, but also a totality. To experience the east was to have immediate access to its past, and many Victorians represented themselves as in the presence of the past—a past that they preserved by making ahistorical. In "A Day at the Dead Sea" Cobbe describes the "immobility of the East" and writes that "after four thousand years the Sheikh of Hebron has probably not varied an iota from the costume, the habits, or the acquirements of Abraham" (113). For many travelers to the region, the past led, by implication, to all of human history. In "From Ocean to Sea," one of his *Prose Idylls*, Charles Kingsley described the Mediterranean as "the sacred sea; the sea of all civilisation and almost all history."[14] And in a letter written on a return journey to Cairo, Martineau meditated on "what new and unthought of knowledge comes to one in the presence of [the] past."[15] Although typical to writing about the Middle East, the tendency to find in foreign lands sources of history was not limited to place, or, indeed, genre. Just as in *Romola* George Eliot created a Florence that could serve both as a "certain historical spot" and as "an almost unviolated symbol,"[16] so too did others need to find regional pockets protected from the march of time that was hurrying England along. This was especially true for the work of art historians. Lady Eastlake once remarked, "We live in the past— the pictorial past—as we walk about Bruges, Ghent, and Antwerp," (*Journals and Correspondence*, II, 281). John Pemble concludes that this tendency was a reflection of the widespread Victorian "quest for oblivion," an impulse that led them to find refuge in a "womb-like past." He goes on to suggest that "their desire to stop the flow of history suggests the despair of men and women confronting the existential Nothingness: the void where there is no imperative save choice and where every choice reveals to the chooser that he is created and abandoned, free to choose because forsaken."[17]

In a sense, though, both believing and doubting Victorians traveled to the Middle East less as questors than as pilgrims of history. Having ascended the Mount of Olives, Martineau proclaimed in *Eastern Life, Present and Past*: "No one spot of the Holy Land can be more interesting to a pilgrim than this" (I, 436). To Frances Power Cobbe the idea of a pilgrimage appealed in its implicit rebuke of Protestant England. She explains in "A Day at the Dead Sea," another *Cities of the Past* essay: "What a pleasant thing it would be, after all, if in our day we could only believe in a pilgrimage! It is a common reproach against us modern English that we are all home-sick (i.e., sick of our homes!); and if we could but imagine that it were possible to combine a holy "work" and a pleasure-trip, the question is, not who would go, but who would stay behind" (134). Later in the same essay, she describes with glee her "real full day's pilgrimage" and remarks: "A journey in the desert is like reading a series of parables. We are then truly 'pilgrims and sojourners on earth,'" (112). Travelers on a pilgrimage could "read" the landscape for its history and be morally the better for it.

The Holy Land was for Cobbe as for many others the ultimate destination, less a place to be visited than an experience to be attained. In "The City of Peace," she describes Jerusalem as "the bourn of all pilgrimage, the most sacred spot of all earth" (177). The "sacred spots" that Martineau and Cobbe discovered were invariably the familiar places of the Bible—for example, the Garden of Gethsemane, the Pool of Hezekiah, the Mount of Olives, and the Mountains of the Temptation. More interesting than the places they chose to find and explore, though, was how they chose to render them. Arrival at the sacred spot afforded ample opportunity for imaginative role playing. Again and again in their work, they sought to recreate—often at length—the biblical episodes they associated with these places. Visiting Mount Sinai, for example, prompted Harriet Martineau to speculate on the feelings of Moses: "How intense must have been his sense of solitude here!" (*Eastern Life, Present and Past*, 319). She later explained, "It is impossible to avoid endeavoring to enter his mind, when on the spot of his meditations" (*Eastern Life, Present and Past*, 320). Here Martineau effectively collapses the boundaries between past and present when she arrives on the sacred spot; she seeks instead to create a sense of ahistorical space, a place free from association with the local, the everyday.

In their tendency to locate the sacred spot and to imaginatively recreate there what had been felt in the past, both Martineau and Cobbe redirected their travel accounts into something like histories. In this sense, both clearly perceived history to be an interpretive practice—not strictly an objective, neutral science. In essence, they represented themselves as historical fieldworkers, as historians whose fieldwork took them to the sacred spots of Middle Eastern history. In his work on the evolution of ethnography, James Clifford describes the range of nineteenth-century "fieldworkers," for example, missionaries, administrators, traders, and travelers. He sees all of these as variations of what James Frazer first called the "man on the spot," the man whose authority issued out of his presence on the "spot" of another culture. He argues that the written work of the ethnographer established a special kind of authority based on the ethnographer's ability to take the reader to the place of interest and to share his observational standpoint.[18]

Many of the Victorian women who wrote about their experiences abroad tapped into similar sources of authority. Victorian adventuresses quite clearly piqued the interest of their readers by featuring their close contact with native populations, their experiences "on the spot" of foreign culture. The art historians who garnered the most authority were those who, like Anna Jameson and Lady Eastlake, had acquired their knowledge of art "on location" as it were and who were consequently able to describe these works in context. Similarly, the travelers to America, discussed in the next chapter, took their readers with them to witness the democratic experiment in process.

Although Harriet Martineau and Frances Power Cobbe participated in this tradition, their orientation differed in that the interest of the "sacred spot" was its past and its relation to human history, not its present state. Thus, whereas adventuresses, cultural tourists, and travelers to America could witness and objectively record what they observed on a day-to-day basis on the spot of foreign culture, the historian's task instead was to record everyday experiences only insofar as they helped to represent what once was there.

Martineau and Cobbe rose to the challenge. Rendering their accounts as variations on the classic ethnographic formula of participant-observation, they attempted to recreate for their readers moments of participation in an assumed past. And they sought to objectify their moments of participation by placing them within an observational context—by claiming to "witness" the past and by recording their observations. Although more commonly associated with the traditional ethnography that concerns Clifford, these methods served Martineau and Cobbe well and enabled them to occupy positions within

and outside of the pasts that they explored—to be both subjects and
agents of a process of recovery.

The Glorious Sterile Valley: Harriet Martineau's East

In 1846, Harriet Martineau began her eastern travels in northern
Africa. Although she carried with her compass and pencil, ready to
record, her impressions on first seeing the continent from her boat
suggested a different kind of experience, one that she would be
unable to measure:

> What we saw was the island of Zembra, and the neighboring coast of
> Tunis. Nothing in Africa struck me more than this its first phantom ap-
> pearance amidst the chill and gathering dusk of evening and with a vast
> expanse of sea heaving red between us and it. (*Eastern Life, Present and
> Past*, 17)

In the beginning of *Eastern Life, Present and Past* Martineau set up an
Africa as illusory as it was real, and though she anxiously awaited
arrival, her description of its phantom appearance in the chill evening
indicates not just anticipation but fear. Furthermore, the language
she chose to convey context—her heaving expanse of red sea—suggests that she likened her travel to a birthing experience, a metaphorical return to the womb. Martineau was not simply beginning a
standard tour of the Middle East; she was commencing a quest for
her origins.

When Martineau set out in 1846 for northern Africa she was still
in a sense recovering from some of the most difficult years of her life.
The early years of the 1840s were marked for her by an increasing and
painful loss of religious conviction and a corresponding need to separate herself from the Unitarian doctrine she had for many years embraced—feelings made more painful because of the rift they caused
with her brother James. The emotional strain of this situation coupled
with a debilitating stomach ailment was enough to prompt Martineau—never at a loss for the dramatic—to confine herself to a sickroom for nearly five years. The direction she would take in *Eastern
Life, Present and Past* was in large measure determined by these years
of personal crisis. Although the process that led to Martineau's renun-
ciation of Christianity was gradual, most of her biographers agree
that with *Eastern Life, Present and Past* she "crossed the threshold
of unbelief."[19] Given this assumption, it is especially interesting to
consider the impact of the sickroom experience on her identity as
a traveler.

Addressed to her "fellow sufferers," *Life in the Sickroom* was published in 1844, just two years before *Eastern Life, Present and Past*. It documents the anguish she experienced for an extended period when she thought she was dying. Martineau was what might be called a robust invalid. *Life in the Sickroom* is as much about recovery as it is about invalidism or pain. As she worked her way out of the sickroom, she came to view invalidism as having a "peculiar privilege," one "of seeing and feeling something of the simultaneous vastness and minuteness of providential administration."[20] Martineau's sickroom was "the scene of intensest convictions" (1) and "a sanctuary of confidence. . . . a natural confessional" (211). There she came to believe intensely in the powers of the mind, and toward the end of her book she proclaimed for all invalids: "We may be excluded from much observation of the outer life of men; but of the inner life, which originates and interprets the other, it is scarcely possible that in any other circumstances we could have known so much" (211). The seclusion afforded by her sickroom enabled Martineau to exercise her interpretive skills, to give full rein to the inner life. Just as she here claims an ability to bring the "inner" life of men to bear on the "outer," so would she in the Middle East see its past as an "inner life" that could help interpret the present. Feeling that her sickness had empowered her with these skills in no small measure accounted for her recovery.[21]

Martineau left on her relatively soon travels after emerging from her sickroom. With three other companions, she traveled first through Egypt, where she went up the Nile to Philae. From Egypt, she crossed the desert through Sinai to Palestine—the Holy Land—and from there went into Syria. When she journeyed east, she took with her an enormous confidence in the interpretive skills with which sickness had empowered her. She believed in her power to recover her self and to access the inner life and past that surrounded her. In many ways, the east became for her a second sickroom, and to ensure its status as such Martineau insisted that she be left to experience it alone. Although she traveled with three companions, she insisted on riding ahead or behind the group. After her group's evening meal she took long walks alone; when others gathered round a fire to chat, she retreated to her tent and her journal. This posture enhanced the privacy she already relished by virtue of her deafness. Hence, it is not surprising that Martineau felt as if her travels were an entirely private experience. The "sacred spots" she discovered became her "scenes of intensest convictions," its deserts and wastelands her "sanctuaries of confidence."

"Alone" in the east, Martineau could recover its past with the same skills that worked in the sickroom. In her autobiography Martineau describes her impulse to write about her eastern travels in language that is curiously akin to that which she had used to explain her need to write about her years in the sickroom: "The book itself had been determined on from the time when I found the influx of impressions growing painful, for want of expression" (I, 537). From the very first, she became engrossed with deducing from her surroundings "evidence" with which to reconstruct a history, and she was particularly concerned with recovering from it a pattern of spiritual development. As she recalled in her autobiography, "Step by step as we proceeded, evidence arose of the true character of the faiths which ruled the world; and my observations issued in a view of their genealogy and its results which I certainly did not carry with me, or invent by the wayside" (I, 537).

Martineau's genealogy began in Egypt, where the Nile and the desert became emblematic of what she considered the universal spiritual struggle between hope and fear. Read together, they helped to explain the country's singular spirituality. Explaining the centrality of Egyptian ideas of life and death to their faith, she wrote:

> The imagery before their eyes had perpetually sustained these modes of thought. Everywhere they had in their presence the symbols of the world of death and life;—the limited scene of production, activity and change;—the valley with its verdure, its floods, and its busy multitudes, who were all incessantly passing away, to be succeeded by their life; while, as a boundary to this scene of life, lay the region of death, to their view unlimited, and everlastingly silent to the human ear. (*Eastern Life, Present and Past*, 48)

Martineau represents herself here as a historical fieldworker who envisions and records what people in the past ostensibly saw, and her perspective might be summarized as "I see what they saw; I think what they thought." Although she adopts an authoritative stance very similar to the "you are there because I was there" claim of Clifford's ethnographer, her assumptions about the need to assert such a stance are different. Whereas an ethnographer would adopt this pose to bridge the gulf between cultures for his readers, Martineau does so to argue for a kind of cultural continuity, one that spans national perspective as well as time.

In essence, Martineau wanted to find a Middle East that would include her, and throughout her travels she found a variety of means to accomplish this end. She envisioned an Egypt, for instance, that could serve as a microcosm of all human life. The river and desert for her served as convenient and everywhere visible "symbols of the

world of death and life" (*Eastern Life, Present and Past*, 48). Over and
over again in her account of Egypt Martineau comes back to the Nile
and the desert as metaphors for hope and fear—so often that one
begins to suspect that they helped her to characterize her own
"modes of thought." Indeed, in letters written to friends in England,
Martineau represents her position in terms remarkably akin to those
she identifies in *Eastern Life, Present and Past* with the ancient Egyptians. Describing for Richard Milnes a journey to Cairo, for example,
she wrote: "I rode, day by day, through the glorious sterile valley
which leads one among the population of the dead, feeling the same
ideas and emotions *must* have been in the minds of those before
whose eyes, as before mine, lay the same contrasting scenery of life
and death."[22] By positioning herself within a "sterile valley" and
among "the population of the dead," Martineau likens her experience
to that of Christ's temptation in the wilderness—an analogy that she
would make even more explicitly in the portions of her account devoted to Palestine. Here, as throughout *Eastern Life, Present and Past*,
Martineau makes a direct correlation between scenery (outer life)
and the ideas and emotions (inner life) that can be recovered from
the landscape. Her emphasis ("*must*") suggests not only intensity of
conviction but also her acute need to be the agent of the transition
between inner and outer, the past and the present.

Martineau's comments suggest, furthermore, that part of her strategy as traveling historian of Egypt (and later of the Holy Land) was
at least implicitly to claim that her experience was identical to native
experience—even native experience of many hundreds of years ago.
Not only does she imply that the scenery of Egypt—its contrasting
imagery of life and death—has not changed at all, but also that this
scenery necessarily evokes in her the same ideas and emotions it
once evoked in the ancient Egyptians. The technique enables her to
speak for and about peoples of the past. As a participant-observer,
she takes her readers to the "spot" of inquiry, although in her case
the overt impulse is historical rather than ethnographic.

The strategy evident in Martineau's letter to Milnes is equally
prominent throughout *Eastern Life, Present and Past*, particularly in
and around Jerusalem. Indeed, as her travel account progresses, one
can sense that her priorities become increasingly eastern life past,
rather than present. "We were as sure now as we could feel at Jerusalem of being on the tracks of the Teacher," she wrote outside Naza-
reth, almost as if Christ had just passed through minutes before.
Later in Panias she confidently proclaimed: "To this spot he came—
probably to see the flowing forth of Jordan from the rock. In gazing
at that, he would have seen these niches, and inscriptions which

show in whose honour they were made. What a singular and most interesting union of ideas this is!" (481). Martineau not only takes her readers to the spot of history, but also asks them to follow her vision as if it were Christ's own. She becomes the speaker for his past. She collapses the difference between eastern past and present and creates in its place a "union of ideas," a pocket of ahistoricity in which she recovers for her readers Christ's past.

Writing about the spots of Christian history also enabled Martineau to steer her readers in directions less explicitly related to her own experiences. *Eastern Life, Present and Past* includes both narrative accounts of Martineau's day-to-day impressions and explanatory excursions into religious history. Chapter 2 of "Palestine and its Faith," for example, proceeds on the assumption she must educate her readers on the fundamental elements of Hebrew religious life. "Before going in search of the haunts of Jesus," she wrote, "it seems to me desirable to review, however slightly, the progress which religion had made since the great events which dated from Sinai" (388). She then explained her rationale: "This is necessary in giving a faithful account of my travels, because I found it indispensable on the spot to the true understanding of my journey. We all know something of the beneficent power of knowledge at home, though our knowledge there can be derived only through books" (388).

Martineau wanted her readers to appreciate that her experience on the spot of Christian history has enabled her both to ratify and to exceed the kind(s) of knowledge available to students of history at home. She also strives in her travel account to display her learnedness in both the Bible and the classics. In effect she argues that the legitimacy of her study is twofold: although founded in many ways on the scholarship of England's own "learned men," its authority derives also from her ostensible direct experience of the past. Experience "on the spot," she claims, is as or more valuable to a "true understanding" of history than the limited knowledge that can be obtained from books. When she came several years later to write her autobiography she would reiterate this claim: "It is impossible for even erudite homestayers to conceive what is gained by seeing for one's self the scenes of history" (I, 537).

Martineau also wanted to take advantage of the opportunity travel writing offered her to display her own scholarly prowess, and her account is replete with references to the preparatory reading that she had done at home. Sharpe's account of Egyptian history, Wilkinson's study of the ancient Egyptians, Robinson's study of the Bible, Kitto's history of Palestine, and Hooker's study of ecclesiastical polity are just a few of the works that figure prominently in Martineau's bid for authority. Indeed, part of her achievement with *Eastern Life, Present and Past* was to make such scholarship more accessible to the reader by using it in the context of travel writing. In W. H. Davenport Adams's 1883 study, *Celebrated Women Travellers of the Nineteenth Century*, she is praised for having "given a fresh interest to the beaten track of eastern travel and research, and breathing vitality into the dry bones of Champollini, Wilkinson, and Lane" (409). What Davenport picked up on in her work was her ability to find in the narrative conventions of historical scholarship a tool for explaining her purpose as a travel writer.

Early on in *Eastern Life, Present and Past* she veers from her narrative to speculate on the nature of what she variously calls "historical inquiry" and "modern inquiry." To Martineau, the duty of the eastern traveler was to delineate between fictional and factual dimensions of history:

> It is the business of the philosophical historian to separate the true ideas from their environment of fiction, and to mark the time when the narrative, from being mythical becomes historically true—to classify the two orders of ancient historians—both inestimable in their way—the Poets who perpetuate national Ideas, and the Historians who perpetuate national Facts. (89)

Martineau represents her work as being akin to that of the biblical critics (the "learned men . . up to the mark of historical science" to whom she repeatedly makes reference in *Eastern Life, Present and Past*) who prompted so many believing Victorians to question the basis of their faith. As if to bolster her own credibility as traveler and researcher, Martineau presents a survey of this kind of scholarship in *Eastern Life, Present and Past* (305–8). She seems to sense that "true history" is a repository of facts and that the burden of the "modern inquirer" is to eliminate from this repository all that cannot be empirically proven, to extract from it all legend. Here again her work follows a paradigm of recovery; she weeds out the false from the true in an effort to come closer to—to recover—the original idea untainted by the outer, what in this case is the present. She clearly places her allegiance with the historian, but she acknowledges the value of the poet's work in disseminating what she calls "national Ideas."

On several occasions in *Eastern Life, Present and Past* Martineau steps out of her role as traveler and into that of prospective author concerned only with factual accuracy. Explaining the diligence with which she kept a daily record of her activities, for instance, she wrote: "It is worth any fatigue and annoyance at the moment, to secure certainty for all future time in regard to the knowledge obtained on the spot" (298). At another point she expresses doubts about sending what she considers a "meagre" and "vague" chapter to her publisher and admits:

> I could have made it fuller, and far more interesting and distinct, if I had written down what I was told. . . . But, as I said before, I could not rely on the information, while entirely relying on the honor of those who gave it. I have thought it best to offer only the little I believe to be true. Of this little I cannot say how much might be modified by facts which may lie behind. (276).

Martineau reveals more than her concern that rationality rule the day, even the eastern day. She represents the validity of her work as being—like that of the ethnographer—dependent on her ability to "see through" the fictions perpetuated by native informants. And, like most other middle-class travelers of her time, she was inordinately distrustful of the kinds of information non-Westerners had to offer, at one point even asserting that "it was impossible to obtain any information from the Arabs" (71).

Martineau's concern with turning her travel into a fact-finding mission is borne out in other ways as well. Although she finds herself frequently given over to speculation on the buried treasures of Egypt, she admits that part of her curiosity involved finding a "means for managing that obstinate sand" (46). She takes pains to examine the interiors of native dwellings along the Nile, attempting to form "notions of [their] household economy" that would be valuable to scholars at home (76). And she repeatedly invokes the need for the traveler to approach the country with "clear eyes" and "a fresh mind" to achieve "some clearness of ideas."

Despite Martineau's invocations to rationality, though, one gets the sense throughout her work that she finds rational vision difficult to maintain in the Middle East, that it somehow does not do justice to the experience. Addressing this difficulty at one point in her *Autobiography* she explains: "all is too suggestive and too confounding to be met in the spirit of study. One's powers of observation shrink under the perpetual exercise of thought; and the light-hearted voyager who sets forth from Cairo eager for new scenes and days of frolic, comes back an antique, a citizen of the world of six thousand years ago" (II, 371). The "suggestive" and "confounding" impressions generated on the eastern spot of history overrode the spirit of rational inquiry brought to that spot from the west. Not surprisingly, the rational traveler that Martineau projects in the early portions of

Eastern Life, Present and Past recedes as the narrative progresses. What she discovers along the way is that eastern life does not conform to western ways of thinking. What really piques her imagination is not the obstinate sand or the household interiors but the scenery and monuments, both of which she reads as "illustrations of the eternal" (89). The east she in the end discovers is too vast and shadowy to be met with clear English eyes, and while it intrigues, it also disturbs.

Most disturbing were the temples, which to Martineau led inevitably to "thoughts of death, judgment, and retribution" (151). Recalling for her readers her impressions after leaving a temple at Abu-Simbel, she wrote: "I looked back, and saw beyond the dark halls and shadowy Osirides the golden sand-hill without, a corner of blue sky, and a gay group of the crew in the sunshine. It was like looking out upon life from the grave" (117). Martineau was drawn to the dark and shadowy interiors of eastern life, but she felt oppressed by them as well, trapped as if in a grave. Although she took copious notes of the tombs visited while abroad, these, too, oppressed her: "This black pall of oblivion hanging over all gives one, though a mere stranger, something of the mourner feeling, which is one of the privileges of the speculative, when bringing speculation to bear on the obliterated past, instead of the unrevealed future" (189). Her observations here are in many ways emblematic of her eastern experience as a whole. She represents her skills as Middle Eastern traveler in much the same way as she had represented her "powers" in the sickroom. After all, there too she felt herself looking from a grave out on the life that surrounded but did not include her. In the Middle East, she depicts herself less as an observer than as a meditator, a traveler whose duty was to speculate on the "obliterated" past in much the same way as the sick person had pondered the life that loomed around her. Curiously, in both places (e.g., the Middle East and her sickroom) she identifies her perspective as "privileged." In the sickroom her privilege had been to see and feel "something of the simultaneous vastness and minuteness of providential administration," and this too is what she claims to sense in her encounters with Eastern scenes of history.

Martineau felt acutely the need to conceive of eastern life in terms of the connections, not disruptions, between past and present, vast and minute, and she strove throughout her account to locate and affirm their affinities. Recognition of affinity, she reasoned, was the natural end to historical search. Affinity with the past—as well as a willing acknowledgement of the continuity of "early Ideas" into contemporary life—led not to oppression but to "a cheering efficacy" (229). Describing for her readers the effect of eastern life on the "thoughtful traveller," she wrote: "The more he traces downwards the history and philosophy of religious worship, the more astonished he will be to find to what an extent this early theology originated later systems of belief and adoration, and how long and far it has transcended some of those which arose out of it" (116). Over and over again in *Eastern Life, Present and Past*, Martineau pays tribute to the "solemn" and "serious" enterprise of eastern travel and to the nobility of "the first ideas of Deity known to exist in the world" (116). "There is enough here to teach us some humility and patience about the true history of the world," she at one point concludes (228). As such comments suggest, Martineau thought it her duty to convey that "true history" to her English readers at home and to encourage them to integrate eastern ideas into their ways of thinking.

Martineau's need to establish affinity with the past becomes increasingly evident as *Eastern Life, Present and Past* progresses and is perhaps nowhere more obvious that in her account of "Palestine and its Faith," which begins with her statement that on entering the Holy Land her first thought "was one of pleasure that it was so like home." In this section she expresses concern for travelers entering the region with "anxious mind[s] of superstition":

> Instead of looking before and after, and around them in the broad light of historical and philosophical knowledge, which would reveal to them the origin and sympathy and intermingling of the faiths of men, so that each may go some way in the interpretation of the rest—instead of having so familiarized themselves with the wants and tendencies of men as to recognize in successive faiths what is derived and what is original—instead of being warned that any faith becomes corrupted within a certain length of time by the very zeal of its holders; instead of having the power of setting themselves back to the time when Christ lived and spoke; so as to hear him as if he lived and spoke at this day our travellers may be seen . . . overlooking, more or less consciously—the incompatibilities of the Scriptural narratives—the absolute contradictions which can by no means be reconciled; or so fastening their whole attention upon one narration, to the exclusion of the parallel ones, so to escape the necessity of the recognition of variance. (384)

Taken in its entirety, the passage reveals much about Martineau's project. She distinguishes her inquiry from that of the typical traveler's by virtue of her supposed ability to "look before and after," that is to see eastern life under "the broad light of historical and philosophical knowledge" that exposes the inconsistencies as well as the unities of human forms of faith. Significantly, Martineau draws on her skills as a participant-observer to substantiate her claim. As a traveler directed by historical inquiry, she enjoys the unique privilege of "on the spot" investigation of the past. The typical travelers, she argues, lack (or neglect) the "power of setting themselves back." And it is this power that she throughout her work demonstrates to be essential to the act of recovering history.

Martineau's confidence in her ability to recover the essence of faith from eastern history is nowhere more prominent than in the concluding portions of her work. There she takes her obligatory "last view" of the horizon: "before me lay the sea, our homeward path: and behind lay the East—the birthplace of the Ideas which have hitherto governed mankind. Within me were stirring speculations" (516). Here again Martineau represents her role as traveler to be essentially meditative; her observations lead not to records but to deliberation, speculation, further inquiry. Like the conscientious traveler she had with *How to Observe Morals and Manners* (1838) trained herself to be, Martineau refuses to do more "on the spot" of history than begin to speculate. To truly understand eastern life, she felt, she must wait to invoke the retrospective vision that would only be made possible by a return to western soil.

Although *Eastern Life, Present and Past* incorporates passages from the diary Martineau kept while abroad, much of it was written after she had returned home, where she felt her capacity to recover eastern history assured by the return of English health. Consequently, interspersed throughout the account and binding together excerpts from her diary is retrospective commentary—recollections of her experience given the additional credibility of hindsight. Although Martineau's textual strategy reflects in part the obvious demands of assimilating material from private journals into a publishable—and hence public—form, it also lends structural support to the weight of her argument. In essence, she believed that her experience in the east was only valuable insofar as it could be integrated into her western perspective:

> The reflective and substantiating powers which characterize the Western Mind [must] be brought into union with the Perceptive, Imaginative, and Aspiring Faculty of the East, so as to originate a new order of knowledge and wisdom, and give a continually higher and truer employment to the faculties of Reverence, self-government, and obedience which are common to the whole mind. (517)

On first glance, her projected "new order of knowledge" incorporates equally what she believed to be valuable in eastern and western ways of thinking. But the "Western Mind" enjoys a privileged status in her paradigm; in its substantiating and reflective capacities, it holds the power to authenticate the more ephemeral eastern faculties of perception, imagination, and aspiration. Still, Martineau's paradigm follows the classic Hegelian thesis/antithesis/synthesis pattern, and her "new order" of knowledge reclaims from both eastern and western traditions those qualities which best complement one another.

In many ways, Martineau's pilgrimage to the east adheres in form and content to a traditional quest narrative. It is made complete and meaningful only by virtue of her return to the west, where she ostensibly brings her gleanings from abroad. Like the traditional hero of a quest narrative, she demonstrates on her return an ability to become reacclimated to the local and everyday. *Eastern Life, Present and Past* ends with a vision of reacclimation when Martineau self-consciously interrupts her ruminations on the possibility of a "new order of knowledge": "From out of these speculations now spoke the still small voice of conscience, prescribing the part which every thoughtful person who had accepted the privilege of exploring these Eastern regions should take in the aid of the work of enlightening the human mind" (518). With echoes of Wordsworth, Martineau here juxtaposes speculation with thought, representing the first as part of her now past eastern experience and the second with her present and future in England. She suggests that her ultimate duty as a thoughtful and conscientious English woman is nothing less than to begin the work of human enlightenment. Although eastern experience had enhanced her contemplative nature, Martineau's personal sense of satisfaction is more evidently rooted in western experience—specifically in middle-class Victorian society with its rhetoric of duty.

Not surprisingly, it is with this rhetoric of duty that *Eastern Life, Present and Past* closes: "I could not have accepted the privileges of my travels without accepting also their responsibilities. Having, as well as I could, endeavored to discharge these responsibilities, I can henceforth look back upon the regions of the East with more freedom and pleasure than I could from that Syrian shore, in the light of the last sunset I was ever to watch from the door of our tent" (518). One cannot read Martineau's words without a sense of their ambivalence. Although she speaks to the necessity of her responsibilities as a traveler—and even claims she feels more freedom and pleasure having acted on this sense of duty—her message fails to be wholly convincing. It lacks the vitality of the woman who recalled with glee the times in which she sang aloud while walking alone on the banks of the Jordan River; it lacks the resolve of the woman who marched on ahead of her camel across the Syrian desert. Martineau projects a rational voice at the end of her travel account, but it fails to completely stifle the more sentimental voice of the woman who clearly yearns to return to her sunset vision, the perspective that was afforded looking out of her tent on "that Syrian shore."

That Martineau felt obliged to return to a more wholly rational self in England and in her published work suggests much about the meaning of travel for her. Although her experience in the Middle East evidently allowed her to put to good use the meditative powers she had cultivated in the sickroom, her goal in the end was recovery. And this recovery involved returning to the practical, work-oriented person she had been before her years in the sickroom. The end of both travel and recovery was not to embark on the new but rather to return, reinvigorated to the past. And for Martineau this past was one ruled by the voice of conscience, not by the speculative mind.

Frances Power Cobbe: Capturing the Spirit of the Past

Frances Power Cobbe invites comparison to Harriet Martineau on several grounds. Like Martineau, she established herself as a formidable intellectual woman by challenging very early in her life the ideology that positioned her in a home rather than out in the working world. In a general way, Cobbe's career follows a pattern similar to that of Martineau; both women began by writing on religion, moved later to travel writing, and turned after their travel experiences to social reform. But the interest of comparison lies as much with the personal crises both women underwent as with the public identities that seem to have been inspired by those crises.

Like Harriet Martineau, Frances Power Cobbe chose to travel to the Middle East at a crucial period in her personal history. She left after her father died, committed to beginning anew but at the same time anguished by her sense of isolation. Her isolation stemmed less from his death itself than from the rift that her expression of religious doubts had caused with her father while he was alive. Bothered throughout her childhood by what she felt was an inability to truly believe in the teachings of the church, her sole source of comfort during these years was her mother's willingness to listen to her without hostility. After her mother died, she was left without a confidante and her father apparently felt that her expression of religious doubts—especially in writing—threatened her feminine nature. To the day of his death, Mr. Cobbe refused to read anything that his daughter had written. When she tried to talk with him about her beliefs she was thrown out of her home. Although she later returned, the incident was damaging enough to make her feel strongly that his love was conditional. Instead of blaming him for creating the conditions, however, she found fault with the religious beliefs that had served his purposes.

In a letter written in 1857 after her father died, Cobbe claimed to have felt his death had facilitated the reconciliation that she had yearned for: "At all events the wall of *creed* has fallen down from between our souls forever, and I believe that was the one great obstacle which I could never overthrow entirely."[23] Cobbe's feelings about her father are especially interesting to consider because she left soon after his death for her travels. The "wall of creed" would continue to haunt her while abroad for it would ever serve as her emblem of separation. Travel would become a quest for a life beyond that wall of creed. And although it no longer separated her from her father, death did, and the reality of that sense of separation became increasingly apparent in the weeks and months that followed. Through travel, Cobbe came to terms with the person she would be without a father figuring prominently in her daily life. She looked to the east to recover a sense of her self's place not in Victorian society with its walls of creed but rather in a history she imagined to be "beyond" creed.

Cobbe set off on this first journey outside of England still grieving but nonetheless a self-proclaimed "wilful woman" anxious to prove to doubting friends that she could travel through Egypt and Jerusalem on her own. She published an account of her impressions and experiences in a series of articles for *Fraser's Magazine* (later republished as *Cities of the Past*). She also described her experiences briefly in her autobiography, *The Life of Frances Power Cobbe, by Herself* (1894), a work whose title suggestively points both to Cobbe's independence and to her sense of solitariness. Claiming to have been impressed in her travels by the "enormous amount of pure human good nature" with which she met, Cobbe wrote in her autobiography: "But for viewing human nature *en beau*, commend me to a long journey by a woman of middle age, of no beauty, and travelling as cheaply as possible, alone" (201). Cobbe here represents herself as akin to the kind of woman Charlotte Brontë sought repeatedly to create in her fiction. In the portion of her autobiography devoted to her "long journey," Cobbe appears as a Lucy Snowe–like figure, asking her readers to remain conscious throughout not only of her lack of privilege—the status that youth, beauty, and wealth conferred on other women of her society—but also of her isolation. And she finds occasion throughout *Cities of the Past* to underscore this isolation. In "City of Victory," her account of a visit to Cairo, she reminds her readers: "I was voyaging alone to the East, determined to see Nile and Jordan and Ilyssus before I died; and, woman as I was, to make my way alone if no pleasant company offered" (37). Both here and in her autobiography, Cobbe takes care to emphasize her status as a single woman traveler. The effect is to claim for her journey a unique perspective. Cobbe's quest is set forth not only as a pilgrimage to the Nile and the Jordan, but also as an opportunity to assert her newly discovered independence as a woman.

Cobbe's sense of isolation permeates the essays that comprise *Cities of the Past* in a multitude of ways and reflects more than her awareness of her status as a single woman. To a certain extent, she uses her isolation to imaginatively capture the spirit of the place. In "City of the Sun" for instance she claims: "It was a boon to be alone in Baalbec. The stillness and the calm were most impressive. I remained for hours in the glorious fane so strangely my own, and tried to conceive what had been the thoughts of the worshippers when last the incense had risen from those broken altars to the mysterious Baal" (34). Without the inevitable interruptions and compromise that travel in company necessitates, she could more readily immerse herself in the city's atmosphere. Much like Harriet Martineau, Cobbe uses her isolation to appropriate the place as her own. Just as Martineau traveled ahead of her group to more easily speculate on the thoughts and feelings of the peoples of the ancient past, so too does being alone prompt Cobbe to imagine the workings of the ancient mind. Isolation is requisite to the kind of historical imagining that eastern experience engenders.

Although Cobbe claims in these and other passages that she gained by traveling alone, her *Cities of the Past* essays are nonetheless marked throughout by a sense of loneliness. Indeed, landscape becomes for her, as for the Romantic tourist, an emotional barometer. She writes in "City of the Sun" that Baalbec impresses her with "a sense of desolation no other spot on earth conveyed" (29) and Lebanon appears as "an aged, hoary saint with giant limbs" prompting her to contemplate "the abysses of our own sinful souls" (13). Although momentarily refreshed by the waters of the Jordan, enticed by the incensed air, and fascinated by forms of heathenism she encountered, Cobbe's experience in this region suggestively follows a pattern of descent that one would expect to find in a traditional quest narrative. In nearly every *Cities of the Past* essay, Cobbe moves from a brief celebration of arrival to a more thoroughgoing inquiry into the effects of the place on her state of mind. In Cairo, for example, she is led to speculate on the appeal of the Nile over other points of interest in Egypt and asks: "Is it that, like ourselves, a river only has a beginning, middle, end; the tiny sources, the full strong, flowing stream—the bourn, at last, whence the waters roll not back, nor any traveller may return" (*Cities of the Past*, 52).

Such comments indicate how much her immersion in eastern history was enmeshed with a sense of her own life history. Although doing so less overtly than did Martineau, Cobbe, too, represents herself as a meditative traveler, suggesting that her duty was less to observe and record than to ponder.

Typically, Cobbe's introspective moments occur when writing about enclosed spaces. In "City of the Sun" she describes in great detail the burial sites in Baalbec. At one point they appear almost as microcosms of Dante's inferno:

> The Dead Silence, the thick darkness, and oppressive air of these sepulchre vaults—sepulchres, it might be under a Dead City—are wholly indescribable in their awe. I wandered from one to another, and entered, as I could bear, through doors which seemed like portals of Dante's Hell; till the sense of awe became almost horror, and I could endure no more. (33)

She portrays the experience as nightmarish in its capacity to entrap; although she wanders freely, she seems to do so reluctantly—almost against her will. Just as excursions into the interiors of temples had led Harriet Martineau to speculate on retribution and judgment, so too is Cobbe prompted to conceive of the experience as a trial. With its thick, dark air and dead silence, the sepulchres she describes transport her unwittingly into an area of her own consciousness that she finds painful and, in the end, unendurable.

Such occasions—although momentous—constitute only a small portion of *Cities of the Past*, however. The emphasis in each of Cobbe's essays is not on crisis but rather on the process of recovery. Here again her experience approximates that of Martineau; both women conceived of recovery in both physical and spiritual terms, and both aligned their personal process of recovery with a larger, all-encompassing historical spirit of inquiry.

That recovery was to Cobbe an act of the imagination is evident throughout *Cities of the Past*. She emphasizes throughout not only the necessary workings of her own imagination but also those of her readers. On many occasions she directly addresses her readers and often exhorts them to follow her vision. In "City of Victory," for instance, she asks: "Will you follow me, reader, as I enter Cairo, and strive to convey the impressions of a ride through those dim, wonderful streets?"(55). In a more informal way than Martineau, Cobbe takes her readers with her to the places she associates with the past—to eastern "spots of time."

Curiously, Cobbe on several occasions chooses to identify her readership as specifically female. In "The City of Peace," she urges her fellow countrywomen to "give themselves the delight of beholding the spots of earth round which imagination has hovered from childhood" (173), an appeal that presumes that those spots are as much "made real" by the imagination as they are by history. Over and over again in *Cities of the Past* Cobbe associates her experience with a return to childhood imagination. Almost always described as delightfully liberating, these metaphorical retreats to personal past become central to her overall representation of the act of recovery.

Recovery for Cobbe also involves a celebration of the sensual that is implicitly linked to the freedom she associates with childhood imaginings. Part of her "descent" into eastern experience follows a sort of "sloughing off" of western physicality. In "City of Victory" she describes the process: "We are freed from the vulgar grinding sounds of Western cities, and our senses are all gratified at once; for through the balmy spring atmosphere are constantly stealing the odours of burning cedar, of delicious chibouques and narghilis, of dry Eastern spices, and luscious attar of Mecca" (56). The sensual appeal with which she endows the east marks her escape not only from urban malaise with its "vulgar grinding sounds," but also, and more importantly, from what she conceived to be the overly rigid and dogmatic society in which she was brought up. In "A Day at the Dead Sea" she writes:

> The simple realities of existence, which so rarely approach us at all in the orderly and overly finished life of England, where we slide, without jolt or jar from the cradle to the grave, along the smooth rails laid down by civilization, are present once more in the wilderness of the East. (112)

Cobbe, like many of her compatriots, "orientalizes" her eastern experience, especially in her effort to depict it as free from or outside of history. The east she imagines has escaped the onslaught of progress that has civilized English life and as such it serves as a reservoir of refreshing simplicity. In addition, Cobbe implies that the English, too used to the ease of civilization, could benefit from eastern jolts and jars about "simple reality."

For Cobbe, recovery required more than simply expressing disenchantment with western ways of thinking, though. With *Cities of the Past* she wanted to do more than celebrate the assumed freedoms of the east. Just as Harriet Martineau had moved at the end of *Eastern Life, Present and Past* to suggest the implications that eastern experience had for western ways of thinking, so too did Cobbe introduce into her narrative commentary on the social value of the east. She, too, was very much influenced in this direction of her thought by her reading of biblical critics, although she addressed this influence in her work much less directly than did Martineau. In "City of Victory," for instance, she discusses briefly the effects of biblical criticism on the history of faith and concludes: "Rather must we believe that each advance in knowledge will help forward that nobler faith which is to come—that faith of the future which will not be the extinguishing of past religions, but the essential life of all of them revivified in an immortal resurrection" (62). Like Martineau, she refrains from defining more specifically just what this "nobler faith" entailed. Rather, it exists in her mind and work as an ideal to be approached. Like Martineau's "new order of knowledge," Cobbe's "nobler faith" was a Tennysonian "far-off, divine event," something "to which the whole creation moves" (*Cities of the Past*, 35). In keeping with this train of thought, Cobbe quotes the last stanza of "In Memoriam" toward the end of the same essay.

Expressing her vision of human faith was not just a response to eastern ephemerality. It was central to her own personal program for recovery as well as to her sense of social reform. Stepping briefly out of the role of impressionistic traveler, Cobbe wrote in "City of the Sun":

> The reformers of the world, it would seem, ought to proceed in a far different way. Surely they should take the *spirit* of all that in the past is true and holy, and leave the mere formal blocks of myths and cults to lie where they have fallen; never despised, never desecrated, only disused; visited and studied with a sacred and tender interest, but not forced into unnatural service. (26)

Cobbe's language here reveals something of the extent to which her personal history had become entwined with her sense of eastern history. Although ostensibly expressing her sense of the essence of eastern faith in response to her own society's reform movements, she uses words that resonate with personal meaning. For much of her life she felt "forced into unnatural service" by her religious upbringing. The fallen "blocks of myths of cults" to which she refers here have much in common with the "wall of creed" that for so many years separated her from her father. Her comments suggest, then, that her personal recovery involved finding in her past something she could think of as "true and holy," the "spirit" of her father rather than his reality. To recover this spirit required leaving something behind (those "mere formal blocks") while yet acknowledging their place (as something to be "visited and studied"). More important, it involved recognizing one's self not as abused but as "disused."

To come to such a recognition was not the end of Cobbe's quest, though. Like Martineau, that end came only through reintegration into Victorian society. Cobbe seems to have realized all along that her place was ultimately not in the east, recovering her past, but in England, realizing her future. At the beginning of "City of the Sun," the first essay to appear in *Cities of the Past*, she proclaimed:

> 'Tis a poor choice to give up England in our manhood, and abandon for ever all its purpose and its noble strife for the lotus-eater life of the South. At this hour, when every voice and every arm are needed to grapple with error, and want, and sin . . . it is, I say, a pitiful thing to quit the field and wander away to dream, and gaze, and ponder; and life as perhaps man may have earned the right to live in centuries to come, when Giant Despair and Giant Sin are dead. . . . Yet even for now, for a time, for a passing experience, there is nothing better for us than to cool our fevered lips in the waters of old Nile, and wash our wearied eyes in Jordan. (1–2)

Like the "still small voice of conscience" that at the end of *Eastern Life, Present and Past* reminds Martineau of her duty to the present, Cobbe's voice of conscience from the beginning calls her back to England, and she too counterposes this voice to the meditative mind that her eastern self had cultivated but that her western self had not yet "earned." Positioning her speech in the very beginning of her first essay suggests that she wanted her readers to hear this voice throughout her essays, to know that duty underwrote travel. The natural end of Cobbe's quest was to return from historical inquiry to a life of "noble strife," to reintegrate her self into the everyday, with its inevitable battles against Giant Despair and Giant Sin. Pilgrimage to the past was a necessary but temporary release, a "passing experience."

The other interesting dimension of Cobbe's introductory comment is that she depicts the author-traveler (who is of course also herself) as in his "manhood," a term suggestive of rugged strength and vitality. Cobbe's reference could be part of her appeal to the whole readership—male and female—of *Fraser's Magazine*, where her essays were originally published. But she probably also wanted to identify herself with the life of "purpose" and "noble strife" to which she paid homage. The eastern experience was one that necessarily exacted a more feminine approach, one where her role was to wander, to dream, to gaze, and to ponder. There she "yielded to" experience. At home, in her "manhood," her role was to take control, to "grapple" with the plagues of modern, everyday society.

Both Harriet Martineau and Frances Power Cobbe returned to England from their journeys east to commence very active and highly visible careers in the here and now. After *Eastern Life, Present and Past*, Martineau's next major publication was *Household Education*, an extended treatise on education full of advice for parents raising children. Soon after returning to England she also began to write the lead stories for the *Daily News*. Both of these endeavors suggest that her experience in the east played a major part in facilitating a return to the everyday; it bridged the gap between the sickroom and the newsroom. And, indeed, she admits in her autobiography: "I had little idea what the privilege would turn out to be, nor how the convictions and action of the remnant of my life would be shaped and determined by what I saw and thought during those all-important months that I spent in the East" (I, 536).

Cobbe, too, immersed herself in the everyday on returning to England. Although she made several more trips to Italy after her journey east, she came increasingly to identify herself with social reform. Immediately after her return, for instance, she worked closely with Mary Carpenter in Bristol to bring the conditions of the sick in workhouses to public attention and to improve conditions for workhouse girls. Cobbe also became an outspoken advocate for woman's rights, publishing pamphlets such as "Criminals, Idiots, Women and Minors" (1868) and "Wife Torture" (1878) for the National Society for Woman's Suffrage and working closely with leading feminists like Barbara Leigh Smith Bodichon. She solidified her public reputation by campaigning actively against vivisection, a concern made especially intense because she recognized the connection between man's brutality to animals and his treatment of women. She also—like Martineau—initiated a journalistic career at this time, writing for the newly founded *Echo* and the *Standard*.

Such a cursory glance at the "post-East" careers of Martineau and Cobbe can in no way do justice to the range and intensity of their work as women with public, professional roles in England. But it does suggest that both recovered from earlier periods of personal crisis. For both women, a passionate involvement with their own society—with the everyday—was a central and necessary part of affirming and maintaining complete recovery.

In many ways, the intense involvement with society that Martineau and Cobbe demonstrated on return to England can be seen as a predictable outcome of their eastern experience. For both, work in England was closely interwoven with the sense of historicity that travel had evoked and redirected. The relatively recent scholarship known as "new historicism" can help one appreciate the kind of historical work done by Martineau and Cobbe. In an essay on the Victorian sense of the past, Stephen Bann has argued for a view of Victorian notions of history that encompasses both the work of the amateur and that of the professional.[24] To do so, he works with Foucault's assumption that the nineteenth-century awareness of history was a reaction to an overpowering sense of loss. Bann uses Foucault's dialectical model of loss and retrieval to explain the Victorian historian's methods and intent. He claims both amateur and professional historians responded in their work to "the bare fact that man has found himself to be emptied of history," and the significance of this response lies in the evidence that "he was already at the task of rediscovering in the depths of himself . . . a historicity that was linked to him essentially."[25]

Both Harriet Martineau and Frances Power Cobbe, of course, began their exploration of the eastern past when faced with an acute sense of loss. And for both that loss entailed family connection and support as well as religious sustenance. What is curious is that they did not seek to escape this sense of loss while abroad. On the contrary, they confronted it head on and even embraced it. They immersed themselves in a lifestyle and a landscape that everywhere reminded them of loss, that exacerbated what Martineau referred to as "that mourner feeling" which to her was the privilege of speculation. That Martineau took with her and cultivated "that mourner feeling" is evident throughout *Eastern Life, Present and Past*, as for example when she remarks, "Nothing remains of the monuments but some heaps of stones;—nothing whatever that can be seen from the river" (45). And Cobbe found in "the simple life of tents" a compelling analogy for the irretrievability of her past:

> That very morning at Mar Sabva, as we watched our tents taken down, and all traces of our brief encampment passing away, to be renewed as transitorily elsewhere at night, it forced itself on my mind more clearly than ever before, how the noblest aim of life could only be nightly to pitch our moving tents. . . . A day's march nearer home. (112)

Here Cobbe speaks to more than the appeal of the nomadic. She seems to have discovered in the Middle Eastern landscape and experience "a historicity . . . linked to [her] essentially." Both Harriet Martineau and Frances Power Cobbe transformed their travel accounts into personal explorations of historicity, and both represented the Middle East as a site of and for the "recovery" of this historicity.

In doing so, they took their travel accounts in a different direction than had many of their counterparts. Middle Eastern travel, they implied, demanded a "feminized" approach—a "yielding to" rather than "conquering of" place. They reserved their conquering spirit for the home front.

6

Declarations of Independence:
Victorian Women in America

"I, for one, do not acquiesce. I declare that whatever obedience I yield to the laws of the society in which I live is a matter between, not the community and myself, but my judgment and my will," wrote Harriet Martineau in *Society in America*, her comparative study of America's democratic principles and institutions.[1] *Society in America* is now regarded as one of early Victorian England's most important attempts to apply the as yet undefined principles of sociology to the study of abroad. Significantly, Martineau embeds her proclamation within the ostensibly objective treatise of *Society in America*, not within her more personalized travel account of America, *Retrospect of Western Travel* (1838). In essence, she positions the personal as the professional, and gives her declaration the legitimacy she believes is accorded to a rational, authoritative, and by implication male discourse of sociology.

Harriet Martineau recognized that such overt statements of female independence might compromise the seriousness with which her newly discovered role as social scientist would be taken. She was right. Just after she returned from her two-year trip to America, her colleague at *The Monthly Repository*, Leigh Hunt, wrote the satiric poem "Blue-Stocking Revels; or, the Feast of the Violets." It included the following mock tribute to Martineau:

> Ah! welcome home, Martineau, turning statistics
> To stories, and puzzling your philogamystics!
> I own I can't see, any more than dame Nature,
> Why love should await dear good Harriet's dictature!
> But great is earth's want of some love-legislature.[2]

In a similar vein, a critic for *Fraser's Magazine* welcomed her home from America with the warning: "If Miss Martineau, therefore, or any other maiden malcontent, should again venture to assert the

160

equality of man and woman, our only advice to whomsoever that lady may be, is to turn, before sitting down to her task to the book of Genesis."[3] In addition, a derogatory portrait of Martineau was depicted in the "Gallery of Illustrous Characters," a regular feature of *Fraser's Magazine,* exaggerating Martineau's intellectual inclinations and revealing what Patricia Marks has described as the "prevailing distrust of the bluestocking."[4] The amount of attention Martineau received during the immediate months after she had returned from her travels to America suggests the extent to which her work in social science was viewed as an implicit challenge—and threat—to womanhood.

Martineau was only one of several women prompted by experiences in America to make both personal and professional declarations of independence. For many women travelers, America was a land that cultivated, even demanded, autonomy, and it consequently attracted its fair share of women who traveled in search of physical and emotional independence. In 1854, for instance, Isabella Lucy Bird— twenty-three years old and suffering from a spinal disease and what her doctors called a "nervous debility"—sailed for Liverpool to spend nearly five months in Canada and the United States. She went with great expectations not only of physical recovery but also of intellectual stimulation and published an account of her experiences in the first of what would be many travel books, *The Englishwoman in America* (1856). Recounting for her friends at home her impressions upon arrival there, she wrote:

> We were speedily moored to the wharf at Portland amid a forest of masts; the stars and stripes flaunted gaily overhead in concert with the American eagle; and as I stepped upon those shores on which the sanguine suppose that the Anglo-Saxon race is to renew the vigour of its youth, I felt that a new era of my existence had begun.[5]

As a land that looked to the future, the United States enticed women like Isabella Bird with its promised opportunity of rebirth. Harriet Martineau anticipated "new subjects of research," "new paths of inquiry," and "new trains of ideas." Although no traveler was more reluctant to be rejuvenated by America than Frances Trollope, even she admitted in *Domestic Manners of the Americans* (1832) that "on first touching the soil of a new land, of a new continent, of a new world, it is impossible not to feel considerable excitement and deep interest."[6] And just before her arrival in New York, the Swedish traveler Frederika Bremer proclaimed confidently:

One thing, however, I know: that I shall see something new; learn something new; forget that which was of old; and press onward to that which lies before me. There is much for me to forget, and to be renewed.[7]

Like postlapsarian Eves, Victorian women found in America a new world "all before them," and they were certain only that the experience would be unlike anything that they had known before. Repeatedly emphasizing in their works the capacity of the country to "renew" and "rejuvenate," these women indulged in what they believed to be America's restorative powers.

In *Democracy in America* (1835–40), Alexis de Tocqueville unwittingly addressed the single most commanding source of the country's interest to many of these women. In America, he wrote, "there are no authorities except within itself."[8] In fact, the mark of authority was almost everywhere noticeably lacking, and although travelers for the most part found its absence inviting, they greeted it nonetheless with apprehension. America was both more like home and less like home than any other part of the wider world. Many travelers assumed like Tocqueville that forms of authority familiar to the Old World were not operative in America, and they scoured the country to discover the effects and implications of this difference. Of all the facets of American life affecting their impressions and sensibilities, none was more influential or disturbing than its perceived failure to effectively distinguish between the public and private. "No one dreams of fastening a door in Western America," Frances Trollope observed with discomfort in *Domestic Manners of the Americans*. "I was thus exposed to perpetual, and most vexatious interruptions from people whom I have often never seen, and whose names still oftener were unknown to me" (83). As Trollope's complaint suggests, some women travelers were far from comfortable with America's ostensible unwillingness to observe the rules of propriety. But most were not quite as quick to condemn as she; instead, they turned to the country's institutions to look more closely both at how the public sphere was structured and at where and how women were included.

The absence of authority noted by Tocqueville and felt by Trollope was to many Victorian women evidenced most by the clamoring of voices all claiming an equal opportunity to be heard in America. America, it seemed, offered everyone—including women—a chance to participate in public life, to be a citizen. As Martineau observed in *Society in America*, "In England the idea of an American citizen is of one who is always talking politics, canvassing, bustling about to make proselytes abroad, buried in newspapers at home, and hurrying to vote on election days" (I, 79). Not surprisingly, many of the women who traveled to America wrote accounts of their experiences that were both in focus and in method very different from the kinds engendered by travel to other parts of the world. America seemed to have a more expansive, more accessible public sphere than many of these women had experienced or imagined. Nineteenth-century travelers in general perceived America's essence to be housed in its institutions—its congressional halls, its churches, its town halls, and its newspapers.[9] Victorian women in particular endowed these institutions with the power to give the country's citizens a public voice. "The voice of a whole people goes up in the silent workings of an institution," Harriet Martineau wrote in her 1838 study *How to Observe Morals and Manners*.[10]

Martineau's orientation reflects the imaginative investment that she and other Victorians made in America. America was less a place to be enchanted with than a place to scrutinize and assess. A trip to America demanded that its visitors undertake an exhausting survey of the institutions available to its citizens. Prisons, asylums, markets, shops, and cemeteries were all required reading of America. The entire country was represented as a vast laboratory in which democratic ideals were tested and instituted. In the words of Frederika Bremer, who arrived in America in 1849, it was the "great land of experiment." Its schools, churches, lecture halls, and newspapers flaunted the liberties assumed by public voice, and Victorian women, not surprisingly, listened with intense interest. They also recorded. Travel accounts to America written by Victorian women are replete with lengthy extracts from newspapers, portions of conversations both engaged in and overheard, recollections of lectures and public speeches, paraphrases of sermons. In no other travel literature of the period is as much interest invested in recording the native voice.

In developing ways to represent the variety of voices that made America, Victorian women adopted—and developed—the methods of social study.[11] Nonetheless, their contributions and achievements have not been fully recognized for, as Jane Lewis has argued, "While it is fully acknowledged that women played a major role in the philanthropic world of the late nineteenth century, the part they played as social investigators has often been overlooked," a neglect she attributes to "the fact that female social investigation failed to develop along the quantitative paths pursued by the men."[12] Although Lewis is correct in her judgement that nineteenth-century women have not been adequately credited for their work in social study, her sense that these women "failed" to develop appropriate methodologies is somewhat skewed, as is her assumption that their social investigation was a late nineteenth-century phenomenon.

The social study of Victorian women travelers to America throughout the period provides another story. These women located informants, conducted interviews, inspected facilities, asked questions, and
pursued answers. They compared America's men to its women, its
north to its south, its cities to its country, its ideals to its reality.
Such a rigorous approach to travel was necessary because, as Frances
Trollope explained, America was "hardly better known than Fairy
Land; and the American character has not been much more deeply
studied than that of the Anthropophagi" (82). Her comment points
to the similarities between the sociological perspective adopted by
some of the women who traveled to America and the ethnographic
and geographic perspectives adopted by women travelers discussed
in chapter 4.

In offering up instances of the American voice as evidence with
which to predict the outcome of the democratic experiment, these
women changed the function and shape of the travel account. Much
of their work reads less like conventional travel literature and more
like investigative reporting. America, they reasoned, demanded a
new, more studious approach, and many of their travel accounts accordingly minimize the overtly autobiographical and aspire instead to
render the country from a presumably objective distance. In her preface to *Homes of the New World* (1853), Bremer explains that between
writing the letters that comprised her travel account and publishing
them in book form she had omitted "such passages as refer to [her]
own affairs" and added in their place "historical and statistical
facts."[13] Isabella Bird substantiated her impressions of the country
with "statistical information . . . compiled by the Americans themselves."[14] And Harriet Martineau wrote two separate accounts of her
American experience, one to speculate rationally about its society,
the other to encompass her personal impressions.

These overt attempts to depersonalize their accounts of America
suggest that these women wanted their works to be regarded as authoritative and professional, and they comprise an important piece
of the development of social study in England.[15] They helped to
define the province and methods of sociology, what the Victorians,
following Auguste Comte's lead, were to define as the science of
society. A complete account of the impact of travel writing on the
development of Victorian sociological discourse would also take into
account such influences as that of positivism on Victorian ways of
thinking about the wider world, the rise of statistical research, and
growing concern over the living conditions of the working class both
at home and abroad. Such complexities also suggest how much the
boundaries of what the Victorians considered sociology overlapped

with other developing social sciences—most notably political economy, ethnography, and anthropology.

Travel writing provided a convenient and logical way to bring these interrelated concerns into focus, and—as has already been argued—it was considered an acceptable form in which women could publish. Furthermore, nineteenth-century America—with its claim to be a "new world" and its abundance of institutions designed to ensure its democratic ideals—was ripe for just the sort of investigative approach that the developing discourse(s) of sociology provided. From the early experiments with democracy enacted by Frances Wright and Frances Trollope, to the investigative efforts first of Harriet Martineau and later of Emily Faithfull, and through the turn-of-the-century sociological practice of Beatrice Webb, one can chart a pervasive concern with representing travel to America as social investigation. In short, the New World offered new discursive possibilities and these in turn facilitated new professional opportunities.

Many Victorian women traveled to America alone, and in this sense it served as a testing ground for female independence and enterprise in much the same way as had Africa for Mary Kingsley, Mary Gaunt, and others. Shirley Foster has argued that "in America a woman, even on her own, could travel in ease and safety, untroubled by apprehensions of danger or unwelcome attentions, in a way that would have been quite impossible in Europe."[16] Even before Tocqueville had popularized the country as a land of democratic experiment, Frances Wright had conducted her own experiment with its society as an independent, entrepreneurial women. She traveled there in 1818 with her sister and afterward recorded her experiences and impressions in *Views of Society and Manners in America* (1820), a book that garnered her enough public attention—including praise from Jeremy Bentham and General Lafayette—to enable her a few years later to return and establish an experimental community known as Nashoba near Memphis, Tennessee. She envisioned Nashoba as a kind of halfway house founded on the principles of Owenite cooperation; there the surplus labor of slaves she owned could be applied toward the reimbursement of their original purchase prices plus the cost of replacement in a free country outside the United States. Although her scheme lasted only three years and attracted much criticism, Wright marked America in the minds of many as a land in which women could create opportunities for themselves unheard of in other countries.

Wright is also known for having lured Frances Trollope to America. Planning to join Wright at Nashoba, a debt-ridden but optimistic Trollope left her husband to travel to America with three of her children in 1827. She recognized immediately that Wright's community held out no hopes to her and little for its own residents, describing it in *Domestic Manners of the Americans* as a "forest home" with a "savage aspect." Just days after her arrival in Tennessee, Trollope left for Cincinnati, the prosperous "Queen City" of the West, to try her own hand at conducting business abroad. There she opened an emporium called the Bazaar that was designed to sell European trinkets. This scheme lasted only two years, after which she packed up and traveled through the Middle Atlantic states. Full of resentment, she sailed home and wrote *Domestic Manners of the Americans*, a book that catapulted her to fame as one of America's most mean-spirited visitors from the mother country. After devoting more than three hundred pages to a scathing characterization of Americans as insufferably rude brutes whose widespread lack of manners evidenced a corresponding absence of morals, Trollope magnanimously concluded: "I do not like them. I do not like their principles, I do not like their manners, I do not like their opinions," (358).

Nevertheless, both Wright and Trollope are unique in that they found in America an outpost from which to launch public careers, Wright as an entrepreneurial emancipator of the slave and Trollope as European shopkeeper in the wilderness. Both careers, though short-lived, illuminate something of the power these women thought they could exercise in America. Because America was conceived as an experimental society, it was deemed an appropriate forum for the kind of small-scale social experiments that interested and attracted Wright and Trollope. Wright and Trollope were both, however, principally motivated by an acquisitve spirit—Wright craved publicity for her venture and Trollope needed money to pay off debts at home. America would hold far more appeal to women prompted by an inquisitive interest.[17]

Most of the women who followed Wright and Trollope sought to describe and investigate its social structure(s). In her survey of travelers to America, Shirley Foster describes many of these women as "idealists," whom she defines as "those who went to America with theoretic or visionary ideas which they wished to match against actuality or to implement practically."[18] This description, however, does not do justice to the systematic ways that many self-proclaimed investigators of America went about their work. The challenge first faced by many was to find a form appropriate to the country. In *Homes of the New World*, Frederika Bremer lamented to her American readers that "the realities of your great country could not be compressed into a novel," and decided instead to publish her account as "a faithful transcript of the truth."[19] Similarly, Isabella Bird earmarked *The En-*

glishwoman in America* (1856) not as a comprehensive analysis but rather as "a faithful picture" of what she had "seen and heard."[20] Bird and Bremer were only two of many women to publish lengthy transcripts of what they had experienced in America, replete with detailed descriptions of American life as revealed through its churches, schools, stores, and homes. In 1838, Mrs. Felton published *Life in America* and Sarah Maury's *The Englishwoman in America* came out in 1848. By the middle of the century, travel across the Atlantic was significantly faster and less expensive, and accounts of experiences became more common. Although the 1850s were the high-water mark of travel writing about America, Victorian women continued to publish in this area throughout the rest of the century. Travel accounts of the later Victorian period written by women include Clara Bromley's *A Woman's Wanderings in the Western World* (1863), Lady Mary Anne Hardy's *Through Cities and Prairie Lands* (1881), and Katherine Bates's *A Year in the Great Republic* (1887). The political climate between England and America had also changed considerably. By the 1850s, America's population had overtaken that of England, its economic and military power was tolerated if not enjoyed, and trade between the two countries had reached an all-time high. And though slavery was almost always condemned in Victorian accounts of America, with few exceptions was it a focus for discussion in travel writing.[21] As Martin Crawford notes, "what is impressive about the 1850s is the degree to which open invocation of an Anglo-American identity had pervaded a broad cross-section of the middle- and upper-class opinion across the Atlantic."[22]

This era of good feeling is reflected in much of what Victorian women wrote about America. Although a few midcentury travel accounts—most notably Mrs. C. J. F. Houston's *Hesperos: Or, Travels in the West* (1850)—followed in the vituperative spirit of Mrs. Trollope, most were far less aggressive in their approach. *Travels in the United States: During 1849 and 1850* (1851) records Lady Emmeline Stuart Wortley's daily "impressions of the society and institutions" encountered as she traveled up and down the East Coast. Wortley's daughter Victoria joined in the venture with *A Young Traveller's Journal of a Tour in North and South America during the Year 1850* (1852). Marianne Finch published *An Englishwoman's Experience in America* in 1853 after having immersed herself for several months in the intellectual activities of Boston. One of Queen Victoria's attendants, Amelia Murray, used her *Letters from the United States, Cuba, and Canada* (1856) both as an opportunity to study the position of American women and as a forum for botanical study. Isabella Trotter published *First Impressions of the New World*, a series of letters describing the institutions visited while on a trip to America with her husband in 1859. Bremer's *Homes of the New World* focused on the domestic interior of America but claimed to have been able from "sacred peaceful hearths to contemplate social life beyond."[23] And Barbara Leigh Smith Bodichon wrote detailed letters about her American travels during her visit in 1857 and 1858 and later published articles based on her experiences in the *Englishwoman's Journal*. In her American diary, Bodichon concluded her observations with a call for "all the young men and women in England" to "come for a year of inspection here."[24] Considering that Bodichon was in America on her honeymoon, her rhetoric underscores how much American travel was aligned in spirit with the investigative.

Over and over again in their works, women travelers were drawn to conceive of their observations, impressions, and experiences of America as deliberately neutral, objective, and unemotional. Detailed descriptions of the effects produced by landscape, architecture, and climate—so central to travel writing about other places—are marginalized in the interest of documenting the everyday. Thus, whereas Victorian adventuresses would highlight their close encounters with danger on an African river, women travelers to America would describe the way an American dinner table was set. Whereas cultural tourists would contemplate the various colors blending during an Italian sunset, American travelers would describe the types of hats fashionable on the streets of New York.

Focusing on the seemingly inconsequential details of everyday life in America did not prevent many of these women from addressing concerns not traditionally within the province of the domestic-minded woman writer. As many women discovered, American society was inseparable from its politics, a realm—as Gaye Tuchman and Nina Fortin report in *Edging Women Out*—both theoretically accorded to and in practice monopolized by the male writer. Sensitive to this issue, some women developed strategies to absolve themselves of responsibility for opinions that could be construed as improper to a woman. Trollope, for example, kept her social observations free from the taint of the political (and masculine) by considering the institutional structure of America only insofar as it affected American manners, a focus squarely within the feminine domain. Like others, she seems to have observed these rules for propriety's sake; she was far from uninterested in the political. Nearing the conclusion of her travel account she writes, "Both as a woman, and as a stranger, it might be unseemly for me to say that I do not like their government, and therefore I will not say so" (358). Her rhetorical strategy of negating the implications but not the substance of her remarks was a way to introduce superficial political commentary into her work in an ostensibly innocuous way. As Peter Conrad summarizes, "Though professing only to criticize America for being ill-mannered, she [was] in truth criticizing it for being ill-constituted."[25]

Other women introduced socio-political commentary into their narratives in more direct ways. Nearly every woman who visited America had something to say about its women. As early as 1822, Frances Wright suggested that "perhaps the condition of women affords in all countries the best criterion by which to judge of the character of men."[26] She then concluded:

> Though it is by no means requisite that the American women should emulate the men in the pursuit of the whale, the felling of the forest, or the shooting of wild turkeys, they might, with advantage, be taught in early youth to excel in the race, to hit a mark, to swim, and in short to use every exercise which could impart vigor to their frames and independence to their minds.[27]

Even Frances Trollope had something positive to say about American women, conceding that "the ladies of the Union are great workers" (287). American women did not fare so well in all accounts; Amelia Murray compared the situation of women in America unfavorably to that of English women, claiming that American women wasted precious hours on "personal adornment"—time that their counterparts in England devoted "to drawing, to the study of nature, and to mental cultivation."[28] Despite the variety of conclusions these travelers reached, the significance of their mutual focus of concern should not be underestimated. The condition of American women was almost always regarded as a consequence of its social structure, and in alluding to this relationship, Wright, Trollope, and Murray in essence argued that the American woman was as much a product of her society as she was a biologically determined being. Although none of these women pursued the implications underlying their observation, their orientation nonetheless asserted the necessity of looking at the position of American women as a reflection of its social organization of difference.

These women dabbled at the boundaries of sociology; although they pitched their work in the form of personal diaries, they interspersed their accounts with commentary that was, at least in a rudimentary way, sociological in orientation. They critiqued America's systems of communication and transportation, characterized its men, evaluated the position of its women. Nonetheless, many adopted a regimen of investigation in America—dutifully inspecting its institutions and interrogating its peoples—not to become professional sociologists but simply because that seemed the most appropriate way to explore America.

Their accounts are marked as well by a hesitancy to adopt the rubric of professionalism. More than any of the Victorian women who wrote about experiences in the wider world, those who traveled to America claimed not to have intended to publish their findings. The crux of the issue was not the writing but rather the implied intention to publish a travel account that was more than a diary—that is, that was an effort at professional work. To admit to this was to suggest a craving for publicity that was conceived to be antithetical to womanhood, and to avoid such a charge, some paid excessive homage to the demands of "delicacy" in prefaces and introductions to their work. Others suggested that in their decision to publish they had yielded to the requests of persons who had read their work in private and judged it of public value. Isabella Bird, for example, returned home from America and "was requested by numerous friends to give an account of [her] travels."[29] And though Lady Emmeline Stuart Wortley "left England fully determined against writing a book of travels," once she had returned home, friends, to whose "better judgment" she deferred, convinced her to publish.[30] Other women defended their decision to publish as a demonstration of their overriding concern for public knowledge and the pursuit of truth. In her preface to *Letters from the United States, Cuba, and Canada*, Amelia Murray proclaimed:

> The writer of these letters did not cross the Atlantic to make a book. She has no wish to enter into controversy, or to be supposed a partisan, but facts can never injure truth, on whichever side it may lie; and statements made with fidelity and accuracy ought to be welcome. To shrink from their perusal is to exclude (in the present case) one means of knowing the condition and probable future of that race for whom a deep interest is felt by the British public, as well as by the writer of these pages, however different her convictions may be from the opinions commonly maintained.[31]

Murray's overwrought declaration testifies to the anxiety felt by women who sought to write authoritatively about America. The issue seems not to have been the propriety of the woman's choice of destination (as in the case of the adventuress), but rather the propriety of her choice of vocation. It was implicitly assumed that the woman who wrote about her experiences in America aspired to become a social critic. And—as Murray's carefully worded preface hints—this vocation was ideologically off-limits because it involved participation in public controversy and partisanship, rather than in private peace keeping, a "vocation" more ideologically appropriate to middle- and upper-class Victorian women.

Most of the women who visited America wrote as travelers who, as their prefaces indicate, did not want to compromise their femininity by appearing to "work" as social investigators. Two Victorian women, however, were willing to take these risks, and they experimented with the shape and direction of the conventional travel account to commence careers as social scientists. They won a limited measure of recognition at home as professionals, not as travel writers. These two exceptions were Harriet Martineau and Emily Faithfull.

Harriet Martineau's Appropriation of Social Study

Harriet Martineau brought two fundamental assumptions to her study of American society: that it had to be done systematically and that it was of utmost importance. As she notes in *How to Observe Morals and Manners:*

> Many may object that I am making much too serious a matter of the department of the business of travelling. . . . They do not pretend to be moral philosophers;—they do not desire to be oracles;—they attempt nothing more than to give a simple report of what has come under their notice. But what work on earth is more serious than this of giving an account of the most grave and important things which are transacted on this globe? (28)

Martineau believed that the rational way to approach the country was to test its reality—the everyday working of its institutions, the condition of its peoples—against its ideals, which she assumed to have been articulated by the Founding Fathers. From this test, she reasoned, she could objectively assess the moral progress of the nation.

Insofar as she attempted to adhere to a systematic and unbiased methodology in her investigation, her works represent a major early contribution to the development of sociology. Many critics have argued that what is most noteworthy about Martineau's scheme to examine the country from this standpoint is that she concocted it well before the sociological theories of Comte and, even later, Spencer had been articulated and studied. In *Harriet Martineau: A Radical Victorian*, R. K. Webb claimed that "for years she had been preaching sociology without the name."[32] Alice Rossi wrote "The First Woman

Sociologist: Harriet Martineau" to pay tribute to her ground-breaking mode of analysis.[33] Seymour Lipset in his introduction to *Society in America* credited her as one of "the first to apply explicitly a sociological approach to comparative analysis."[34] And Michael Hill brought out the only edition of *How to Observe Morals and Manners* since its original publication in 1838 because of its status as "the first substantive treatise on sociological methodology."[35] Although correct in their attributions, these studies assume that Martineau's significance derives from her anticipation of a male line of social scientists that includes Comte, Marx, Durkheim, and Weber. More important, they neglect to address two important dimensions of Martineau's approach: (1) that the discourse of sociology appealed to her desire to solidify the authority brought by work in political economy and, (2) that she integrated a concern for the domestic and feminine into a discourse conceived to be public, and by implication, male.

Soon after Frances Trollope had returned home in 1831, Harriet Martineau decided to rescue the ideal of the English woman traveler from the hands of an angry American public resentful of the treatment it had received from Trollope, among others. Other studies of America that were notoriously controversial were Captain Basil Hall's *Travels in North America in the years 1827–28* (1829) and Dickens's *American Notes* (1842). Martineau traveled to America after having achieved widespread public recognition for her popular educational series, *Illustrations of Political Economy* (1832–34), fictional stories she had designed to exemplify the principles of political economists like Malthus, Ricardo, and Bentham. Although she claimed both in her autobiography and elsewhere to have traveled merely because the opportunity had presented itself, she had, with her individual tales of political economy, launched a very successful career as an interpreter of social ills, one who could popularize rather than invent social theory. This career, as Deirdre David has argued in *Intellectual Women and Victorian Patriarchy*, was "defined by [Martineau's] auxiliary usefulness to a male-dominated culture."[36]

Another way to think about Martineau's developing professional interests, though, is in terms of what Robert Colby has called her "zeal for documentation."[37] She enjoyed the new kind of auxiliary authority that documentary study of political economy had provided her and carried this enthusiasm with her across that Atlantic.

Martineau traveled to America neither as an explorer nor as a tourist, but as a social investigator and a professional working woman. To Martineau, the "New World" demanded a new form of travel account, one that measured, studied, assessed, and predicted. It demanded scientific method. The new kind of sociological travel account that she developed to accommodate these beliefs not surprisingly assumed a different kind of traveler, one whose competence was based less on intensity of impression, or ability to look inward—the skills she fine-tuned in the Middle East—than on the skill with which she could describe those outward features of society that would reveal the essence or "meaning" of the country. To cultivate this skill, Martineau argued, the traveler should strive for distance, detachment, "the general view." As she wrote in *How to Observe Morals and Manners*, "To stand on the highest pinnacle is the best way of obtaining an accurate general view, in contemplating a society as well as a city" (60). Martineau was, however, careful to create a vision of the ideal traveler that women could readily fulfill: "The observer must have sympathy; and his sympathy must be untrammelled and unreserved" (52). Although these ideas—the makings of the ideal traveler—were not put into print until *How to Observe Morals and Manners* was published in 1838, they were fleshed out on board ship to America. Martineau went to America determined to fulfill the ideals set forth in *How to Observe Morals and Manners*—and to show the exceptional capacity of women to be investigators of society.

Martineau explains in the beginning of *Retrospect of Western Travel* that she went to America with "a task to do," and after two years abroad she came home with material for three books based on her experiences, *Society in America, Retrospect of Western Travel*, and *How to Observe Morals and Manners*, as well as for a series of articles later republished as *The Martyr Age of the United States* (1839). Martineau wanted her first book to be an investigative inquiry into the theory and practice of American society; she wrote in her autobiography that *Society in America* was intended by her to have been called *Theory and Practice of Society in America* but that she acquiesced to the demands of her publisher and accepted a more generalized title. And only after having returned to England did she decide also to publish a second version of her experiences there, one embellished with more "personal narrative" and interspersed with her impressions of "the lighter characteristics of men" (preface to *Retrospect of Western Travel*). Even if America did not respect the proper divisions between public and private, Martineau urged that her books would. In her introduction to *Society in America* Martineau explained that her object was to "test" America's "Institutions, Morals, and Manners" and that insofar as she had to discuss the people with whom she had become personally involved, her modus operandi was "to speak of the public acts of public persons, precisely as if I had I had known them only in their public character" (55). On the other hand, *Retrospect of Western Travel* would, Martineau imagined, "supply to the English what the Americans do not want—a picture of the aspect of the country, and of its men and manners" (3). *How to Observe Morals and Manners* would chart the way through still different "departments of inquiry," instructing the traveler-reader on the "habits of method" perquisite to apprehending what Martineau called "the science of Morals" (13–15, in passim) as well as theorizing about the public/private distinctions on which her other studies were built.

The kind(s) of authority that Martineau sought to establish through these works are more complicated than her divisions into separate books would suggest. Alice Rossi claims that what distinguishes her work is the "self-consciousness with which she advocated the view that the study of societies constitutes a separate scientific discipline."[38] Yet Martineau's concern for these separations stemmed as much from a concern for her own status as a woman writing in a field more traditionally male as from an awareness of the merits of sociology as a discipline. That she sensed a disjunction between the institutional America that demanded theory and the country's "lighter characteristics" that asked for narration—and that she apportioned her books accordingly—is indicative of her evolving sense of the seriousness of her chosen profession as investigative social scientist, and she thought of her travel writing as essential to this mission. Martineau wanted to avoid tagging her social study of America as too identifiably female, that is, as too "light," unscientific and unprofessional. She appears to have believed that the more anecdotal, narrative, and hence domesticated approach her readers called for could compromise the high seriousness with which she wanted be read. In her preface to *Retrospect of Western Travel* Martineau concedes that "There seems no reason why such a picture should not be appended to an inquiry into the theory and practice of their society" (preface). By tagging the second study as a "picture" that has been "appended to" the more rigorous "inquiry," she unambiguously places her allegiance with the first. She sought to safeguard her public identity as rational, masculine social investigator by overtly separating the spheres of her travel writing according to patriarchal gender ideology, and by suggesting that the "lighter" and hence more feminine book, *Retrospect of Western Travel*, was written only to satisfy the less serious-minded reading public.[39]

To an extent, Martineau wanted to dissociate not only her allegiance but also her authority from *Retrospect of Western Travel*, centering it instead in *Society in America*. As an "inquiry into the theory and practice" of society, this volume promised more to solidify the professional reputation she had already commenced. Some evidence suggests that she was never entirely comfortable with her decision to partition her books into separate domains of inquiry. Indeed, to rein-force the binary oppositions of public and private, description and narration, serious thought and light reading, was to subvert one of Martineau's central missions in all of her work on America—to argue that morals, a feminine domain, was not just compatible with the scientific method but that it depended on it. Linda Peterson has argued that "Martineau sought to make it possible for women to write as sages by demonstrating their competence in masculine rhetoric, then by breaking down common (mis)assumptions about 'masculine' vs. 'feminine' capacities."[40] But her work on America suggests instead that she sought to represent the necessity of the feminine in a mascu-line endeavor. To appreciate how much Martineau's sociological study of America lent credence to this argument entails looking first at her methodological assumptions.

Martineau wrote *How to Observe Morals and Manners* to detail what she regarded as the "philosophical," "moral," and "mechanical" req-uisites to social study. Her intention was to lend to the study of morals and manners the weight of science, and by implication of public, masculine, and serious discourse. As she argues in the open-ing section, "In physical science, great results may be obtained by hap-hazard experiments; but this is not the case in Morals" (23). The gist of this sentence sets the stage for the entire treatise. Throughout the work, Martineau includes in her commentary comparisons be-tween the work of the traveler and other "scientists," such as the geologist and the physiognomist. She rhetorically equates morals with other areas of scientific inquiry and goes one step further by suggest-ing that the student of morals in fact requires more rigor, discipline, and systematic method than that of the physical scientist.

Martineau's strategy was simple. She wanted to map out an area of inquiry for which she as a woman would be uniquely qualified, and she wanted that area to have the same credentials, to be as legitimate, as those from which she would by virtue of her gender be disqualified. To accomplish this end, she proceeds throughout her work on the assumption that travel is scientific investigation. She notes, for example, that "Above all things, the traveler must not despair of good results from his observations" (20). She speaks of the institutions within a social system as "agents . . . known in the gross" and writes: "it is not their nature, but the proportions in which they are combined, which have to be ascertained" (24). Later in her trea-tise she notes:

A traveller must inquire for any public registers which may exist in all districts, and note and reflect upon the facts he finds there. In case of there being none such, it is possible that the physicians of the district may be able to afford information from private documents of the same nature. If not, there remain the cemeteries. (171)

Using the language of social science, Martineau represents America as a laboratory, the Americans as subjects, and, most important, her project as professional work. The traveler who aspires to Martineau's ideals is not just systematic, but also untiring, relentless, ardent.

Martineau not only wanted to establish the import of travel as investigation, but also to suggest that by implication the woman travel writer was performing a useful function and that her work was both necessary and consequential. To her, the critical work of the investigative travel writer was to provide data—data that others were perhaps more qualified to interpret. In her avowal that "every observer and recorder is fulfilling a function," for example, one can sense the boundaries of Martineau's theory of the function of the investigative traveler. As a contributing member of his or her society's intellectual community, the traveler that Martineau delineates in *How to Observe Morals and Manners*, fulfills an ancillary role, one that serves, not directs, social progress. Thus, she believes that "it ought to be an animating thought to a traveler that, even if it be not in his power to settle any one point respecting the morals and manners of an empire, he can infallibly aid in supplying means of approximation to truth" (21). Although couching her comments in the form of inspirational message, she was also arguing for the fundamental value of auxiliary work. She wanted to ensure a place for the work of women travelers within the field of sociology.

Having implicitly established the act of travel as systematic investigation, Martineau claims morals as the primary component of democracy: "It is the traveler's business to learn what is the species of Moral Sentiment which lies deepest in the hearts of the majority of the people" (*How to Observe Morals and Manners*, 113). It follows from her argument that morals are the supreme object of scientific inquiry into democratic society: "To test the morals and manners of a nation by a reference to the essentials of human happiness, is to strike at once to the centre, and to see things as they are" (26). Although never explicitly saying so, Martineau's supposition is that women, as both guardians of and experts in the moral, are singularly qualified to be investigative travelers. Consider, for example, the way in which she justifies her contention that the ideal traveler approach everything encountered with sympathy. Without sympathy, she argues:

He will be amused with public spectacles, and informed of historical and chronological facts; but he will not be invited to weddings and christen-

ings; he will hear no love-tales; domestic sorrows will be kept as secrets
from him; the old folks will not pour out their stores to him, nor the
children bring him their prattle. (54)

Martineau's point is less that the ideal traveler must be female than
that the domestic sphere to which she pays tribute is the essence of
society, and hence that no social scientist can call his or her study
complete without having fully investigated the domestic.

Martineau invokes two voices of authority throughout *How to Observe Morals and Manners*. She legitimizes morals by virtue of its status
as supreme object of scientific inquiry and positions travel as the
appropriate medium through which such inquiry should take place.
In essence, by pursuing this argument through the rhetoric of science, she validates it. At the same time, though, she redirects the
weight of her argument toward the feminine. This redirection is
much more purposeful than what Linda Peterson describes as the
"irruption" of feminine discourse "into Martineau's otherwise 'masculine' texts."[41] She centers morals as the object of her investigation
and implies that women bring to social inquiry a level of understanding exclusive to their gender. Throughout the work, Martineau's argument proceeds on the assumption that these two directions are
theoretically compatible. Both *Society in America* and *Retrospect of
Western Travel* were, in a sense, Martineau's testing of her own hy-
potheses.

The identity Martineau sought to establish with *Society in America*
is evident in the way she introduces her mission: "I determined to
go to the United States, chiefly because I felt a strong curiosity to
witness the actual workings of republican institutions" (50). By explaining her attraction to America as one of intellectual curiosity, she
unwittingly aligns her motives with those of Tocqueville, who had
traveled to the United States just one year ahead of her. In the
first of his two-part *Democracy in America*,[42] Tocqueville explains the
predispositions that he took abroad:

> In America I saw more than America; I sought there the image of de-
> mocracy itself, with its inclinations, its characters, its prejudices, and
> its passions, in order to learn what we have to fear or to hope from its
> progress. (15)

His remarks provide instructive insight into the kind of liberty he
enjoyed as a male travel writer visiting America at almost the same
time as Martineau. He enjoys the imaginative flexibility to move
his focus from the actualities of democracy to their more emotional
counterparts—inclination, prejudice, and passion. Martineau, on the

other hand, is more attuned to the necessity of paying attention to the everyday, the "actual workings" of the democratic experiment. Her concern is founded on an assumption that the traveler who aspires to pronounce a theory of the society she visits must protect herself from just the sort of predisposition that Tocqueville readily admits to. As she cautions in *How to Observe Morals and Manners,* "The traveller must deny himself all indulgence of peremptory decision, not only in public on his return, but in his journal, and in his most superficial thoughts" (17). Martineau's approach to travel is excessive in its asceticism and reflects more than her professed concern to enunciate the "science" of observation. One can sense in such comments a fear of the impressionistic, the immediate, the spontaneous. These and other qualities—the prejudices and passions that Tocqueville admits to—are anathema to Martineau because they fall short of the scientific standards she believes she should stand by. Moreover, admission to such subjective biases would implicate her position as a woman in a way that contradicted her overarching argument for the rational scrutiny of national morals.

Society in America was to be Martineau's exercise in applying the principles of observation she had sketched out in *How to Observe.* What is most noteworthy about this inquiry is that she attempts to maintain the balance between the rational observer who systematically examines American society to obtain "results" and the investigator who relies on her familiarity with the domestic to give the fullest and most accurate account of the country's moral essence. Aware that her gender compromised rather than enhanced her authority, she wrote:

> I am sure I have seen much more of domestic life than could possibly have been exhibited to any gentlemen travelling through the country. The nursery, the boudoir, the kitchen, are all excellent schools in which to learn the morals and manners of a people: and, as for public and professional affairs, those may always gain full information upon such matters, who really feel an interest in them—be they men or women.[43]

Martineau's need to defend herself in anticipation of rather than in reaction to criticism reflects a certain fear of the very domesticity that she claims to acknowledge. In characteristic fashion, though, she overcomes her own hesitation within the same breadth. She brings America's standards of free and open inquiry to her own defense, arguing that her authority extended equally in both public and private directions.

Martineau follows the standards she had elaborated in *How to*

Observe in other ways as well. To accommodate her belief that "the institutions of a nation" and "records of any society" both "afford more information on Morals," she took on an exhausting and stringent schedule of activities while abroad. In the introduction to *Society in America* she provides her readers with evidence of the breadth of her experiences:

> In the course of this tour, I visited almost every kind of institution. The prisons of Auburn, Philadelphia, and Nashville: the insane and other hospitals of almost every considerable place; the literary and scientific institutions; the factories of the north; the plantations of the south; the farms of the west. I lived in houses which might be called palaces, in log-houses, and in a farm-house. I travelled much in wagons, as well as stages; also on horseback, and in some of the best and worst of steam boats. I saw weddings, and christenings; the gatherings of the richer at watering places and of the humbler at country festivals. I was present at orations, at land sales, and in the slave market. I was in frequent attendance on the Supreme Court and the Senate; Above all, I was received into the bosom of many families, not as a stranger, but as a daughter or sister. (52–53)

By providing her readers with a condensed inventory of her experiences, Martineau argues that her authority derives from the range of her social investigation. The best traveler, she reasons, is the most democratic traveler—the one as comfortable in the presence of the humble as the rich, the one as concerned with what was happening at the slave market as the Supreme Court. Yet, as with so many of her observations, she steers her readers toward a recognition of the value that she brought to the investigation as a woman. The last "institution" she catalogues is the domestic sphere; there, "above all," she is received "as a daughter or sister." In *Society in America,* as in *How to Observe Morals and Manners,* Martineau makes her authority depend equally on her ability to play the detached observer of society and the daughter or sister who makes her way into the homes and hearts of the families who greet her.

It would do Martineau's efforts as investigative author of *Society in America* and narrator in *Retrospect of Western Travel* a disservice to imply that her agenda as a working woman was limited to finding a place for the domestic within the developing discourse(s) of sociology. Rather she sought to represent morals as the all-encompassing context within which to place sociological or political investigation. Although her contemporary Frances Trollope chose to refrain from overt political commentary, Martineau structures her study around it. *Society in America* investigates what she called "the morals of politics," an orientation that leads her to such topics as "newspapers," "apathy in citizenship," "allegiance to law," "citizenship of people of colour," and "the political non-existence of women." By arguing that all of these issues are symptomatic of America's moral state, she brings them into a feminine domain and, by implication, appropriates them for her own use.

In both *Society in America* and *Retrospect of Western Travel*, Martineau sought to represent herself as a public spokesperson for democratic values; the oppressed position of women as democratic citizens was one of several issues on which she spoke and wrote eloquently. She made her voice heard in America. In one of the most vivid and theatrical essays of *Retrospect of Western Travel*, for example, she recounts for her readers an episode in which she magnanimously took the public stage in Boston in defense of the abolitionist movement—amidst a crowd of angry listeners. In "Signs of the Times in Massachusetts" she appropriates Carlyle's language to her own use, clearly reveling in the role of the passionate defender of the oppressed. Remembering the motives that prompted her move, Martineau ruminates:

> If I had been a mere stranger, attending with a mere stranger's interest to the proceedings of a party of natives, I might and ought to have declined mixing myself up with their proceedings. But I had long before published against slavery, and always declared my conviction that this was a question of humanity. . . . Having thus declared on the safe side of the Atlantic, I was bound to act up to my declaration of the unsafe side (*Retrospect of Western Travel*, 163).

Martineau collapses the boundaries between objective data gatherer and humanitarian emissary and in doing so takes recourse to both her humanitarian convictions and her status as a published opponent of slavery. Although she chastises America as "the unsafe side" on which to proclaim her position, she clearly feels authorized to do so. Here, as elsewhere, she willingly—even eagerly—assumes public responsibility for her public writings. In *Retrospect of Western Travel* she recounts her "First Sight of Slavery" and concludes: "I . . . was glad that my having published against its principles divested me altogether of the character of a spy, and gave me an unquestioned liberty to publish the results of what I might observe" (140). Here Martineau openly makes use of the "cultural capital" her published work has brought her, using its authority to legitimize her status as an investigative traveler. She is as much reminiscing about how she felt at the time of her "first sight" as reminding her readers of her authority as a professional working woman, authority that she intends to extend in new, more political directions.

One of the most compelling reasons that Martineau felt appalled by American slavery was that she saw it as analogous to America's treatment of women. American women and slaves were akin in that their status as democratic citizens was withheld. In *Society in America* she dismisses many of the issues about the position of slaves in American society with the following: "The common argument, about the inferiority of the coloured race, bears no relation whatever to this question. They are citizens" (100). To Martineau, black women were doubly oppressed. In *Retrospect of Western Travel* she finds "something inexpressibly disgusting in the sight of a slave woman in the field" (218). Elaborating on her reaction, she writes: "I do not share the horror of the Americans at the idea of women being employed in outdoor labour. . . . But a negro woman behind the plough presents a very different object from the English mother with her children in the turnipfield, or the Scotch lassie among the reapers" (218). To fully address the analogy, she devotes a section of *Society in America* on "the political nonexistence of women" to a comparison between the conditions of women and slaves in the United States. Although Martineau pays homage to the middle-class domestic ideal in much of her work, her impulse to conformity was almost always at odds with what Deirdre David labels her "spirited confrontation of male privilege" (32). Nowhere was this impulse so tried as when she was abroad; in America and elsewhere she saw and felt acutely the limited power of women to voice their opinions, to exercise their minds. America everywhere offered evidence of its failure to live up to the principles of equality on which the country was founded. After accusing America of having "fallen below" the standards of "the Old World," Martineau scathingly writes: "While woman's intellect is confined, her morals crushed, her health ruined, her weaknesses encouraged, and her strength punished, she is told that her lot is cast in the paradise of women: and there is not a country in the world where there is so much boasting of the chivalrous treatment she enjoys" (291). She notes further that America, like England, has created a situation in which marriage is the only reasonable "occupation" available to women and concludes that in America "the morals of women are crushed" (293).

Here, as elsewhere, Martineau was careful to place her highly charged polemic in the context of the moral investigation that she was conducting. Although she claims to have exposed herself to a wide range of American people and institutions in conducting her study, she draws on those institutions and people selectively. In *How to Observe Morals and Manners*, she asserts that "the Marriage compact is the most important feature of the domestic state on which the observer can fix his attention" (172). Although she couches her claim in the language of science, she does little to hide her predisposition: "If he be a thinker, he will not be surprised at finding much imperfection in the marriage state wherever he goes" (173). Similarly, in the portion of *Society in America* devoted to a study of "Civilisation," Martineau chooses as her focal points the "Idea of Honour," "Women," "Children," "Sufferers," and "Utterance." Women, children, and sufferers were all, to Martineau, special populations whose lack of "utterance," or liberty of speech—and, by implication, power—reflected poorly on that civilization's idea of honor.

To Martineau, all of America's great expectations were centered in its promise to give to its citizens the power to express themselves. The judgement that she, in the end, renders ("The civilisation and the morals of the Americans fall far below their own principles") was largely due to what she saw as its failure to live up to this promise, the promise to grant all citizens—men and women, blacks and whites—utterance. As a deaf woman, she felt more acutely than most the necessity of this power, and, to pay homage to its personal significance claimed in a self-prepared obituary: "Her stimulus in all she wrote from first to last, was simply the need for utterance."[44]

Martineau began her work on America assuming that its authority would derive from one voice, the voice of the social investigator who knew how and what to observe. But in the end America inspired in her not one but many voices, and her authority derived less from the dominance of one than from the skill with which she projected many. In creating a sociology that allowed for—indeed demanded—an interplay of voices, Martineau's project provided a paradigm on which at least one future woman sociologist sought to build.

The Example of Emily Faithfull

In several ways, Emily Faithfull's work in America provides an instructive gloss on that of Martineau. That Faithfull was cognizant of Martineau's work is suggested by the fact that she devotes chapter 18 of *Three Visits to America* to "Occupations Open to Women in 1836, when Harriet Martineau visited America, contrasted with Those of Today."[45] Yet, while Faithfull shared some of Martineau's assumptions, she went about the "practice" of social study in a different, more directed way. Of the many women who traveled to America after Martineau, none was more interested in capturing the voices of

American women than Faithfull. Founder of the Victoria Press, her primary purpose in *Three Visits to the United States* (1884) was to document the possibilities that American institutions offered to its working women. Faithfull went to America with a political purpose—to search out and make contact with its women achievers. She intended to publicize their achievements and thereby to garner support for the contributions women made to public life.

Well before Emily Faithfull traveled to America she had established a reputation as an outspoken advocate of work for women of any class and her concern for the relationship of women to industry had led her already to the investigation of social structure. She worked closely with Jessie Boucherett and Bessie Parkes in the founding in 1859 of the Society for Promoting the Employment of Women, a branch of the National Association for the Promotion of Social Science (NAPSS). Faithfull's association with the NAPSS enabled her to found the Victoria Press in 1860, and in 1863 she established *Victoria Magazine*, which also sought to publicize the claims of women for remunerative employment. Even after she had ceased to be directly involved with the Victoria Press, Faithfull continued to lend her name to the cause of working women—actively supporting the causes of Women's Trade Union League and the Women's Printing Society and founding *The West London Express* to provide work for women typesetters.

Emily Faithfull traveled to America as a self-proclaimed advocate for the working woman. Like Martineau, she envisioned her trip as an investigative mission. As she explains in the preface to *Three Visits to America*:

> Throughout my three visits I had one object specifically before me, namely, to supplement the experience gained during twenty years of practical work in England, in regard to the changed position of women in the nineteenth century, by ascertaining how America is trying to solve the most delicate and difficult problem presented by modern civilisation. (preface)

Faithfull's objectives bear some consideration. Like Martineau, she sees the position of women as central to the state of the nation. She also represents her primary task as one of social study but relies less explicitly on the rhetoric of the social scientist than on her own "practical work." The authority that Faithfull brings to her study of America is clearly her own; she is less dependent on articulating her objectives in language that she assumes to be objective, scientific, and hence "legitimate." She underscores her source of authority by reminding her readers that she has twenty years of work to her credit.

Emily Faithfull probably did not need to remind her readers of her work, because by the time she made the first of her three visits in 1872 (her later visits were made in 1877 and 1882), she enjoyed a solid reputation on both sides of the Atlantic as a leader of the women's reform movement. One measure of her reputation is reflected in the numerous invitations she received to lecture before a variety of audiences while abroad, and she spoke almost exclusively in the area of women and work, choosing topics such as the changes in English domestic economy, woman's work out of the house, and woman's involvement in the manufacturing industry.[46] Her presence and activities were monitored by the American press, and her travel account includes excerpts from these notices. Aware of her status as a representative of the English working woman, Faithfull wanted her travels to provide their own evidence of a woman's capacity to be successful both at womanhood and at working.[47]

Not surprisingly, then, Faithfull projects several distinct voices in her work that at times seem to contradict one another. She is variously the amiable travel writer, the rational social investigator, the crusty feminist, the cultural sage. Like Harriet Martineau, she wanted to evince both the breadth of her coverage of the country and the seriousness of her mission. She refered to her travels as a "programme," a term chosen to underscore both the stringent schedule that she kept and the rigor of her approach. She, too, wanted to project the authority of the social scientist. Over the course of her three trips, she traveled throughout every region of America, made extended stays in New Orleans and California as well as in the northeast, and "penetrated as far as the borders of Minnesota" (*Three Visits*, 120). The widespread recognition she had achieved for her successful enterprises at home enabled her to obtain almost unlimited access to American institutions, and these she tirelessly inspected for information about the status and condition of woman's work in America. She interviewed women physicians, clergywomen, women teachers and students, women writers and editors, women perfume manufacturers and pottery makers, housewives, laundresses, draughtswomen, and women lobbyists. She seemed to sense that the validity of her criticisms would be measured by the scope of her research. To meet these criticisms (like Martineau, ones which she anticipated), Faithfull wrote near the end of *Three Visits to America:*

> I have . . . had an opportunity granted to few, of seeing American cousins as they really are—not as they are supposed to be! Every facility was afforded me for visiting all the public institutions, the methods of the public schools and colleges were duly explained to me by the leading

authorities, the factories and workshops were thrown open to me. Personal interviews were accorded by most of the eminent public characters, including the President, senators, journalists, college professors, and artists, and I was cordially welcomed into the houses of people. (376–77)

In both tone and scope, Faithfull's litany cannot help but remind one of several of Martineau's speeches. Both women felt the need to underscore those experiences that would lend credibility to their conclusions and, though Faithfull puts more emphasis on her contact with America's most eminent citizens than did Martineau, she concludes her inventory in similar fashion, making reference to her experiences in the homes of Americans. Like Martineau, she wrote with an awareness of the need to articulate a concern for the domestic as an integral feature of the sociological approach.

What is most captivating about Faithfull's remarks, however, is how much she flaunts the opportunities her public recognition had brought her, exaggerating both her welcome and her status by claiming that institutions were opened and factory doors "thrown open" for her inspection. Touring Riverside Press in Boston, for example, she writes: "On concluding the tour of inspection, Mr. Houghton reminded me of a visit paid to my London printing establishment, adding that the idea of introducing women compositors into his own office had been due to what he had seen and heard at the Victoria Press" (*Three Visits*, 23). Although such self-congratulatory commentary on occasion seem gratuitous, it suggests that to Faithfull the power of work was not limited to financial independence. The successful working woman, she implies, can peddle influence. In a variety of similar vignettes, she depicts her working self as the object of American male interest and admiration. And in almost every such situation, she takes advantage of the opportunity to lobby for women's work. Reporting her trip to Washington, for example, she recalls: "In a private audience accorded me by the President, he assured me of his anxiety to promote the industrial interests of women, and the 'better pay,' but confessed he was opposed to female suffrage" (*Three Visits*, 38). Here she suggests that her "private audience" with the most powerful man in America has enabled her to garner for all of working womanhood a guarantee that their interests as wage earners, if not as voters, would be served. Faithfull supported the suffrage movement, but focused much of her energy and attention on reform movements oriented around labor issues.

Faithfull sought to project authority as a social scientist in other ways as well. Throughout *Three Visits to America* she substantiates both her observations and her evaluations by citing statistics that support her point. By situating her statistical evidence within her narrative (rather than in notes or appendices) she suggests that it is part of the working knowledge she brings to her investigation. Consider, for example, one of her many discussions of the incongruities between opportunities afforded to men and women for remunerative work:

> It still requires the publication of the figures of the census to induce some people to realise that a great disparity exists between the sexes numerically. . . . The census of 1881 showed 188,954 more women than men aged twenty, 116,502 more aged thirty, and this inequality continues up to the age of fifty-three, when the men numerically exceed the women. (*Three Visits*, 286)

Although the figures she quotes effectively confirm her argument, one can sense the frustration that Faithfull feels in taking recourse to statistical data, discourse presumed to constitute "real" knowledge and marked in the minds of many of her contemporaries as male. The implication of her remarks is that she does so only to convince those people who would otherwise be unwilling to recognize what she considers obvious and rampant inequality.

As a travel account that adopted the methods and objectives of sociology, *Three Visits to America* is innovative in its incorporation of voices other than Faithfull's own. In many ways, the text is a study of collaboration, and Faithfull's method is to pay homage to what she has learned from fellow feminists. Throughout her account she features the words and wisdoms of her fellow English women. She quotes Frances Power Cobbe's aphorism that "'a woman is generally at the beck and call of somebody, generally of everybody'" (*Three Visits*, 64). On another occasion she remembers Elizabeth Barrett Browning having said, "'I worked with patience, which means almost power'" (*Three Visits*, 288). More important, Faithfull intersperses her narrative with recollections of what American women had to say while she was there. She pays tribute to the "earnest and dignified utterances" of such luminaries as Mrs. Julia Ward Howe. But her purpose was also to illustrate feminist voices in the common worker. To do so, she renders for her readers the spontaneous commentary she overheard, commentary that to her illuminated some essential aspect of the American woman as worker.

Snippets of conversation are quoted throughout her account to add not only a sense of American women's voices, but also to evidence the power of the American woman to be heard. For example, toward the end of *Three Visits*, she recalls: "'What would you do in time of war if you had the suffrage?' said Horace Greeley to Mrs. Stanton. 'Just what you have done, Mr. Greeley,' replied the ready lady, 'stay at home, and urge others to fight!'" (328). In the Midwest, she remembers that "Grace Greenwood once told me she regarded Chicago as 'New York with the heart left in'" (52). The effect of Faithfull's method is not only to enliven her account and give it a more conversational tone, but also to create a patchwork of women's voices. In doing so, Faithfull implies that these voices contribute as much to a sociological portrait of America as do the kinds of information obtained from inspections, formal interviews, and statistical surveys.

In a sense, Faithfull's goal was to produce an account of America whose authenticity was a direct result of its documentary methods. Like most documentary makers, she had a political agenda. Whereas Martineau had self-consciously attempted to adhere to the standards of objectivity outlined in *How to Observe Morals and Manners*, Faithfull openly embraced the bias implicit in her stated objective to investigate "the changed position of women." She took advantage of the opportunity to meet with the leaders of the emancipation movement in America and records in her work not only admiration for but also productive meetings with Julia Ward Howe, Elizabeth Stanton, Lucretia Mott, and others. Faithfull was as concerned with documenting the various success stories of women whose names had not yet reached English ears. She wanted to show that feminism in America had advanced beyond the level of the reform movement and had affected and improved the position of the everyday working woman.

Wherever she went, Emily Faithfull found an exemplary American woman, someone she could depict as embodying both the industrious and feminine spirit. Interspersed throughout *Three Visits to America* are vignettes of individual American women that are almost without exception laudatory. Miss Maria Mitchell, a professor of astronomy at Vassar College and director of its observatory, is held up as a "remarkable" example of the working intellectual. After meeting the journalist Lillian Whiting, Faithfull gushes in *Three Visits to America* that her "piquant magnificent letters are not only known to the readers of the *Boston Traveller*, but her signature is familiar to those who see the papers published in New Orleans, Chicago, Philadelphia, and Washington" (343). The actress Mary Anderson "represents what the stage still wants in both countries" (*Three Visits*, 364). In San Francisco she discovers a Mrs. Sarah Cooper, whose work in the formation of kindergartens prompts her to conclude: "If one woman alone is enough to redeem a whole nation, that woman is Mrs. Cooper" (*Three Visits*, 218). In southern California she meets Miss Austin, whose ranch "produced 20,000 pounds of raisins . . . worth about

30,000 dollars" (*Three Visits*, 239). And after a stay with Mrs. Bullard in Boston, Faithfull concludes:

> To anyone who associated the idea of a literary woman with the picture drawn of "the strong-minded blue-stocking" of olden days, with her outre manners, masculine ways, and total absence of all feminine grace, Mrs. Bullard must indeed have been a revelation. (*Three Visits*, 5)

Faithfull gives her readers the impression that successful working women were the rule and not the exception in America. Yet, as her last comment suggests, she was eager to dispel the notion that a woman who worked had somehow relinquished her hold on femininity.

To ensure this, Faithfull often followed her descriptions of American women's achievements with summations of their accomplishments in the domestic sphere, summations that sometimes appear to have been hastily added on to the end of her illustrations rather than earnestly incorporated into Faithfull's idea of the woman's character. Hence, for example, she describes Mrs. Cooper as "surrounded by her books; a devoted husband and daughter complete the circle" (*Three Visits*, 219). Although Faithfull pays tribute to the middle-class ideology that defined a woman as incomplete without husband and child, her own allegiances throughout *Three Visits to America* are with the woman—single or married—whose life is felt as incomplete without work.[48]

It is when she is addressing this issue that Faithfull's voice is most earnest, determined, convincing, and authoritative. Sensitive to the powerful influence of her society's ideologies of class, Faithfull tried to wage an argument that would include all women:

> I fail to see why women should be first taught to place an undue value upon social status and then asked to relinquish it. . . . I cannot admit that domestic service is a reasonable channel for the employment of educated ladies, although I consider that no honest work is as derogatory as idleness. (*Three Visits*, 277)

Every woman has the right to want to work, she reasoned. Even the most routine work, she argued, provides women with ammunition to overcome the powerful ideologies that position them—often unwittingly—at home: "Genius, and even talent, is given to few, and the idea that brain-work is alone fitted for a lady compelled to work has made shipwreck of the life and happiness of many women. Naturally they shrink from vocations, foolishly made a badge of social inferiority" (*Three Visits*, 15–16). Here and elsewhere she argues that work is necessary for a woman's emotional well-being, and hence that to restrict a woman's access to work in any way is to compromise her ability to function as a human being.

Emily Faithfull targeted the limited education of women as the central barrier to working equity: "To this hour, in both countries, a woman's claim to equal educational advantages, in order that she may worthily fulfill her own place in the world, and prove a real help-meet for man, is met by the charge that she is 'ruthlessly shattering household gods'" (*Three Visits*, 105). Here she positions a woman's right to "fulfill her own place" as a complementary goal of her responsibility to be man's "help-meet." Although she felt strongly about the necessity of providing women with opportunities to work, she recognized that her argument would garner widespread criticism and she structured her arguments to conform to the ideology that would engender the kind of criticism she anticipated. In Faithfull's mind, a woman could satisfy her own ambitions and needs without compromising those qualities that rendered her a help to others. At the same time that she seems to accommodate middle-class ideology, however, she also advocates change: "Surely it is time for us all to help in breaking down the false notions by which women are still hampered—to testify against the indolence which is not only regarded as a permissible foible, but as feminine and refined" (*Three Visits*, 286). She argues forcefully that such a change in her society's fundamental attitude about the position of women would enable women to live lives of "wholesome activity" and to enjoy the "repose which comes after fruitful toil" (*Three Visits*, 286).

Two things are particularly noteworthy about Faithfull's commentary on the needs of women to have access to education and work, commentary that periodically comes to the forefront and recedes throughout the narrative portions of *Three Visits to America*. One is that the issue seems to empower her to adopt overtly a commanding rhetorical stance. She expresses her opinions, and she expresses them powerfully and without reservation. She assumes the voice of a cultural critic. To a certain extent, Faithfull strays beyond the boundaries of sociology. Rather than draw dry conclusions based on a systematic assessment of her observations, her experiences instead incite her to react, to judge, to criticize. Although she veers away from the model offered by Martineau in *How to Observe Morals and Manners*, she offers another response to the challenge of the country and establishes her own standards for social investigation. Faithfull's notion of social investigation incorporates into it the features of a political campaign.

The other important dimension of Faithfull's commentary on women and work is that it leads her to question some of her society's (and, indeed, Western society's) most fundamental assumptions. And in this outcome, Faithfull's work most resembles that of Martineau. Considering how some of her contemporaries had chosen to interpret the Bible, for example, prompts her to conclude:

> Christianity, in truth, was the signal for the breaking down of false and artificial barriers, though it has proved a signal some of its professors . . . resolutely refuse to see. They indulge in confusing discourses on broad lines of demarcation . . . forgetting that the very highest thought of God includes the blending of those elements which, in common speech, we call masculine and feminine. (*Three Visits*, 107)

Faithfull here has taken her reader far beyond the sociological framework she originally set forth. Although embedded within her discussion of the state of Massachusetts, this particular discussion forms one piece of a larger part of *Three Visits to America* that, in its entirety, invites its readers to question the social constructions of gender that regulate their lives. In essence, Faithfull argues that to accept the idea of separate spheres is not only to contradict Christian intention but also to do a fundamental disservice to everyday life:

> It is time to reject as heathenish the notion of separate codes of virtue, and to look for modesty in men and courage in women, and then we shall find that what is true of highest humanity is true of the world at large, and that for the service of that world the spirit and power of woman is as much needed as the spirit and power of man. (*Three Visits*, 107)

This is a more forthright proposition than her claim that "classes and sexes must sink or swim together" (*Three Visits*, 277). She is in effect asking her readers to reassess the ideologies that have compelled them to think and believe in ways that encourage the discrete and divisive.

Harriet Martineau was also of course prompted by her experiences in America to rethink the assumptions of separate spheres. In her examination of the position of American women in *Society in America*, she writes:

> The truth is, that while there is much said about "the sphere of woman," two widely different notions are entertained of what is meant by the phrase. The narrow, and, to the ruling party, the more convenient notion, is that sphere appointed by men, and bounded by their ideas of propriety;—a notion from which any and every woman may fairly dissent. The broad and true conception is of the sphere appointed by God, and bounded by the powers which he has bestowed. This commands the

assent of man and woman; and only the question of powers remains to be proved. (154)

Although more pointed in her assignation of blame, Martineau's comments are similar to those of Faithfull in that she legitimizes her reinterpretation of separate spheres by representing it as that "appointed by God." Both of them believe in a broader, more powerful conception of womanhood that allows for a wider range of interpretation.

What is equally interesting to consider, though, is that both Martineau and Faithfull embed their speculation on the highly controversial issue of separate spheres within their social investigation of America. That they did so is in part a reflection of the flexibility of travel writing to encompass a variety of narrative strategies and voices. It also suggests that both women found in travel to America the liberty not only to open themselves up to the new, but also to reconsider the old. Both women saw in a sociological approach the opportunity to explore and capture the variety and range of voices that made America, and both were led to experiment with their own variety and range of voice. Finally, and most important, both made in America declarations of independence not only for themselves but also for all women—really for all men and women.

Beatrice Webb's Working Womanhood

For both Martineau and Faithfull travel to America provided the incentive to bring together complex ideas about the position of women in society. In doing so both sharpened their sense of their professional selves. But while they found in America compelling ideas to take home, there is surprisingly little evidence to suggest that their work provided paradigms on which other women modeled their careers. Indeed, a brief glance at some of the assumptions Beatrice Webb brought to her career at the turn of the century serves as a tonic antidote to the powerful stories of Martineau and Faithfull.

Webb traveled to America relatively early in her career as a social investigator; she left with her husband in 1897, just six years after her first book on the cooperative movement in England was written. Her decision to work in fields traditionally associated with men was instead a product of a variety of experiences, what in her autobiography *My Apprenticeship* (1926) she calls the "weight of circumstance."[49] Providing compelling incentives were both her childhood association with Herbert Spencer and, more notably, her rebellion against the ideologies that would have her take up fiction writing rather than some form of writing she perceived to be more serious, informative, and worthy.

Other features of Webb's career choice bear consideration as well. Before she was married, for example, she was like many other upper-class women actively involved in the Charity Organisation Society (COS), working first as an unpaid visitor and rent collector and eventually editing *The Charity Organisation Society Review*.[50] As Barbara Caine observes, "it was primarily the desire to understand the structural and economic basis of social problems which led first to the COS and then to [Webb's] own social investigation."[51] Coupled with this desire was what Jane Lewis has described as Webb's "delight in first-hand observation," which "is obvious from the pages of her diary."[52]

All of these experiences led Webb to see herself as both different from and better than the ordinary woman. Spencer taught her the value of scientific method, which she describes in *My Apprenticeship* as the ability "to look on all social institutions exactly as if they were plants or animals—things that could be observed, classified, and explained" (37). But more important, Spencer encouraged her to aspire beyond her own sex. In *My Apprenticeship* she writes: "What he taught me to discern was not the truth, but the relevance of facts; a gift said to be rare in a woman and of untold importance to the social investigator" (27).

Whereas Martineau and Faithfull had sought to demonstrate the superior capacity of woman to function as a social investigator, Webb does just the opposite. She implies that the analytical abilities she brings to study not only mark her as a skilled investigator, but also separate her from the rest of her sex. Over and over again in her diary Webb reveals not only a suspiciousness of the abilities of her own sex, but also a disregard for them. Although she took delight in Spencer comparing her to George Eliot (28), she saw socially constructed definitions of womanhood as disabling: "But however useful intellectual curiosity and concentrated purpose may be to the scientific worker, they are not attractive gifts in a child or in a marriageable young woman, and they are therefore apt to be hidden" (*My Apprenticeship*, 60).

Although Webb very early on accepted her decision to be what her sister Mary called a bluestocking, she was never really able to shake the very assumptions that she here and elsewhere so clearly condemns. Rather than turn her critical energies to attacking the institutions and ideologies that defined womanhood in ways that restricted, if not eliminated, her ability to embrace intellectual curiosity, she seems instead to have turned from her gender—to implicitly endorse the judgements that she found derogatory.

Webb's assumptions about late Victorian womanhood and writing shaped more than her decision to be a social investigator instead of a domestic novelist. They also directed her feelings about the goals and methods of social study; they prevented her from aligning herself with the tradition that she could have found in Martineau and Faithfull. The intellectual and emotional heritage that she traces in *My Apprenticeship* begins with her father, continues through Spencer, Joseph Chamberlain, and Charles Booth and ends with her father's death and her marriage to Sidney Webb, whom she calls "the man of my destiny" (xii). The strictly male lineage that Webb situates herself in suggests her acute sense that gender was something to be overcome.

Webb's investigation of America is marked throughout by the sense that she and her husband were the first to bring with them a methodology with which to interview, assess, and conclude. To an extent she was radically unable to acknowledge the accomplishments of two women who had conducted investigations before her, because to do so would have forced her to rethink her entire sense of self. Webb traveled to America already having commenced her career with *The Cooperative Movement* (1891) and with *The History of Trade Unionism* (1894), cowritten with her husband. While there, they focused their attention on urban America and in the process of their investigation interviewed those whom they considered the country's best and brightest, a roster that included Theodore Roosevelt, Woodrow Wilson, Jane Addams, Lillian Wald, among many others. By the time she had arrived in America, Webb felt that she had mastered the techniques of the sociologist, and under the tutelage of her cousin Charles Booth she had developed interviewing skills and studied statistical methods.

Although she never published her work on America, there is some evidence that she had originally intended to. Tacked on to the final portions of the diary are two sections subtitled "General Impressions of America" and "Superficial Notes on American Characteristics," both of which evidence Webb's attempt to gather her material into a working sociology of the country.[53] Why the material on America was never gathered into book form is telling, though, and is suggested in "General Impressions of America," where Webb writes:

> We cannot pretend to have studied America or the Americans. We have
> focussed our attention on Municipal Government, but even here our
> enquiry has been superficial. We have interviewed individuals and ob-

served the working of the machine, but our information has been for the
most part unverified and some of the details given in our notes are certain
to be incorrect. (142)

She suggests that because their study failed to adhere to their own
rigorous standards, it was without value. She represents herself not
as a traveler, and much less as a woman, but only as a social scientist.
She requires systematic inquiry and accurate note taking and demands verification. And without meeting these requirements her observations in America were, it seemed, not worth publishing.

In her enunciation of the high standards to which the observer who
aspires to write authoritatively about another country must adhere,
Webb reveals something of her own limitations. Although she pays
homage to the very qualities of method that Martineau had nearly
sixty years earlier proposed in *How to Observe Morals and Manners*,
she nowhere credits these or any other works by women on America.
In fact, she hastily dismisses Martineau's work on America as just
one of several instances of an early Victorian novelistic (and hence,
inferior) approach to travel. She asks, "Who would recognize as dis-
tinctively American the essentially eccentric and ugly individuals por-
trayed by Dickens, Trollope and Martineau?" (*American Diary*, 142).
And, more pointedly, Webb represses from her work any sense of
her own, personal impressions of the country.

How much Webb represses her personal self in the interest of
nurturing a public, authoritative self is nowhere more evident than
in her autobiography. Although Webb did keep extensive diaries,
often detailing intense anxiety and pain, she limits her autobiography
to an elaboration of her working womanhood. *My Apprenticeship* is
both an autobiographical retrospective of her life as a social investigator and a history of the development of sociology up until the time
that she and Sidney Webb became principal players (at which point
her second autobiographical volume, *Our Partnership*, begins). Situ-
ated within *My Apprenticeship*, for example, is Webb's account of
Charles Booth's enquiry to obtain a statistical assessment of "the
number and proportion of families living in a state of misery, poverty,
decent comfort and luxury respectively" (225). Included within this
section is a table listing Booth's famous "eightfold classification of
people" as well as tables documenting classification by family income
and by number of rooms occupied. Although all of these help Webb
to explain their "map of poverty," what she believed to be a crowning
achievement of her early working womanhood, their inclusion at all
suggests something of Webb's monotonic approach to her life. *My
Apprenticeship* is replete with statistical data, tables, and excerpts from

her own and others' working papers. In addition, Webb includes in her appendix essays on such topics as the interconnection between personal observation and statistical enquiry, the interview method, the art of note taking, and the nature of economics. Such materials suggest Webb's extreme need to validate her professional self—in a sense to prove it real. One can read Webb's anxiety of authorship as an inevitable reaction to her culture, but—as with Martineau and Faithfull—one must at the same time see her as endorsing fundamental features of the culture that constricted her.

Although Harriet Martineau, Emily Faithfull, and Beatrice Webb each brought to her sense of social investigation different assumptions and different priorities, certain similarities between them bear consideration. Martineau and Faithfull in particular redirected their travel account from a record of private experience into a document of public study, and, in a sense, one can read Webb's autobiography this way. As women struggling at different times within the Victorian era to be intellectuals, each was led at some point to make a declaration of independence from the traditions in which they were positioned as women and as writers. Most important, each found within the discourse of sociology the capacity to cultivate—and market—a professional self, and although the process entailed a good deal of what one might call "gender anxiety," the experience in some way proved liberating for all three. The study of society enabled all to see more clearly how much their womanhood was as at least in part socially, not essentially, constructed. Doing so opened new ground for alternate readings—of America, of society, and of themselves.

Conclusion
Victorian Women and the Spirit of Place

In 1899, the poet and essayist Alice Meynell published a collection of prose works titled *The Spirit of Place and Other Essays*.[1] It was not her first book of essays, nor would it be her last, but it nonetheless marked an important stage in her professional development. Meynell had up to this point distinguished herself primarily as a poet and art critic; she had published several volumes of poetry as well as a study of William Holman Hunt and two collections of essays. With their emphasis on color, line, sound, and texture, both *The Colour of Life and Other Essays on Things Seen and Heard* (1893) and *The Rhythm of Life and Other Essays* (1893) illustrate Meynell's developing sense of the applicability of aestheticism not only to art but also to life. As its title suggests, *The Spirit of Place* was also a venture in aestheticism; it was Meynell's first sustained effort at applying an aesthetic approach to the study of travel.

Several of the essays collected in *The Spirit of Place* are specifically devoted to evoking Meynell's sense of the "feel" of travel, its colors, smells, sights, and sounds. Meynell, like so many of her contemporaries, had spent substantial portions of her formative years abroad. As a young girl she had traveled extensively with her family through Italy and had lived for months at a time in Sori, near Genoa. As Catherine Cantalupo has written, "Alternating chiefly between Italy and England, the Thompsons usually spent no longer than a season in one place."[2] Curiously, though, at the time she composed the essays for *The Spirit of Place*, she had not left England for several years. None of the seventeen essays included in *The Spirit of Place* make much direct reference to Italy or, indeed, to any of her experiences abroad. Nevertheless, in essays such as "Solitude" and "The Horizon," as well as in her title piece, "The Spirit of Place," Meynell addresses forcefully the psychological needs served by travel. In each of these essays, she focuses almost exclusively on depicting the various ways in which the identities of traveler and place are reciprocally related. Her goal is not so much to describe either the traveler or

196

place, but rather to impressionistically evoke a sense of distance and discovery.

The subject of "Solitude," for example, is an unidentified park that Meynell endows with human qualities: "A park insists too much, and, besides, does not insist very sincerely" (21). What interests her are its boundaries, which by definition pose artificial restrictions on the (to her) natural tendency of its visitors to yearn for areas beyond those circumscribed. Meynell values, however, the park's propensity to cultivate seclusion and solitude: "To keep the published promise of a park, the owner thereof should be a lover of long seclusion or of a very life of loneliness" (21). Speculating on this state of solitariness, which she terms "a condition of life," leads her to consider solitude as a function of travel:

> The traveler who may have gone astray in countries where an almost life-long solitude is possible knows how invincibly apart are the lonely figures he has seen in desert places there. Their loneliness is broken by his passage, it is true, but hardly so to them. They look at him as though they were invisible. Their unself-consciousness is absolute; it is in the wild degree. (21)

The place that Meynell here imagines is made a "desert place" not by virtue of its landscape, but rather by the psychological state of the people—the "lonely figures"—who inhabit it, however transitorily. They, in turn, are identified by their relationship to place; they live in psychological wildernesses, in areas where Meynell's imaginary traveler goes astray. Meynell's allegiance, however, is less with this temporary visitor who wanders into the deserted landscape, one who significantly is figured as male, than with the "lonely people," the permanent inhabitants of this wild zone. As passive recipients of the traveler's gaze, they function within this landscape as symbolically female. But they establish their power by not responding to this gaze, thus remaining "invincibly apart." The traveler in this scenario learns to associate place with a psychological state, in this case "unselfcon-sciousness."

"The Horizon," another essay from *The Spirit of Place*, focuses in a similar way on the mutually constitutive relationship between the traveler and place. In the unidentified landscape featured in this essay, "the eye and the horizon answer one another" (280). Here, too, the place Meynell depicts is one that cannot be located spatially or temporally; its status as a geographical site is unimportant. She simply asks her reader to let her imaginatively recreate the sensation

of mounting a hill and looking out over the horizon. As with "Soli-
tudes," her goal is to represent the psychological state of the traveler:
"To mount a hill is to lift with you something lighter and brighter
than yourself or than any meaner burden. You lift the world, you raise
the horizon; you give a signal for distance to stand up" (280).

The situation that Meynell imagines in "The Horizon" is one in
which landscape empowers the traveler: "You summon the sea, you
bring the mountains, the distances unfold unlooked-for wings and
take an even flight" (280). The attraction of the horizon is that it
simultaneously represents a boundary and the potential for life beyond boundaries. To "capture" the horizon, then, is to take control
of distance:

> It is to uplift the horizon to the quality of your sight that you go high.
> You give it a distance worthy of the skies. There is no distance, except
> the distance in the sky, to be seen from the level earth; but from the
> height is to be seen the distance of this world. The line is sent back into
> the remoteness of light, the verge is removed beyond verge, into a dis-
> tance that is enormous and minute. (280–81)

Meynell values the horizon because it provides perspective and can
be controlled with position. By keeping an eye always on the horizon,
the traveler she imagines is one who can live contentedly on the
"verge removed beyond verge," the omnipresent margin or border
of life from which distance can be seen both as "enormous and minute." To Meynell, the traveler's position becomes the most important
identifying feature. She does not explicitly identify her traveler as a
woman, because she does not have to. Her interest is not with the
gender of the traveler but rather with her position, and she clearly
wants to convey to her readers the value of perspective afforded to
one who occupies a decentered, marginal position. Seeing the world
from her position "on the verge" enables Meynell's traveler to feel
uncircumscribed by boundaries; she sends the lines (or markers of
boundaries) "back into the remoteness of light" and controls her own
sense of distance.

The idealized and unidentified traveler who Meynell envisions in
these and other essays is in many ways akin to the "Sentimental
Traveller" that Vernon Lee describes in several of her essays, written
a few years after *The Spirit of Place*. In 1908, Lee published a collection of thirty-three essays titled *The Sentimental Traveller: Notes on
Places*.[3] The bulk of the collection is divided according to region;
individual essays are devoted to Lee's impressions of Germany, Italy,
France, and Switzerland. But set off as a division unto itself is her

title essay, "The Sentimental Traveller." The central topic of this essay—the relationship between what Lee calls the "Genius Loci" and the Sentimental Traveller—reappears in the last essay of the volume, "The Keepsake," as well. Lee goes farther than Meynell in openly identifying herself with the traveler of her essay. She begins the essay by dispelling the notion that her "childhood of romantic roamings" accounts for her identity as a sentimental traveler. "I have grown into a Sentimental Traveller because I have travelled not more, but less, than most folk," she writes (4). It is not the experience of travel itself but rather one's psychological processing of the experience that concerns her:

> For the passion for localities, the curious emotions connected with lie of the land, shape of buildings, history, and even quality of air and soil, are born, like all intense and permeating feeling, less of outside things than of our own soul. (4)

In a manner very similar to that of Meynell, Lee concerns herself with the interaction of place and person, not simply with place itself. Such phrases as "the passion for localities" and "feeling for places" reoccur throughout "The Sentimental Traveller." Hence, although she on several occasions makes reference to her fascination with Rome, the basis for her interest is less with the actualities of its churches and monuments than with the variety of perspectives it affords her:

> And beyond this Rome, which seemed to exist for those unlike ourselves, appeared dim outlines of other parts of the world, with magic Alhambras and Temples of Paestum and Alpine forests; a Europe occupying other dimensions than that network of railways blobbed with hotels and custom-houses across which I was periodically hurried from inventory to inventory. (13–14)

Here Lee focuses, like Meynell, not on place but on an imagined world beyond that immediate place; her eyes follow "dim outlines" and lead to "other parts of the world," magic places where her imagination is both fortified and exercised. Her sense of travel is not one to be fostered by the gleanings of a guidebook but by "other dimensions" of abroad. Lee later identifies this sense of a place's other dimensions as the "Genius Loci." Describing her love for Rome, for example, she writes: "And in the nostalgic longing for that city, unknown though looked down on during each daily walk, began my secret worship of the Genius Loci, of the spirit immanent in those cupolas and towers and hilly pinegroves which seemed as far beyond

my reach almost as the sun setting behind them" (14). Here again
our perspective is directed beyond the actual physical boundaries of
the city; we look down on Rome as if walking in the hills surrounding
it, look up toward its cupolas and towers, and finally look with Lee
beyond the horizon as the sun sets. Although Lee seems to feel
disempowered by the majesty of her surroundings that stretch "beyond [her] reach," she at the same time comes away from the experience confident in her self. The passage—and essay—ends: "Thus I
became a Sentimental Traveller" (14).

The connection between the experience of travel and the making
of identity is the subject of many of Lee's essays. Whereas in "The
Horizon" Meynell only hints that the traveler she envisions is female,
Lee is somewhat more direct. She argues in her essay that passion
for travel is born of inexperience with the world, "of repression and
short comings" (4), and that "this unimpaired zest for travel is but
the accumulated thwarted longing of . . . sedentary lives" (6).
Women, she implies, are by virtue of their socially restricted lives
destined to become sentimental travelers:

> Thus among our mothers and grandmothers there arose a breed of Senti-
> mental Travellers, insatiate, indefatigable, some of whom still survive
> (and may they long do so!) to show our puny generations what the passion
> for localities can do at threescore and ten. (5)

Lee suggests that the sentimental traveler originates from a hardy
line of matriarchs, women who are distinguished by their unremitting
passion for activity. Lee endows her narrative with the power of myth;
her sentimental travelers become "wondrous priestesses of the Genius Loci" who awe others with their "sacred fury of travel" (10).
She focuses in the essay on a "Mrs. S," who functions as her prototypical female traveler; she is variously referred to as "the high priestess
of them all," "the most favoured and inspired votary of the Spirit of
Localities," and the "most wisely fantastic of Wandering Ladies"
(10–11). Lee's "Mrs. S" is both real and unreal; she is a woman Lee
has encountered, met with, and admired on her travels, but at the
same time she is never anywhere. "Mrs. S" is "for ever lifting the
other foot . . . in the direction of distant lands" (11). She travels "not
elsewhere on our earth, but journey[s] a longer way" (11). By situating this figure of her imagination at the center of "The Sentimental
Traveler," Lee suggests the centrality that the imaginary traveler will
have in the remainer of essays in *The Sentimental Traveller: Notes on
Places*. She returns to the theme in the volume's final essay, "The
Keepsake."

Lee uses "The Keepsake" to underscore what she hopes her essays have conveyed—a sense that imagination—not money, or railways, or roads—makes travel possible. She returns in the essay to speak of the "stay-at-home" life that taught her "to make what [she] wanted in [her] imagination, out of whatever lay nearest at hand" (273). The places that Lee most remembers traveling to are not the "real" places but rather those that she has imagined. For example, she recalls at length poring over a "Keepsake" volume of northern Italian cities and writes: "Among these I rambled with a delight such as no real places (I had seen but few interesting ones) had as yet given me" (276). Her aside is especially curious, coming as it does after thirty-some essays about specific places in Germany, Italy, and Switzerland. But it suggests that the kind of travel she has in mind is in no sense limited to the literal. She qualifies her sentence to this effect immediately afterwards: "'Rambling' is the wrong word; it was no active living, but a sort of brooding sense of the existence of those places" (276).

Lee returns also in this final essay to address the importance of perspective: "The passionate feeling for places depends very largely on a habit of craving for the *beyond: beyond* the plain which intervenes between us and the mountain range; *beyond* the hill, the pass between us and the seashore" (273). In her repeated emphasis on the impulse to look to the beyond, Lee almost seems to be preaching, and it is impossible not to believe that her intended audience consisted of women, especially given her earlier emphasis on the female identity of the sentimental traveler. The yearning for the beyond, she later argues, "is largely connected to the poverty of experience in those early years" (277). The sense of place to which all of her essays are addressed is one "for ever sovereign and sacred to us" (277). The places governed by the imagination are realms over which she—and the other women she refers to as sentimental travelers—has complete control.

In some ways, the emphasis both Meynell and Lee place on the interior interest of place and travel might be read as typical to the early modernist work of women writers in general. In her discussion of the female aesthetic in *A Literature of Their Own*, Elaine Showalter argues that Virginia Woolf's generation "tried to create a power base in inner space, an aesthetic that championed the feminine consciousness and asserted its superiority to the public, rationalist masculine world."[4] Although interiority empowers the female figures that occupy the attention of Woolf and others, it also serves as a retreat from the very world over which it looked. Although both Meynell and

Lee clearly found travel empowering, they, too, can be said to have retreated from the active involvement with the world evidenced in the work of other Victorian and late Victorian women travelers. In their works they showed none of the physical finesse and sheer activity of the adventuress; none of the dynamic involvement with the everyday of the sociologist; none of the concern for the past of the historian and art historian. And whereas they shared some of the interests and concerns of the tourist—for example, the attentiveness to landscape—their goal was less to authentically evoke the foreign place than to foreground and highlight personal response. Although Lee in particular claimed to stake out for her sentimental travelers a "sovereign" sphere, this sphere is isolated, seemingly unrelated to and uninvolved with the material world. Finally, despite all of her claims for the mythic powers of the wandering woman, it is difficult to see this figure as commanding any kind of real force—as capable of effecting change in her world.

To recognize the limitations of the kind of traveler envisioned by Meynell and Lee is not to disparage their achievements as travel writers. They were among the first to openly address the psychological implications of travel and to argue in an indirect way for its necessity. They were also among the first to recognize that travel enabled women to have some control over their *position*—their position in relation to the wider world and their position in relation to others in that world. To an extent, then, their works evidence what Patricia Yaeger in *Honey-Mad Women: Emancipatory Strategies in Women's Writing* describes as the woman writer's "capacity for transforming boundaries, for defining her own loci of power."[5] Certainly Meynell did so by suggesting in her essays that the perspective afforded by one's position "on the verge" was an empowering perspective—one that enabled her traveler to see what boundaries created her sense of distance and to experiment with exerting control over her position. Meynell translated this concern with perspective into her very late poetry, where in poems such as "Winter Trees on the Horizon" she embraces a marginal position as "her own."

Similarly, Lee created her "sentimental traveller" to be a woman whose imagination allowed her to control her position, one whose eyes forever looked "to other parts of the world." By representing the woman traveler in terms of her control over perspective and position, both Lee and Meynell avoided the risk of a more essentialist description of her achievements, one which might depict her work as the "natural" product of her gender rather than as a consequence of her socially constructed position.

Another important and related dimension of Meynell's and Lee's work is suggested by their seeming unwillingness to render the woman traveler in any kind of tangible detail. In failing or, more likely, refusing to do so, both women acknowledge the difficulty of recognizing the achievements of women travelers. To attempt to delineate those achievements in concrete language is necessarily to limit them—to represent them as "contributions" to some ostensibly "larger," more inclusive tradition or to depict them as the isolated accomplishments of a few exceptional women.

In many ways, achievement recognition is a problem that all who try to write about women and history face, as the work of the historian Joan Scott and others has shown, and it continues to trouble those of us who study the lives and work of Victorian women. In an essay in *Gender & History*, "Writing Inside the Kaleidoscope: Re-Representing Victorian Women Public Figures," Kali Israel uses the image of the kaleidoscope to "suggest some of the complexities of 'seeing' women historically."[6] She argues that the historian has only fragments of material to work with and that these fragments are, for the most part, only refractions of public representations. Israel's work may help to remind us as well of the difficulties of attempting to "see," much less to summarize, Victorian women travelers, for they, too, are only partially accessible to us. Given the inevitable limitations of the historical perspective, though, what can be said of them?

In the course of documenting women's activities and achievements in the wider world, certain important issues arise. Among them is the legitimacy of separating their accomplishments from those of their male counterparts. Victorian women did not have different intellectual capabilities that somehow caused them to experience their travels differently or to write about their experiences differently. But the dominant gender ideologies that encouraged women to identify with their emotional propensities over intellectual capabilities certainly influenced how many women chose to represent their experiences in their works. One can also argue that the significantly different social statuses and cultural roles of Victorian men and women influenced the shape and direction of their travel writing. These disparities can be measured in many ways. The unequal opportunities for education and employment available to men and women at home, for example, are just two barometers of socially constructed and maintained difference in Victorian England, but class differences were also critical to this nexus. All of these differences undoubtedly affected how women represented the significance of their travels. Clearly, no simple description of the differences between male and female travel writing exists. One needs instead to ask how Victorian men and women let perceived differences between genders, classes, races, and nationalities affect what they experienced abroad and how they conveyed those experiences to their readers.

These questions, though, invite another series of questions, ultimately ad infinitum, for one's response varies with each individual woman traveler and depends as well on when and where she traveled. Many of the women who toured Italy, for instance, brought with them certain assumptions about what constituted taste, what was culturally valuable. They sometimes attempted to align their work to a high culture tradition of writing about Italy; in other discernible ways (e.g., in their attentiveness to nature), though, they marked their work as different. For other women Italy (and other European countries) offered the opportunity for professional development and credibility and many correspondingly created ways to "overcome" the limitations of gender by redirecting travel writing into the more respectable field of art history. The women who traveled to regions considered remote from England were clearly prompted by a still different sense of what the wider world had to offer them as women. And although many could be said to "escape" the confines of gender by acting out lives of adventure and heroism abroad, many also took advantage of their opportunities to invoke domestic ideology to advantage. The women who directed their travel accounts into histories in some ways adopted a posture in blatant contrast to that of the adventuress; they often represented themselves as passive recipients of the place rather than as aggressors. This posture in some ways represents a more traditionally "feminized" approach to travel, but the women who fashioned histories out of travel also participated in a tradition of writing that was very much linked in the public mind with the sage figure. Finally, the women who traveled to America responded to their sense of their position as women in different ways as well. Martineau argued that as a woman she was particularly suited to social study but on occasion invoked the essentialist explanation that women were inherently moral to justify her claim. Faithfull for the most part avoided such reasoning and chose instead to focus on the social position of women because it helped to advance her claims for remunerative employment for women in England. Nonetheless, both women looked to America as a land of professional opportunity, both for its women and for themselves. Even such a cursory glance at the subjects of this study suggests the fallacy of identifying and describing "the Victorian woman traveler" as a homogenous entity. To even begin to acknowledge their breadth of experience and range of emphasis, one must think instead of "Victorian women travelers."

Each region of the wider world clearly offered, or at least seemed to offer, different kinds of opportunities for Victorian women travelers. And each woman responded to these opportunities in a different way. But notwithstanding the differences of perspective that each woman brought to her travels, certain claims can be made for what they learned from abroad and what they taught their readers. I argue that nearly all of the women who traveled abroad discovered that the gender differences that had seemed definitive at home were capable of being reimagined and reworked in some way. Because travel writing by implication decentralized the domestic, it necessarily enabled women to foreground the issues of professional and cultural identity that had been marginalized in the service of domestic realism. Travel writing therefore provides a record nowhere else available of Victorian women's efforts to construct and reconstruct these identities. It also suggests the fallacy of assuming that such a project follows a clearly discernible pattern—that is, that Victorian women travelers "evolved" as a species, beginning as tourists, advancing to adventuresses, and ending as professionally successful historians, art historians, and sociologists. Instead, their achievements in each of these areas spanned the period, took many different shapes, and, at different times, various approaches to travel writing appealed to different segments of the reading public for different reasons. And it would be a mistake to assume that the backdrop of this story of achievement is one of historical homogeneity; the socio-economic and political status of Victorian women of all classes changed throughout the nineteenth century in different ways and to different degrees, as Mary Poovey has demonstrated in *Uneven Developments*. Taken in its totality, the work of Victorian women travel writers calls into question the widely held doctrine of separate spheres that continues even today to influence and in some cases restrict what can be said about middle-class Victorian women and their work. For the women examined in this study, travel was a way to rethink those spheres, to forge links to broader social, intellectual, and political movements, and to create a wider range for their activity.

Notes

Preface

1. William E. Buckler, ed., *Prose of the Victorian Period* (Boston: Houghton Mifflin, 1958).
2. Virginia Woolf, *A Room of One's Own* (New York: Harcourt Brace and World, 1929), p. 83; subsequent citations from this work are noted parenthetically in the text.
3. Elaine Showalter, *A Literature of Their Own: British Women Novelists from Brontë to Lessing* (Princeton: Princeton University Press, 1977).
4. Mary Poovey, *Uneven Developments: The Ideological Work of Gender in Mid-Victorian England* (Chicago: University of Chicago Press, 1988).
5. Martha Vicinus, ed., *A Widening Sphere: Changing Roles of Victorian Women* (Bloomington: Indiana University Press, 1977).

Chapter 1. Voyagers Out: Victorian Women Abroad

1. Constance Larymore, *A Resident's Wife in Nigeria* (London: Routledge, 1908), p. 54.
2. Ibid., p. 2.
3. Frances Elliot, *Diary of an Idle Woman in Italy*, 2 vols. (New York: Brentanos, 1871), 1: 318–19.
4. Ibid., 2: 279.
5. That Sarah Ellis and Sarah Lewis consigned their fellow English women to the domestic sphere is ironic, because both women actively pursued a public forum for their views.
6. George Eliot, *Middlemarch: A Study of Provincial Life* (1871–72; reprint, Harmondsworth, England: Penguin, 1984); references from this edition of *Middlemarch* will hereafter be cited parenthetically in the text. Curiously, Frances Elliot's *Diary of an Idle Woman in Italy* came out in the same year as *Middlemarch*.
7. Charlotte Brontë, *Shirley* (1849; reprint, Harmondsworth, England: Penguin, 1982), p. 384; subsequent citations from this work are noted parenthetically in the text.
8. *The George Eliot Letters*, ed. G. Gordon Haight, 9 vols. (New Haven: Yale University Press, 1954–78), 2: 165. For further discussion of Eliot's reasons for making reference to Labassecour see Deirdre David's "'Getting Out of the Eel Jar': George Eliot's Literary Appropriation of Abroad," in *Creditable Warriors*, ed. Michael Cotsell (Atlantic Highlands, N.J.: Ashfield Press, 1990) pp. 257–72.
9. For a full discussion of Brontë's intellectual relationship with Constantin Heger, see Sue Lonoff's essay, "Charlotte Brontë's Belgian Essays: The Discourse of Empowerment," in *Victorian Studies* 32 (Spring 1989), 386–409.
10. Elizabeth Eastlake, "Lady Travellers," *Quarterly Review* 76 (June 1845), 136.

11. John Pemble, *The Mediterranean Passion: Victorians and Edwardians in the South* (London: Clarendon, 1987), p. 96.

12. Ibid., p. 96.

13. Sir Charles Petrie, *The Victorians* (London: Eyre and Spottiswoode, 1960), p. 168.

14. Amelia Edwards, *Untrodden Peaks and Unfrequented Valleys* (1873; reprint, Boston: Beacon Press, 1987), p. 1.

15. John Pemble, *The Mediterranean Passion*, p. 46.

16. Frances Power Cobbe, *Cities of the Past* (London: Trubner and Co., 1864), p. 173; subsequent citations from this work are noted parenthetically in the text.

17. Amelia Edwards, *A Thousand Miles Up the Nile* (London: George Routledge, 1889), pp. 1–2; subsequent citations from this work are noted parenthetically in the text.

18. An example of an exceptionally early traveling English woman is Margery Kempe, who records her visit to Jerusalem and Rome in her autobiography, *The Book of Margery Kempe*, thought to date from 1436.

19. In addition, early women novelists made use of their experiences abroad. Aphra Behn, for example, wrote *Oroonoko* after having lived in Surinam. Charlotte Lennox incorporated some of her American experiences in *Harriot Stuart* and *Euphemia*.

20. Quoted by Cecil Woodham-Smith in *Florence Nightingale*. (New York: McGraw-Hill 1951), p. 266.

21. Elizabeth Gaskell, *The Life of Charlotte Brontë* (1857; reprint, Harmondsworth, England: Penguin, 1985), p. 225.

22. Cobbe, *Cities*, p. 176.

23. Harriet Martineau, *Retrospect of Western Travel*, 2 vols (New York: Lohman, 1838), 2: 18–19; subsequent citations from this work are noted parenthetically in the text.

24. Mary Kingsley, *Travels in West Africa: Congo Francais, Corisco, and Cameroons* (1897: reprint, Boston: Beacon Press, 1982), p. 6; subsequent citations from this work are noted parenthetically in the text.

25. Pemble, *Mediterranean Passion*, pp. 77–78.

26. Catherine Barnes Stevenson, *Victorian Women Travel Writers in Africa* (Boston: Twayne, 1982), p. 3.

27. Jihang Park, "Women of Their Time: The Growing Recognition of the Second Sex in Victorian and Edwardian England," *Journal of Social History* 21 (Fall 1987), 49.

28. For examples of work on the public/private dichotomy in Victorian life see Janet Siltanen and Michelle Stanworth's collection of essays *Women and the Public Sphere: A Critique of Sociology and Politics* (New York: St. Martin's Press, 1984) and Catherine Hall's "Private Persons Versus Public Someones: Class, Gender and Politics in England, 1780–1850" in *Language, Gender and Childhood*, ed. Carolyn Steedman, Cathy Urwin, and Valerie Walkerdine (London: Routledge and Kegan Paul, 1985), p. 10–33.

29. Susan Morgan, "Victorian Women, Wisdom, and Southeast Asia," in *Victorian Sages and Cultural Discourse: Renegotiating Gender and Power*, ed. Thais Morgan (New Brunswick, N.J.: Rutgers University Press, 1991), p. 223.

30. Ibid., p. 223.

31. Sarah Lewis, *Woman's Mission* (London: John W. Parker, 1839).

32. Quoted in Stevenson, *Women Travel Writers in Africa*, p. 87.

33. Mary Poovey, *Uneven Developments*, p. 8–9.

34. Pemble, *The Mediterranean Passion*, p. 53.

35. Gabriele Annan, "Roughing It," *The New York Review of Books* (22 December 1988), p. 3.

36. Joanne Shattock, and Michael Wolff, *The Victorian Periodical Press: Soundings and Samplings* (Leicester, England: Leicester University Press, 1982), p. xiv.

37. In her article "'The Hero as Man of Letters': Masculinity and Victorian Nonfiction Prose," Carol T. Christ notes that women account for only thirteen percent of those authors indexed in *The Wellesley Index to Victorian Periodicals* (21). Not surprisingly, many of the women she mentions were travel writers, among them Frances Power Cobbe, Lady Eastlake, and Vernon Lee.

38. Pierre Bourdieu, *Distinction: A Social Critique of the Judgement of Taste*, trans. Richard Nice (Cambridge: Harvard University Press, 1984).

39. Ibid., p. 317.

40. Martha Vicinus, *Independent Women: Work and Community for Single Women, 1850–1920* (Chicago: University of Chicago Press, 1985), p. 7.

41. Anne Radcliffe, *A Journey made in the Summer of 1794 Through Holland and the Western Frontier of Germany* (1795; reprint, Hildesheim, N.Y.: G. Olms Co., 1975), p. v.

42. Frances Elliot, *Diary of an Idle Woman in Constantinople* (Leipzig, Germany: Bernhard Tauchnitz, 1893), n.p.

43. Amelia Edwards, *Untrodden Peaks*, p. 242.

44. Carol Christ, "The Hero as Man of Letters," in *Victorian Sages and Cultural Discourse: Renegotiating Gender and Power*, ed. Thais Morgan (New Brunswick, N.J.: Rutgers University Press, 1991), p. 230.

45. Gaye Tuchman, and Nine Fortin, *Edging Women Out: Victorian Novelists, Publishers, and Social Change* (New Haven: Yale University Press, 1989), p. 215.

46. Ibid., p. 3.

47. Ironically, one of the most influential pieces of "woman writer" criticism was written by a woman: "Silly Novels by Lady Novelists" by George Eliot was published in *The Westminster Review* in October of 1856.

48. Tuchman and Fortin, *Edging Women Out*, p. 73.

49. Viola Klein, *The Feminine Character: History of an Ideology* (New York: International Universities Press,1949), p. 42.

50. Pinney, Thomas, p. 334.

51. Michael Cotsell, ed., *Creditable Warriors, 1830–1876* (Atlantic Highlands, N.J.: Ashfield Press, 1990), p. 14.

52. Their research shows that most Victorian nonfiction can be categorized according to gender. Whereas "male specialties" included the natural sciences, physical sciences, classics, geography, and economics, "female categories" were limited to women's topics and children's books. "High-prestige" specialties, those accorded the most cultural status, included philosophy, history, politics, social theory, and public policy—many of the same areas that Deirdre David would identify as the province of the traditional intellectual.

53. Nancy Armstrong, "The Rise of Feminine Authority in the Novel," *Novel: A Forum on Fiction* 15 (Winter 1982), p. 129.

54. Deirdre David, *Intellectual Women and Victorian Patriarchy* (Ithaca: Cornell University Press, 1987).

55. Janet Murray, *Strong-Minded Women and Other Lost Voices from the Nineteenth Century* (New York: Pantheon Books, 1982).

56. Phillipa Levine, *Feminist Lives in Victorian England* (Cambridge: Basil Blackwell: 1990).

57. Vernon Lee, *The Enchanted Woods: And Other Essays on the Genius of Places*

(London: John Lane, 1905), p. 3; subsequent citations from this work are noted parenthetically in the text.

58. Annan, "Roughing It," p. 3.

59. James Buzard, *The Beaten Track: European Tourism, Literature, and the Ways to "Culture," 1800–1918* (New York: Oxford Press, 1993).

60. Sara Mills, *Discourses of Difference: An Analysis of Women's Travel Writing and Colonialism* (New York: Routledge, 1991).

61. Billie Melman, *Women's Orients: English Women and the Middle East, 1718–1918* (New York: Macmillan, 1991).

62. Anna Leonowens, *The Romance of The Harem*, ed. Susan Morgan (Charlottesville: University Press of Virginia, 1991).

63. Shirley Foster, *Nineteenth-Century Women Travellers and Their Writings* (London: Harvester Wheatsheaf, 1990).

64. Jane Robinson, *Wayward Women: A Guide to Women Travellers* (Oxford: Oxford University Press, 1990).

Chapter 2. Into the Temple of Taste: Victorian Women in Italy

1. Charlotte Eaton, *Rome in the Nineteenth Century*, 5th ed. 2 vols. (London: Henry G. Bohn, 1852), 1: p. 91; subsequent citations to this work are noted parenthetically in the text.

2. Eaton was, of course, not the first or the last to explicitly associate her trip to Italy with the cultivation of taste. In *Italian Hours*, Henry James wrote of Italy's "great artistic deeds" that as "you spend a constant portion of your days among them the sense of one of the happiest periods of human Taste—to put it only at that—settles upon your spirit." (London: William Heinemann, 1909), p. 274.

3. Paul Fussell, *Abroad: Literary Traveling Between the Wars* (New York: Oxford University Press, 1980), p. 39.

4. Elizabeth Eastlake, "Lady Travellers," p. 136.

5. E. M. Forster, *A Room With a View*, (1908; reprint New York: Bantam Books, 1988), pp. 15–16; subsequent citations from this work will be noted parenthetically in the text.

6. In this sense Forster represents Lucy as something of a "new woman." Writing about "new women" abroad, Eva-Maria Kroller has noted, "The 'new woman' often considered the routes and sights prescribed by the guidebooks as paternalistic straightjackets" (74).

7. Elizabeth Eastlake, Untitled Review, *Quarterly Review* 91 (June 1852): p. 1.

8. Mary Shelley, *The Letters of Mary Shelley*, ed. Betty T. Bennett, 3 vols. (Baltimore: Johns Hopkins University Press, 1988), 2: 202; subsequent citations from this work are noted parenthetically in the text.

9. Helen Heineman, *Mrs. Trollope: The Triumphant Feminine in the Nineteenth Century* (Athens: Ohio University Press, 1979), p. 16.

10. Debra Edelstein, "Vernon Lee," in vol. 57 of *Dictionary of Literary Biography*, ed. William Thesing (Detroit: Gale Research Company, 1987), pp. 156–57.

11. Valene Smith, ed. *Hosts and Guests: The Anthropology of Tourism*, (Philadelphia: University of Pennsylvania Press, 1977): pp. 1–14.

12. Mary Shelley, "The English in Italy," *Westminster Review* 6 (October 1826), p. 334; subsequent citations from this work are cited parenthetically in the text.

13. Eastlake, "Lady Travellers," p. 101.

14. Hester Lynch Piozzi, *Observations and Reflections Made in the Course of a Journey Through France, Italy, and Germany*, 2 vols. (London: A. Strahn, 1779), 1: iv.

15. Elliot, *Diary of an Idle Woman in Italy*, preface.

16. Lady Marguerite Blessington, *The Idler in Italy*, 2 vols. (London: Henry Colburn, 1839), 2: 326.

17. Vernon Lee, *For Maurice: Five Unlikely Stories* (London: Lane, Bodley Head, 1927), p. xxxvi. By featuring Symonds in her comment, Lee ironically calls attention to the male monopoly of cultural taste and criticism.

18. Vernon Lee, *The Spirit of Rome: Leaves from a Diary* (London: John Lane, 1906), p. 66; subsequent citations from this work are noted parenthetically in the text.

19. Mary Shelley, *Rambles in Germany and Italy in 1840, 1842, and 1843*, 2 vols. (London: Edward Moxon, 1844), 1: 45.

20. Curiously, one of Eaton's most favorable reviewers was Mary Shelley, who in her *Westminster Review* article called the work "an inestimable guide to all who visit the Eternal City, and even to those at home; more than any other work on the same subject, it gives a faithful account of that metropolis of the world" ("The English in Italy," *Westminster Review* 6 [October 1826]), p. 337.

21. Frances Trollope, *A Visit to Italy* (London: R. Bentley, 1842), p. 22; subsequent citations from this work are noted parenthetically in the text.

22. Review of *Italian Highways* by Mrs. R. M. King, *The Athenaeum* (30 January 1897), p. 147.

23. Anne Buckland, *The World Beyond the Esterelles* (London: Remington, 1884), p. i; subsequent citations to this work are noted parenthetically in the text.

24. Mary Shelley, *Letters* 3: 96.

25. Mariana Starke, *Letters from Italy*, 2 vols. (London: Bentley, 1800); 2: 93.

26. There are, however, some noteworthy exceptions to this trend. Frances Power Cobbe's *Italics* treats the country from both historical and socio-political perspectives.

27. Elizabeth Barrett, and Robert Browning, *The Letters of Robert Browning and Elizabeth Barrett, 1845–1846*, 2 vols., ed. Elvan Kintner (Cambridge: Cambridge University Press, 1969), 1: 189.

28. Cotsell, *Creditable Warriors*, p. 8.

29. Pemble, *The Mediterranean Passion*, p. 149.

30. Charles Dickens, *Pictures from Italy* (1846; reprint, New York: Coward, McCann, and Geoghegan, 1974), pp. 60–61.

31. Vernon Lee, "On Modern Travelling," *Macmillan's Magazine* 96 (February 1894): p. 309; subsequent citations from this work are cited parenthetically in the text.

32. Review of *The Spirit of Rome* by Vernon Lee in *The Atlantic* (April 1906): pp. 559–60.

33. Blessington, *The Idler in Italy*, 2: 121.

34. Gaston Bachelard, *The Poetics of Space* (Boston: Beacon Press, 1965), p. 183.

35. Frances Power Cobbe, *Italics: Brief Notes on the Politics, People, and Places in Italy* (London: Trubner and Co., 1864), p. 373.

Chapter 3. The Professionalization of Taste: Art Historians Abroad

1. *The Journals and Correspondence of Lady Eastlake*, ed. Charles E. Smith, 2 vols. (London: John Murray, 1895), 1: 91; subsequent citations from Lady Eastlake's

correspondence are from these volumes and are cited parenthetically by volume and page number in the text.

2. See *The History of Our Lord as Exemplified in Works of Art*, commenced by the late Mrs. Jameson, continued and completed by Lady Eastlake, 2 vols. (London: Longmans, Green, 1864). When Jameson died in 1860, her family asked Eastlake to complete her work-in-progress.

3. Shirley Foster summarizes this tendency in *Across New Worlds* as a consequence of the individuality of women travelers: "As individual travellers, each with her own aspirations and goals, the women did not see themselves as a group" (viii). In *A Voyager Out: The Life of Mary Kingsley* (Boston: Houghton Mifflin, 1986) Katherine Frank documents Mary Kingsley's troubled relationship with fellow African traveler, Mary Lugard. Other women travelers were known to have problematic relationships as well: Marianne North and Florence Dixie shunned Isabella Bird Bishop's attempts at friendship.

4. Louisa Twining, *Symbols of Early and Mediaeval Christian Art* (London: Longman, Brown, Green, and Longmans, 1852), preface.

5. *A Bright Remembrance: The Diaries of Julia Cartwright, 1851–1924*, ed. and with an intro. by Angela Emanuel (London: Weidenfeld and Nicolson, 1989); subsequent citations from this work are noted parenthetically in the text.

6. Julia Ady, "The New Art Criticism," *Quarterly Review* (1896): 466.

7. Mary Heaton, *Masterpieces of Flemish Art, Including Examples of the Early German and Dutch Schools* (London: Bell and Daldy, 1869), p. 1.

8. In addition to her many articles on Renaissance art, Ady published several biographies of the period's prominent figures. One of her most successful was of Isabella d'Este, a fifteenth-century Italian princess.

9. See Colin Eisler's "Lady Dilke (1840–1904): The Six Lives of an Art Historian," in *Women as Interpreters of the Visual Arts, 1820–1979*, ed. Claire Richter Sherman with Adele M. Holcomb (Westport, Conn.: Greenwood Press, 1981), p. 154.

10. Of her doctor's diagnosis Cartwright wrote in her diary: "The worst is that he maintains that I must not work my brain, only indulge in the lightest literature, which I think horrible. What am I to do when work is my life?" (77).

11. Anna Jameson, *Letters and Friendships, 1812–1860*, ed. Mrs. Steuart Erskine (London: T. Fisher Unwin, 1915), p. 246; subsequent citations from this work are noted parenthetically in the text.

12. Claire Richter Sherman provides a concise and valuable discussion of the impact of historiography on art scholarship in the first chapter of *Women as Interpreters of the Visual Arts, 1820–1979*, ed. Claire Richter Sherman and Adele M. Holcomb (Westport, Conn.: The Greenwood Press, 1967), pp. 3–26.

13. Julia Ady, "English Art in the Victorian Age," *Quarterly Review* 187 (1898): pp. 212–13.

14. Later in the century Ady paid tribute to the woman connoisseur with her biography of Isabella d'Este, which focused on her significance as a patron of the arts.

15. Ady, "English Art," p. 213.

16. Francis Sheppard, *London 1808–1870: The Infernal Wen* (Los Angeles: University of California Press, 1971), pp. 361–62.

17. Ibid, p. 362.

18. Eastlake pursues this theme throughout her essay "The British Museum," *Quarterly Review* 124 (January 1868): 147–179.

19. Ellen Moers, *Literary Women* (New York: Doubleday and Co., 1976), p. 188.

20. Clara Thomas, *Love and Work Enough: The Life of Anna Jameson* (Toronto: University of Toronto Press, 1967), p. 29.

21. Ibid., p. 53.

22. Moers, *Literary Women*, p. 188.

23. Anna Jameson, *Diary of an Ennuyee*, (1826; reprinted in *Visits and Sketches at Home and Abroad, with Tales and Miscellanies* New York: Harper Brothers, 1834), p. 104; subsequent citations from this work are noted parenthetically in the text.

24. Adele Holcomb, "Anna Jameson (1794–1860): Sacred Art and Social Vision," in *Women as Interpreters of the Visual Arts, 1820–1979*, ed. Claire Richter Sherman and Adele Holcomb. (Westport, Conn.: Greenwood Press, 1981), pp. 93–121.

25. Anna Jameson, *Visits and Sketches at Home and Abroad, with Tales and Miscellanies* (New York: Harper Brothers, 1834); subsequent citations from this work are noted parenthetically in the text.

26. Holcomb, "Anna Jameson," p. 99.

27. Anna Jameson, *Companion to the Most Celebrated Private Galleries of Art in London* (London: Saunders and Otley, 1844), p. xi.

28. Hawthorne is quoted by Giuliana Treves in *The Golden Ring: The Anglo-Florentines, 1847–1862*, trans. Sylvia Sprigge (London: Longmans, Green, and Co., 1956), p. 115.

29. Anna Jameson, "Female Criticism," reprinted in *Commonplace Book of Thoughts, Memories, and Fancies* (London: Longman, Brown, Green, and Longmans, 1852), p. 309.

30. Jameson's interest in the figure of the virgin later took another direction. In 1852 she published *Legends of the Madonna as Represented in the Fine Arts* (Reprint; Boston: Houghton Mifflin, 1895), a work whose focus was on the historical impact of the cult of the virgin.

31. Jameson, *Letters and Friendships*, p. 157.

32. She also wanted to attack the commission's assertion that working mothers were to blame for opium poisoning among the children of Nottingham lacemakers. Holcomb writes: "Her fury with the investigators' incomprehension approached more closely to a bellow of despair than anything in her previous or later writings, though it remained controlled" (Holcomb, "Anna Jameson," p. 106).

33. Anna Jameson, "Report of the Commissioners on the Employments of Children, &c.,: Condition of the Women and the Female Children," *The Athenaeum*, no. 871 (24 June 1843): p. 588.

34. The educated middle-class woman restricted to governessing was also the subject of her work, *On the Relative Social Position of Mothers and Governesses*.

35. Jameson, *Companion*, p. v.

36. Ibid., p. vi.

37. Anna Jameson, *Handbook to the Public Galleries of Art in and near London*. (London: John Murray, 1842), p. ix.

38. Ibid., p. 98.

39. Ibid., p. 172.

40. Both essays are reprinted in *Sketches of Art, Literature, and Character* (Boston: Ticknor and Fields, 1858).

41. Ibid., p. 61.

42. Ibid., pp. 61–62.

43. Her entire statement is reprinted in *Letters and Friendships*, pp. 332–34. This particular quotation occurs on p. 334.

44. Jameson, *Handbook*, p. 4.

45. Harriet Martineau, "Mrs. Jameson," in *Biographical Sketches* (New York: Leypoldt and Holt, 1869), p. 118.

46. Here, too, I draw on the work of Deirdre David. For a full elaboration of this theme, see David on Martineau in *Intellectual Women and Victorian Patriarchy*.

47. Anna Jameson, *Sacred and Legendary Art*, (1848; reprint, London: Longmans, Green, 1857), p. vi.

48. John Steegman, *Consort of Taste: 1830–1870* (London: Sidgwick and Jackson, Limited, 1950), p. 187.

49. Elizabeth Eastlake, "Evangelical Novels," *Quarterly Review* 72 (May 1843): p. 32.

50. In *Politics and Reviewers: The Edinburgh and the Quarterly in the Early Victorian Age*, Joanne Shattock identifies the readership of the *Quarterly Review* as composed of the "so-called intelligentsia, almost certainly, the educated upper-middle classes, the professional classes, and some of the lower-middle classes," (London: Leicester University Press, 1989), p. 158.

51. Elizabeth Eastlake, "Michael Angelo," *Quarterly Review* 103 (April 1858): pp. 436–483; subsequent citations from this work are noted parenthetically in the text.

52. Elizabeth Eastlake, "Review of *Modern Painters*," *Quarterly Review* 98 (March 1856): p. 389; subsequent citations from this work are noted parenthetically in the text.

53. Elizabeth Eastlake, "Modern Photography," *Quarterly Review* 101 (April 1857): pp. 442–61; subsequent citations from this work are noted parenthetically in the text.

54. Elizabeth Eastlake, "The Englishwoman at School," *Quarterly Review* 146 (July 1878): pp. 40–69.

55. Ibid., p. 69.

56. Quoted by Betty Askwith in *Lady Dilke, A Biography* (London: Chatto and Windus, 1969), p. 77.

57. Quoted by Edelstein, "Vernon Lee," p. 161.

Chapter 4. Fair Amazons Abroad: The Social Construction of the Victorian Adventuress

1. *London Figaro* (8 February 1881), p. 4.

2. Paul Fussell, *Abroad: Literary Traveling Between the Wars* (New York: Oxford University Press, 1980), p. 203.

3. W. H. Davenport Adams, *Celebrated Women Travellers of the Nineteenth Century* (London: W. Swan Sonnenschein, 1883), p. 12.

4. Florence Dixie, *Across Patagonia* (London: R. Bentley, 1880), p. 3; subsequent citations from this work are noted parenthetically in the text.

5. Edwards, *Untrodden Peaks*, p. xxix.

6. Isabella Bird Bishop, *The Yangtze Valley and Beyond*, 2 vols. (London: John Murray, 1899), 1: 159; subsequent citations from this work are noted parenthetically in the text.

7. Constance Gordon Cumming, *At Home in Fiji* (New York: Armstrong, 1882), p. 10. Subsequent citations from this work are noted parenthetically in the text.

8. Mary Seacole, *The Wonderful Adventures of Mrs. Seacole in Many Lands* (1857; reprint, intro. William L. Andrews and a preface by W. H. Russell (New York: Oxford University Press, 1988), p. 71; subsequent citations from this work are noted parenthetically in the text.

9. Isabella Bird Bishop, *Six Months Among the Palm Groves, Coral Reefs, and Volca-*

noes of the Sandwich Islands, 2d ed. (London: John Murray, 1876), p. 237. Subsequent citations from this work are noted parenthetically in the text.

10. For a fuller elaboration of this topic, see Sara Mills's *Discourses of Difference.*

11. Martin Green, *Dreams of Adventure and Deeds of Empire* (New York: Basic Books, 1979), p. 3.

12. George Eliot, *Daniel Deronda* (1876; reprint, Harmondsworth, England: Penguin, p. 171.

13. Joseph Conrad, *The Heart of Darkness* (1902; reprint, New York: Penguin, 1973), p. 69.

14. For fictional instances of this process one thinks, for example, of Amelia Sedley in *Vanity Fair* (1848) who, though unaware of her brother's activities abroad, eagerly awaits the cashmere sweaters that Jos regularly sends.

15. Isabella Bird Bishop, *A Lady's Life in the Rocky Mountains* (London: John Murray, 1880; reprint, London: Virago, 1982), p. 113; subsequent citations from this work are noted parenthetically in the text.

16. Constance Gordon Cumming, *In the Himalayas and On the Indian Plains* (London: Chatto and Windus, 1884), p. 460; subsequent citations from this work are noted parenthetically in the text.

17. *The Scottish Geographical Magazine* 20 (1904): p. 596.

18. *The Athenaeum,* no. 3615 (6 February 1896): p. 174.

19. *The Scottish Geographical Magazine* 12 (1896): p. 41.

20. *The Athenaeum,* no. 3615 (6 February 1896): p. 174.

21. W. G. Blaikie, "Lady Travellers," *Blackwood's Magazine* 160 (July 1896): p. 49.

22. Ibid., p. 51.

23. George Curzon, "Ladies and the Royal Geographic Society," Letter to the editor of *The Times* (31 May 1893): p. 11.

24. "To the Royal Geographic Society," *Punch* (6 October 1893): p. 269.

25. *The Gentlewoman* (16 June 1900): p. 771.

26. Such labeling was, of course, applied not only to the adventuress but also to all women who seemed to compromise their natural womanhood. Gilbert and Gubar report in the first volume of *No Man's Land,* for instance, that Victorian moralists like Nicholas Cooke argued that granting a woman political rights would cause her to "become rapidly unsexed and degraded" and "to cease to be the gentle mother, and become the Amazonian brawler" (13).

27. Nina Auerbach, *Woman and the Demon: The Life of a Victorian Myth* (Cambridge: Harvard University Press, 1982), p. 8.

28. Mary Gaunt, *Alone in West Africa* (London: T. Werner Laurie, 1911), p. 2.

29. Mary Tinling, *Women in the Unknown: A Sourcebook on Women Explorers and Travelers* (New York: Greenwood Press, 1989), p. 48.

30. Lucy Broad, *A Woman's Wanderings the World Over* (London: Headley Brothers, 1909), p. 12.

31. Birkett, *Spinsters Abroad,* p. 198.

32. Lucie Duff Gordon, *Letters from Egypt: To Which are Added Letters from the Cape* (London: Macmillan, 1876), p. 29; subsequent citations from this work are noted parenthetically in the text.

33. T. S. Clouston, *Female Education from a Medical Point of View* (Edinburgh: Macniven and Wallace, 1882), p. 41.

34. Florence Dixie, *In the Land of Misfortune* (London: Bentley, 1884), p. 2; subsequent citations from this work are noted parenthetically in the text.

35. Quoted in Cecil Woodham-Smith, *Florence Nightingale, 1820–1910* (New York: McGraw-Hill, 1951), p. 301.

36. Harriet Martineau, *Eastern Life, Present and Past*, 2 vols. in 1 (Philadelphia: Lea and Blanchard, 1848), p. 40; subsequent citations from this work are noted parenthetically in the text.

37. Curiously, Dea Birkett reports in *Spinsters Abroad* that even after images of the "noble savage" were no longer a regular feature of anthropological and ethnological scholarship, women travellers "persisted in recording savages, cannibals and ferocious tribesmen in countries where the wilderness had long been tamed" (145).

38. *The Athenaeum*, no. 3618 (27 February 1897): p. 278.

39. Marc Manganaro, "'The Tangled Bank' Revisited: Anthropological Authority in Frazer's *The Golden Bough*," *The Yale Journal of Criticism* 3 (Fall 1989): p. 109.

40. That Edwards is able to indulge in her attraction at all reveals how much she believed—or pretended—that she looked on them unseen.

41. Pemble, *The Mediterranean Passion*, p. 273.

42. Elaine Showalter, "Feminist Criticism in the Wilderness," *Critical Inquiry* 8 (Winter 1981): pp. 179–205.

43. Ibid., p. 201.

44. *St. James Gazette* (3 July 1882), n.p.

45. Ironically, the sponsorship of excavations to Egypt and the destruction of its antiquities went hand-in-hand. Edwards displays surprisingly little self-consciousness when she exclaims in *A Thousand Miles Up the Nile*, "What treasures of sculptured history, what pictured chambers, what buried bronzes and statues may here await the pick of the excavator!" (163).

46. *The Spectator* (16 June 1900): p. 834.

47. *The Athenaeum*, no. 3618 (27 February 1897): p. 278.

48. Mary Kingsley, *West African Studies*, 1899, 3d ed. (New York: Barnes and Noble, 1964), p. vii.

49. *The Athenaeum*, no. 3618 (27 February 1897): p. 278.

50. *The Spectator* (8 November 1879): p. 1415.

51. Blaikie, "Lady Travellers," p. 66.

Chapter 5. Spots of Time: Victorian Women in the Middle East

1. Thomas Carlyle, "On History," (1830; reprint, *A Carlyle Reader*, ed. G. B. Tennyson (New York: Cambridge University Press, 1984).

2. Thomas Carlyle, "Count Cagliostro in Two Flights," in *The Centenary Edition of The Collected Works*, 28 (New York: 1899), pp. 259–60.

3. Carlyle, "On History," pp. 60–61.

4. Peter Allen Dale, *The Victorian Critic and the Idea of History* (Cambridge: Harvard University Press, 1977), p. 3.

5. Margaret Oliphant, *Jerusalem the Holy City: Its History and Hope* (New York: Macmillan, 1891), p. ix (note).

6. Harriet Martineau, *The Autobiography of Harriet Martineau*, ed. with an intro. by Maria Weston Chapman, 2 vols. (Boston: Houghton, Osgood & Co.: 1879), 2: 537; subsequent citations from this work are noted parenthetically in the text.

7. Rosemary Jann, *The Art and Science of Victorian History* (Columbus: Ohio State University Press, 1985), p. xi.

8. Levine, *The Amateur and the Professional*, p. 1.

9. Dale, *The Victorian Critic*, p. 2.

10. For a full discussion of this theme see J. H. Buckley's *The Triumph of Time: A*

Study of the Victorian Concepts of Time, History, Progress, and Decadence (New York: Oxford University Press, 1980).

11. Levine, *The Amateur and the Professional*, p. 9.

12. Augusta Klein, "Sketches of Eastern Travel," In *Blackwood's Magazine* 151 (January 1892): p. 59.

13. Frances Power Cobbe, *Cities of the Past* (London: Trubner and Co., 1864), p. 14; subsequent citations from this work are noted parenthetically in the text.

14. Charles Kingsley, "From Ocean to Sea," (Reprint; in *Prose Idylls* London: n.p., 1882), p. 205.

15. Quoted in Valerie Pichanick, *Harriet Martineau: The Woman and Her Work, 1802–76* (Ann Arbor: University of Michigan Press, 1980), p. 176.

16. George Eliot, *Romola* (Edinburgh: Blackwood and Son, 1863), p. 2.

17. Pemble, *The Mediterranean Passion*, p. 275.

18. James Clifford, Intro. to *Writing Culture: The Poetics and Politics of Ethnography*, ed. James Clifford and George Marcus (Berkeley: University of California Press, 1986), p. 22.

19. Pichanick, *Harriet Martineau*, p. 175.

20. Harriet Martineau, *Life in the Sickroom: Essays by an Invalid* (London: Edward Moxon, 1844), p. xiv; subsequent citations from this work are noted parenthetically in the text.

21. Martineau would later write that she was cured through mesmerism, a claim that substantiates my own feeling that her sickroom experience fundamentally shaped the paradigm of recovery that informed most of what she wrote after *Life in the Sickroom*.

22. Quoted in Pichanick, *Harriet Martineau*, p. 176.

23. Frances Power Cobbe, *The Life of Frances Power Cobbe, By Herself*, 2 vols. in 1. (Cambridge, Mass.: Riverside Press, 1894), p. 194; subsequent citations from this work are noted parenthetically in the text.

24. Stephen Bann, "The Sense of the Past: Image, Text, and Object in the Formation of Historical Consciousness in Nineteenth-Century Britain," in *The New Historicism*, ed. H. Aram Veeser (London: Routledge and Kegan Paul, 1989), pp. 102–15.

25. Bann, "The Sense of the Past," p. 103.

Chapter 6. Declarations of Independence: Victorian Women in America

1. Harriet Martineau, *Society in America*, 2 vols. (Paris: Baudry's European Library, 1873), 1: 204; references are to this edition and hereafter will be cited parenthetically by volume and page number in the text.

2. Leigh Hunt, "Blue Stocking Revels; or the Feast of the Violets," (1837; reprint, *The Poetical Works of Leigh Hunt*, ed. H. S. Milford [New York: Oxford University Press, 1923]), p. 183.

3. The critic responsible for this passage has not been identified in the *Wellesley Index*. *Fraser's Magazine* (19 May 1839), pp. 557–92.

4. For further discussion of this "ad hominem attack based on a prevailing distrust of the bluestocking," see Patricia Marks's essay, "Harriet Martineau: *Fraser's* 'Maid of [Dis]Honour,'" *Victorian Periodicals Review* 19 (Spring 1986), 28–34.

5. Isabella Bird Bishop, *The Englishwoman in America* (1856; reprint, Madison: University of Wisconsin Press, 1966), pp. 88–89.

6. Frances Trollope, *Domestic Manners of the Americans* (1832; reprint, New York:

Oxford University Press, 1894), p. 4; subsequent citations from this work are noted parenthetically in the text.

7. Frederika Bremer, *Homes of the New World*, trans. Mary Howitt, 3 vols. (London: Arthur Hall, Virtue, and Co., 1853), 1: 11.

8. Alexis de Tocqueville, *Democracy in America*, trans. George Lawrence (New York: Anchor, 1969), p. 66.

9. See Peter Conrad's *Imagining America* (New York: Oxford University Press, 1980), for an elaboration of this theme. He focuses on the English traveler who was also a practiced novelist—for example, Frances and Anthony Trollope and Charles Dickens. As trained "anatomists of society," he argues, they were predisposed to explore the social structures they encountered.

10. Harriet Martineau, *How to Observe Morals and Manners* (1838; reprint, intro. Michael R. Hills (New Brunswick, N.J.: Transaction Books, 1988), p. 73.

11. Kathryn Kish Sklar has analyzed thoroughly the contribution that American women of the Victorian period made to the enterprise of social science as well. For more discussion of the gendered features of early social science see her article "Hull-House Maps and Papers: Social Science as Women's Work in the 1890s" in *The Social Survey in Historical Perspective, 1880–1940*, ed. Martin Bulmer, Kevin Bales, and Kathryn Kish Sklar (New York: Cambridge University Press, 1991), pp. 111–47.

12. Jane Lewis, "The Place of Social Investigation, Social Theory and Social Work in the Approach to Late Victorian and Edwardian Social Problems: The Case of Beatrice Webb and Helen Bosanquet," in *The Social Survey in Historical Perspective, 1880–1940*, ed. Martin Bulmer, Kevin Bales, and Kathryn Kish Sklar (New York: Cambridge University Press, 1991), pp. 148–69.

13. Bremer, *Homes of the New World*, p. xii.

14. Bird Bishop, *The English Woman in America*, p. 5.

15. For a good discussion of the evolution of sociology as both discipline and profession see Philip Abrams's *The Origins of British Sociology* (Chicago: University of Chicago Press, 1968).

16. Shirley Foster, *Across New Worlds*, p. 82.

17. One might argue that the women who went to study in America were no less "acquisitive" than were Wright or Trollope. They simply enacted a more subtle and, hence, more acceptable form of labor, the intellectual work of observing and recording the foreign character.

18. Shirley Foster, *Across New Worlds*, p. 73.

19. Bremer, *Homes of the New World*, pp. x–xi.

20. Bird Bishop, *The Englishwoman in America*, p. 2.

21. Frances Butler Kemble's travel account was one such exception. Her *Journal of a Residence on a Georgia Plantation* (1861) included a high-spirited attack on American slavery and garnered a fair amount of public attention. The subject of slavery also forms an essential component of Martineau's work on America.

22. Martin Crawford, *The Anglo-American Crisis of the Mid-Nineteenth Century* (Athens: University of Georgia Press, 1987), p. 9.

23. Bremer, *Homes of the New World*, p. ix.

24. Barbara Leigh Smith Bodichon, *An American Diary: 1857–58*, ed. Joseph W. Reed (London: Routledge and Kegan Paul, 1972), p. 161.

25. Conrad, *Imagining America*, p. 38.

26. Frances Wright, *Views of Society and Manner in America*, 2d ed., (London: Longman and Co., 1820), p. 219.

27. Ibid., p. 222.

28. Amelia Murray, *Letters from the United States, Cuba, and Canada* (New York: Putnam, 1856), p. 35.

29. Isabella Bird Bishop, *The Englishwoman in America*, p. 1.

30. Lady Emmeline Stuart Wortley, *Travels in the United States During 1849 and 1850* (New York: Harper Brothers, 1851), preface.

31. Murray, *Letters*, preface.

32. R. K. Webb, *Harriet Martineau: A Radical Victorian* (New York: Columbia University Press, 1960), p. 308.

33. Alice Rossi, "Harriet Martineau: The First Woman Sociologist," in *The Feminist Papers: From Adams to de Beauvoir*, ed. Alice S. Rossi (New York: Columbia University Press, 1973), pp. 118–24.

34. Seymour Martin Lipset, "Harriet Martineau's America," in *Society in America*, ed. S. M. Lipset (New Brunswick, N.J.: Transaction Books, 1981), p. 37.

35. Hill, intro. to *How to Observe Morals and Manners* (New Brunswick, N.J.: Transaction Books, 1988), p. xi.

36. Deirdre David, *Intellectual Women*, p. 31.

37. Robert Colby, "'Rational Amusement': Fiction versus Useful Knowledge in the Nineteenth Century," in *Victorian Literature and Society: Essays Presented to Richard Altick*, ed. James R. Kincaid and Albert Kuhn (Columbus: Ohio State University Press, 1984), p. 56.

38. Alice Rossi, "Harriet Martineau," p. 119.

39. For more on Martineau's beliefs about personal writing and her attempts at "masculine discourse" see Linda Peterson's article "Harriet Martineau: Masculine Discourse, Female Sage," in *Victorian Sages and Cultural Discourse: Renegotiating Gender and Power*, ed. Thais E. Morgan (New Brunswick, N.J.: Rutgers University Press, 1991), pp. 171–86.

40. Ibid., p. 175.

41. Ibid., p. 183.

42. Tocqueville allegedly refused to read Martineau's *Society in America*, published three years before the second portion of his work.

43. Quoted in Lipset, "Harriet Martineau's America," p. 53.

44. To Martineau "utterance" was also connected to her sense of self-control. Thinking that she was going to die, she prepared her obituary for the *Daily News* nearly twenty years before she actually did pass away. It is a measure of how much utterance meant to her that she kept what she had originally written and insisted that it be used.

45. Emily Faithfull, *Three Visits to America*, (Edinburgh: D. Douglas, 1884); subsequent citations from this work are noted parenthetically in the text.

46. Faithfull nurtured this reputation as a speaker by inviting many of America's most prominent women, including Susan B. Anthony, to attend her lectures. Faithfull wanted her message to be disseminated as widely as possible.

47. She also traveled aware of her position as a representative English traveler and makes reference on several occasions to Frances and Anthony Trollope and Dickens, among others.

48. Faithfull reinscribed the very ideology that she sought to subvert in other ways as well. For example, she suggests that one of the positive effects of introducing more women into the workplace is that "bad language and bad habits had been banished" (23).

49. Beatrice Webb, *My Apprenticeship* (London: Longmans, Green and Company, 1926), p. 106; subsequent citations from this work are noted parenthetically in the text.

50. Webb was, however, dissatisfied with some of the practical aspects of work for the COS. For more information, see Jane Lewis's "The Place of Social Investigation, Social Theory, and Social Work in the Approach to late-Victorian and Edwardian Social Problems: the Case of Beatrice Webb and Helen Bosanquet," pp. 151–57.

51. Barbara Caine, "Beatrice Webb and the 'Woman Question,'" *History Workshop Journal* 14 (Autumn 1982), p. 30.

52. Jane Lewis, "The Place of Social Investigation," p. 156.

53. Beatrice Webb, *American Diary, 1898*, ed. David Shannon (Madison: University of Wisconsin Press, 1963), p. 142; subsequent citations from this work are noted parenthetically in the text.

Conclusion: Victorian Women and the Spirit of Place

1. Alice Meynell, *The Spirit of Place and Other Essays* (London: John Lane, 1898); citations from this work are noted parenthetically in the text.

2. Catherine Cantalupo, "Alice Meynell," in vol. 19 of *Dictionary of Literary Biography*, ed. Donald E. Stanford (Detroit: Gale Research Company, 1983), p. 314.

3. Vernon Lee, *The Sentimental Traveller: Notes on Places* (London: John Lane, 1908); subsequent citations from this work are noted parenthetically in the text.

4. Elaine Showalter, *A Literature of Their Own*, p. 298.

5. Patricia Yaeger, *Honey-Mad Women: Emancipatory Strategies in Women's Writing* (New York: Columbia University Press, 1988), p. 5.

6. Kali Israel, "Writing Inside the Kaleidoscope: Rerepresenting Victorian Women Public Figures," *Gender and History* 2 (Spring 1990), p. 40.

Bibliography

Primary Sources

Adams, W. H. Davenport. *Celebrated Women Travellers of the Nineteenth Century.* London: W. Swan Sonnenschein, 1883.

Ady, Julia Cartwright. *A Bright Remembrance: The Diaries of Julia Cartwright, 1851–1924.* Edited by Angela Emanuel. London: Weidenfeld and Nicolson, 1989.

———. "English Art in the Victorian Age." *Quarterly Review* 187 (1898): 209–33.

———. *The Life of Isabella d'Este.* 1903. Author's original manuscript. 2 vols. Huntington Manuscript 17248.

Barker, Lady Mary Anne. *A Year's Housekeeping in South Africa.* London: Macmillan and Co., 1877.

Barrett, Elizabeth, and Robert Browning. *The Letters of Robert Browning and Elizabeth Barrett, 1845–1846.* 2 vols. Edited by Elvan Kintner. Cambridge: Cambridge University Press, 1969.

Bates, Katherine. *A Year in the Great Republic.* New York: Macmillan, 1887.

Baxter, Lucy [Leader Scott, pseud.]. *The Renaissance of Art in Italy.* New York: Scribner and Welford, 1883.

———. *Tuscan Studies and Sketches.* New York: Scribner and Welford, 1887.

Behn, Aphra. *Oroonoko; or, The Royal Slave.* 1695. Reprint. Edited by Adelaide P. Amore. Lanham, Md.: University Press of America, 1987.

Bishop, Isabella Bird. *The Englishwoman in America.* London: John Murray, 1856. Reprint. Madison: University of Wisconsin Press, 1966.

———. *A Lady's Life in the Rocky Mountains.* London: John Murray, 1880. Reprint. London: Virago Press, 1982.

———. *Six Months Among the Palm Groves, Coral Reefs, and Volcanoes of the Sandwich Islands.* 2d ed. London: John Murray, 1876.

———. *Unbeaten Tracks in Japan.* 1880. Reprint. With an Introduction by Pat Barr. London: Virago, 1984.

———. *The Yangtze Valley and Beyond.* 2 vols. London: John Murray, 1899.

Blaikie, W. G. "Lady Travellers." *Blackwood's Magazine* 160 (July 1896): 49–66.

Blessington, Lady Marguerite. *The Idler in Italy.* 2 vols. London: Henry Colburn, 1839.

Bodichon, Barbara Leigh Smith. *An American Diary: 1857–58.* Edited by Joseph W. Reed. London: Routledge and Kegan Paul, 1972.

Braddon, Mary. *Lady Audley's Secret.* 1862. Reprint. New York: Oxford University Press, 1987.

Brassey, Annie. *Around the World in the Yacht "Sunbeam".* New York: Henry Holt and Co., 1889.

Bremer, Frederika. *Homes of the New World.* Translated by Mary Howitt. 3 vols. London: Arthur Hall, Virtue and Co., 1853.

Broad, Lucy. *A Woman's Wanderings the World Over.* London: Headley Brothers, 1909.

Bromley, Clara. *A Woman's Wanderings in the Western World.* London: Saunders, Otley, and Co., 1863.

Brontë, Charlotte [Currer Bell, pseud.]. *Jane Eyre.* 1847. Reprint. New York: W. W. Norton, 1971.

———. *Shirley.* 1849. Reprint. Harmondsworth, England: Penguin, 1982.

———. *Villette.* 1853. Reprint. Oxford: Clarendon Press, 1984.

Buckland, Anne. *The World Beyond the Esterelles.* London: Remington, 1884.

Burton, Isabel. *The Inner Life of Syria, Palestine, and the Holy Land.* London: H. S. King, 1875.

Butler, Josephine. *Woman's Work and Woman's Culture.* London: Macmillan, 1869.

Carlyle, Thomas. "Count Cagliostro in Two Flights." 1833. Reprint. In *Critical and Miscellaneous Essays,* vol. 28 of *The Works of Thomas Carlyle: Centenary Edition,* 249–318. London: Chapman and Hall, 1896–99.

———. "On History." 1830. Reprint. In *A Carlyle Reader,* edited by G. B. Tennyson, 55–66. New York: Cambridge University Press, 1984.

Clouston, T. S. *Female Education from a Medical Point of View.* Edinburgh: Macniven and Wallace, 1882.

Cobbe, Frances Power. *Cities of the Past.* London: Trubner and Co., 1864.

———. *Italics: Brief Notes on Politics, People, and Places in Italy.* London: Trubner and Co., 1864.

———. *The Life of Frances Power Cobbe, By Herself.* 2 vols. Cambridge, Mass.: Riverside Press, 1894.

Conrad, Joseph. *The Heart of Darkness.* 1902. Reprint. New York: Penguin, 1973.

Cruttwell, Maud. *A Guide to the Paintings in the Florentine Galleries: The Uffizi, the Pitti, the Academia: a Critical Catalogue, with quotations from Vasari.* London: J. M. Dent and Co., 1907.

Cumming, Constance Gordon. *From the Hebrides to the Himalayas.* 2 vols. London: Sampson Low, Marston, Searle, and Rivington, 1876.

———. *At Home in Fiji.* New York: Armstrong and Son, 1882.

———. *In the Himalayas and On the Indian Plains.* London: Chatto and Windus, 1884.

———. *A Lady's Cruise in a French Man-of-War.* 2 vols. Edinburgh: Blackwood and Sons, 1882.

Curzon, George. "Ladies and the Royal Geographic Society." *The Times* (31 May 1893): 11.

Dickens, Charles. *Little Dorrit.* 1857. Reprint. Harmondsworth, England: Penguin, 1981.

———. *Pictures from Italy.* 1846. Reprint. New York: Coward, McCann, and Geoghegan, 1974.

Dilke, Emilia Pattison. *Claude Lorrain, sa vie et ses oeuvres.* Paris: Rouam, 1884.

———. *French Architects and Sculptors in the Eighteenth Century.* London: G. Bell and Sons, 1900.

———. *French Engravers and Draughtsmen of the Eighteenth Century.* London: G. Bell and Sons, 1902.

————. *French Furniture and Decoration in the Eighteenth Century*. London: G. Bell and Sons, 1901.

————. *French Painters of the Eighteenth Century*. London: G. Bell and Sons, 1899.

————. *The Renaissance of Art in France*. 2 vols. London, 1879.

Dixie, Florence. *Across Patagonia*. London: R. Bentley, 1880.

————. *Aniwee; or, The Warrior Queen*. London: Henry and Co., 1890.

————. *A Defence of Zululand and its King*. London: Chatto and Windus, 1882.

————. *Gloriana; or the Revolution of 1900*. London: Henry and Co., 1890.

————. *In the Land of Misfortune*. London: Bentley, 1884.

————. *Towards Freedom: An Appeal to Thoughtful Men and Women*. London: Watts, 1904.

————. *The Young Castaways; or the Child Hunters of Patagonia*. London: Shaw, 1890.

————. "Woman's Mission." *Vanity Fair* (16 August 1884): 114–15.

[Eastlake, Elizabeth.] "The British Museum." *Quarterly Review* 124 (January 1868): 147–79.

————. "The Englishwoman at School." *Quarterly Review* 146 (July 1878): 40–69.

————. "Evangelical Novels." *Quarterly Review* 72 (May 1843): 25–53.

————. "*Jane Eyre* and *Vanity Fair*." *Quarterly Review* 84 (December 1848): 153–85.

————. "Crowe and Cavalcaselle on the History of Painting." *Edinburgh Review* 135 (January 1872): 122–49.

————. "Lady Travellers." *Quarterly Review* 76 (June 1845): 98–136.

————. *Letters from the Shores of the Baltic*. London: John Murray, 1844.

————. *The Journals and Correspondence of Lady Eastlake*. Edited by Charles E. Smith. 2 vols. London: John Murray, 1895.

————. "Michael Angelo." *Quarterly Review* 103 (April 1858): 436–83.

————. "Photography." *Quarterly Review* 101 (April 1857): 442–68.

————. "Treasures of Art in Great Britain." *Quarterly Review* 94 (1854): 467–508.

Eaton, Charlotte. *Rome in the Nineteenth Century*. 5th ed. 2 vols. London: Henry G. Bohn, 1852.

Edwards, Amelia. *Pharoahs, Fellahs, and Explorers*. New York: Harper Brothers, 1891.

————. *A Thousand Miles Up the Nile*. London: George Routledge, 1889.

————. *Untrodden Peaks and Unfrequented Valleys*. 1873. Reprint. Boston: Beacon Press, 1987.

Eliot, George. *Daniel Deronda*. 1876. Reprint. Harmondsworth, England: Penguin, 1987.

————. *The George Eliot Letters*. 9 vols. Edited by G. Gordon Haight. New Haven: Yale University Press, 1954–78.

————. *Middlemarch: A Study of Provincial Life*. 1871–72. Reprint. Harmondsworth, England: Penguin, 1984.

————. *The Mill on the Floss*. 1860. Reprint. New York: Signet, 1981.

————. *Romola*. Edinburgh: Blackwood and Sons, 1863.

————. "Silly Novels by Lady Novelists." 1856. Reprint. *The Writings of George Eliot* 22 Boston: Houghton Mifflin Co., 1908: 186–220.

Elliot, Frances. *Diary of an Idle Woman in Constantinople*. Leipzig, Germany: Bernhard Tauchnitz, 1893.

———. *Diary of an Idle Woman in Italy.* 2 vols. in 1. New York: Brentanos, 1871.

———. *Diary of an Idle Woman in Sicily.* 2 vols. London: Bentley and Son, 1871.

———. *Diary of an Idle Woman in Spain.* 2 vols. London: F. V. White, 1884.

Faithfull, Emily. Letter to Susan B. Anthony. Huntington Manuscript 10548.

———. *Three Visits to the United States.* Edinburgh: D. Douglas, 1884.

Felton, Mrs. *Life in America.* London: Hull, 1838.

Finch, Marianne. *An Englishwoman's Experience in America.* 1853. Reprint. New York: Negro University Press, 1981.

Forster, E. M. *A Room with a View.* 1908. Reprint: New York: Bantam Books, 1988.

Frazer, Sir James. *The Golden Bough: A Study of Comparative Religion.* 2 vols. London: Macmillan, 1890.

Gaskell, Elizabeth. *The Life of Charlotte Brontë.* 1857. Reprint. Harmondsworth, England: Penguin, 1985.

Gaunt, Mary. *Alone in West Africa.* London: T. Werner Laurie, 1911.

Gissing, George. *The Emancipated.* 1890. Reprint. Edited by Pierre Coustillas. Rutherford, N.J.: Fairleigh Dickinson University Press, 1977.

Gordon, Lucie Duff. *Letters from Egypt: To Which are Added Letters from the Cape.* London: Macmillan, 1876.

Hall, Captain Basil. *Travels in North America in the Years 1827 and 1828.* 3 vols. Edinburgh, 1829.

Hardy, Lady Mary Anne. *Through Cities and Prairie Lands.* New York: A. Worthington, 1881.

Hardy, Thomas. *The Return of the Native.* 1878. Reprint. Harmondsworth, England: Penguin, 1986.

Heaton, Mary. *Masterpieces of Flemish Art, Including Examples of the Early German and Dutch Schools.* London: Bell and Daldy, 1869.

Houston, Mrs. C. J. F. *Hesperos: or, Travels in the West.* London: J. W. Parker, 1850.

Hunt, Leigh. "Blue Stocking Revels; or the Feast of the Violets." 1837. Reprint. In *The Poetical Works of Leigh Hunt,* edited by H. S. Milford, 176–92. New York: Oxford University Press, 1923.

James, Henry. *Italian Hours.* London: William Heinemann, 1909.

Jameson, Anna. *Characteristics of Women, Moral, Poetical, and Historical.* 1832. Reprint. London: G. Bell, 1879.

———. *A Commonplace Book of Thoughts, Memories, and Fancies.* London: Longman, Brown, Green, and Longmans, 1854.

———. *Companion to the Most Celebrated Private Galleries of Art in London.* London: Saunders and Otley, 1844.

———. *Diary of an Ennuyee.* 1826. Reprint. In *Visits and Sketches at Home and Abroad, with Tales and Miscellanies.* 2 vols. New York: Harper Brothers, 1834.

———. *Handbook to the Public Galleries of Art in and near London.* London: John Murray, 1842.

———. *The History of our Lord as Exemplified in Works of Art.* Continued and completed by Lady Eastlake. 1864. 2d ed. 2 vols. London: Longmans, Green, 1890.

———. *Legends of the Madonna.* Reprint. Boston: Houghton Mifflin, 1895.

———. *Letters and Friendships, 1812–1860.* Edited by Mrs. Steuart Erskine. London: T. Fisher Unwin, 1915.

————. *Memoirs of Celebrated Female Sovereigns.* 2 vols. London, 1831.

————. "Report of the Commissioners on the Employments of Children, &c.,: Condition of the Women and the Female Children." *The Athenaeum* No. 871 (24 June 1843): 588.

————. *Sacred and Legendary Art.* 1848. Reprint. London: Longmans, Green, 1857.

————. *Sketches of Art, Literature, and Character.* Boston: Ticknor and Fields, 1858.

————. "Some Thoughts on Art: Addressed to the Uninitiated." *The Art Journal* 2 (1849): 69–71.

————. *Studies, Stories, and Memoirs.* Boston: Ticknor and Fields, 1859.

————. *Winter Studies and Summer Rambles.* London: Saunders and Otley, 1838.

Kemble, Frances Butler. *Journal of a Residence on a Georgia Plantation.* New York: Harper Brothers, 1861.

Kempe, Margery. *The Book of Margery Kempe.* 1436. Reprint. Translated by D. A. Windeatt. Harmondsworth, England: Penguin, 1985.

Kingsley, Charles. "From Ocean to Sea." Reprint. In *Prose Idylls.* London: 1882.

Kingsley, Mary. *The Story of West Africa.* London: Horace Marshall, 1900.

————. *Travels in West Africa: Congo Francais, Corisco and Cameroons.* 1897. Reprint. Boston: Beacon Press, 1982.

————. *West African Studies.* 1899. 3d ed. New York: Barnes and Noble, 1964.

Klein, Augusta. "Sketches of Eastern Travel." 4 installments. *Blackwood's Magazine* 151 (January, March, April, May 1892): 50–72, 399–413, 518–36, 722–45.

Larymore, Constance. *A Resident's Wife in Nigeria.* London: George Routledge, 1908.

Lee, Vernon. *The Enchanted Woods: And Other Essays on the Genius of Places.* London: John Lane, 1905.

————. *For Maurice: Five Unlikely Stories.* London: Lane, Bodley Head, 1927.

————. *Genius Loci: Notes on Places.* London: G. Richards, 1899.

————. "On Modern Travelling." *Macmillan's Magazine* 69 (February 1894): 306–11.

————. *The Sentimental Traveller: Notes on Places.* London: John Lane, 1908.

————. *The Spirit of Rome: Leaves from a Diary.* London: John Lane, 1906.

Lennox, Charlotte. *Euphemia.* 1790. Reprint. Las Vegas: Scholars' Facsimiles and Reprints, 1989.

————. *The Life of Harriot Stuart. Written by Herself.* 1751.

Leonowens, Anna. *The English Governess at the Siamese Court.* Boston: Field, Osgood, and Co., 1870.

————. *The Romance of the Harem.* 1873. Reprint. Edited by Susan Morgan. Charlottesville: University Press of Virginia, 1991.

Lewis, George Henry. "The Lady Novelists." *Westminster Review* 58 (July 1852): 129–41.

Lewis, Sarah. *Woman's Mission.* London: John W. Parker, 1839.

Lott, Emmeline. *Harem Life in Egypt and Constantinople.* London: Bentley, 1865.

Martineau, Harriet. *Eastern Life, Present and Past.* 2 vols. Philadelphia: Lea and Blanchard, 1848.

————. *Household Education.* 1848. Reprint. Boston: James R. Osgood and Co., 1877.

————. *How to Observe Morals and Manners.* 1838. Reprint. With an Introduction By Michael R. Hill. New Brunswick, N.J.: Transaction Books, 1988.

————. *Illustrations of Political Economy.* 9 vols. London: Charles Fox, 1834.

————. *Life in the Sickroom: Essays by an Invalid.* London: Edward Moxon, 1844.

————. *The Martyr Age of the United States.* 1839. Reprint. New York: Arno Press, 1969.

————. "Mrs. Jameson." In *Biographical Sketches.* New York: Leypoldt and Holt, 1869.

————. "Preface" to *The Positive Philosophy of Auguste Comte. Freely Translated and Condensed.* New York: Calvin Blanchard, 1855.

————. *Retrospect of Western Travel.* 2 vols. New York: Lohman, 1838.

————. *Society in America.* 2 vols. Paris: Baudry's European Library, 1837.

Maury, Sarah. *An Englishwoman in America.* London: T. Richardson and Sons, 1848.

Meynell, Alice. *The Colour of Life and Other Essays.* London: John Lane, 1893.

————. *Essays.* London: Burns, 1923.

————. *Essays of Today and Yesterday.* London: G. G. Harrap, 1926.

————. *The Rhythm of Life and Other Essays.* London: Elkin Mathews and John Lane, 1893.

————. *The Spirit of Place and Other Essays.* London: John Lane, 1899.

Montagu, Lady Mary Wortley. *Embassy to Constantinople: The Travels of Lady Mary Wortley Montagu.* Edited and compiled by Christopher Pick. London: Century, 1988.

————. *Letters of the Right Honourable Lady Mary Wortley Montagu, Written During Travels in Europe, Asia, and Africa, to persons of distinction, men of letters, &c. in different parts of Europe.* 3 vols. in 1. London: Becket and P. A. Hondt, 1763.

Morgan, Lady. *Italy.* 2 vols. London: H. Colburn, 1821.

Murray, Amelia M. *Letters from the United States, Cuba, and Canada.* New York: G. P. Putnam, 1856.

Nightingale, Florence. *Cassandra.* Reprint. Old Westbury, N.Y.: The Feminist Press, 1979.

————. *Letters from Egypt: A Journey on the Nile, 1849–50.* Selected by Anthony Sattin. New York: Weidenfeld and Nicolson, 1987.

Oliphant, Margaret. *Jerusalem the Holy City: Its History and Hope.* New York: Macmillan, 1891.

————. *The Makers of Florence: Dante, Giotto, Savonarola.* London: Macmillan, 1876.

————. *The Makers of Modern Rome.* 4 vols. New York: Macmillan, 1895.

Piozzi, Hester Lynch. *Observations and Reflections Made in the Course of a Journey Through France, Italy, and Germany.* 2 vols. London: A. Strahn, 1779.

Radcliffe, Ann. *The Italian.* 1796. Reprint. London: Oxford University Press, 1968.

————. *A Journey Made in the Summer of 1794 Through Holland and the Western Frontier of Germany.* 1795. Reprint. Hildesheim, N.Y.: G. Olms, 1975.

————. *The Mysteries of Udolpho: A Romance: interspersed with some pieces of poetry.* 4 vols. London: G. G. and J. Robinson, 1794.

Seacole, Mary. *The Wonderful Adventures of Mrs. Seacole in Many Lands.* 1857. Reprint. With an Introduction by William L. Andrews and a Preface by W. H. Russell. New York: Oxford University Press, 1988.

Sewell, Elizabeth Missing. *Impressions of Rome, Florence, and Turin.* London: Longman, Green, Longman, and Roberts, 1862.

Shannon, David, ed. *Beatrice Webb's American Diary*. 1898. Reprint. Madison: University of Wisconsin Press, 1963.

Shelley, Mary. "The English in Italy." *Westminster Review* 6 (October 1826): 325–41.

———. *The Letters of Mary Shelley*. Edited by Betty T. Bennett. 3 vols. Baltimore: Johns Hopkins University Press, 1988.

———. *Rambles in Germany and Italy in 1840, 1842, and 1843*. 2 vols. London: Edward Moxon, 1844.

———. "Recollections of Italy." *London Magazine* 9 (1824): 21–26.

Smiles, Samuel. "Miss Martineau." In *Brief Biographies*, 499–510. Chicago: Belford, Clarke and Co., 1883.

Stael, Madame de. *Corinne, or Italy*. 2 vols. in 1. 3d American ed. Philadelphia: E. L. Carey and A. Hart, 1836.

Starke, Mariana. *Letters from Italy*. 2 vols. London: Bentley, 1800.

———. *Travels in Europe for the Use of Travellers on the Continent and Likewise in the Island of Sicily to which is added on Account of the Remains of Ancient Italy*. 9th ed. Paris: A. and W. Galigani and Co., 1839.

Taylor, Catherine. *Letters from Italy to a Younger Sister*. 2 vols. London: John Murray, 1840–41.

Thackeray, William. *Vanity Fair: A Novel without a Hero*. 1848. Reprint. Edited by Peter L. Shillingsburg, New York: Garland, 1989.

Tocqueville. Alexis. *Democracy in America*. Translated by Henry Reeve. London: Saunders and Otley, 1835–40.

Trollope, Frances. *Domestic Manners of the Americans*. 1832. Reprint. New York: Oxford University Press, 1984.

———. *Fashionable Life: Or, Paris and London*. 3 vols. London, 1856.

———. *Paris and the Parisians in 1835*. 2 vols. London, 1836.

———. *The Robertses on Their Travels*. 3 vols. London, 1846.

———. *Travels and Travellers: A Series of Sketches*. 2 vols. London, 1846.

———. *Vienna and the Austrians*. 2 vols. London, 1838.

———. *A Visit to Italy*. London: R. Bentley, 1842.

Trotter, Isabella. *First Impressions of the New World*. London: 1859.

Twining, Louisa. *Symbols of Early and Mediaeval Christian Art*. London: Longman, Brown, Green, and Longmans, 1852.

Tylor, Edward Burnett. *Primitive Culture: Researches into the Development of Mythology, Philosophy, Religion, Language, Art and Custom*. New York: Holt, 1889.

Waitz, Theodor. *Introduction to Anthropology*. Edited by J. F. Collingwood. London: Anthropology Society Publications, 1863.

Ward, Mrs. Humphry. *Robert Elsmere*. 1888. Reprint. New York: Oxford University Press, 1987.

Westermarck, Edward. *The History of Human Marriage*. London: Macmillan, 1891.

Webb, Beatrice. *American Diary, 1898*. Edited by David Shannon. Madison: University of Wisconsin Press, 1963.

———. *The Cooperative Movement in Great Britain*. London: S. Sonnenschein, 1891.

———. *My Apprenticeship*. London: Longmans, Green, 1926.

Webb, Beatrice, and Sidney Webb. *The History of Trade Unionism*. London: Longmans and Co., 1894.

————. *Methods of Social Study.* 1932. Reprint. London School of Economics and Political Science: Cambridge University Press, 1975.

Wollstonecraft, Mary. *Letters Written During a Short Residence in Sweden, Norway, and Denmark.* 1796. Edited by Carol H. Poston. Lincoln: University of Nebraska Press, 1976.

Wood, Mrs. Henry. *East Lynne.* 1861. Reprint. New Brunswick, N.J.: Rutgers University Press, 1984.

Woolf, Virginia. *A Room of One's Own.* New York: Harcourt, Brace, and World, 1929.

Wortley, Lady Emmeline Stuart. *Travels in the United States During 1849 and 1850.* New York: Harper Brothers, 1851.

Wortley, Victoria. *A Young Traveller's Journal of a Tour in North and South America during the Year 1850.* London: Macmillan, 1852.

Wright, Frances. *Views of Society and Manners in America.* 1820. 2d. ed., London: Longman and Co., 1822.

Secondary Sources

Abrams, Philip. *The Origins of British Sociology: 1834–1914.* Chicago: University of Chicago Press, 1968.

Alexander, Caroline. *One Dry Season: In the Footsteps of Mary Kingsley.* New York: Knopf, 1990.

Annan, Gabriele. "Roughing It." *The New York Review of Books.* (22 December 1988): 3–4.

Armstrong, Nancy. "The Rise of Feminine Authority in the Novel." *Novel: A Forum on Fiction* 15 (Winter 1982): 127–45.

Askwith, Betty. *Lady Dilke, A Biography.* London: Chatto and Windus, 1969.

Auerbach, Nina. *Woman and the Demon: The Life of a Victorian Myth.* Cambridge: Harvard University Press, 1982.

Bachelard, Gaston. *The Poetics of Space.* 1958. Translated by Maria Jolas. Boston: Beacon Press, 1969.

Bann, Stephen. "The Sense of the Past: Image, Text, and Object in the Formation of Historical Consciousness in Nineteenth-Century Britain." In *The New Historicism*, edited by H. Aram Veeser, 102–15. London: Routledge and Kegan Paul, 1989.

Birkett, Dea. *Spinsters Abroad: Victorian Lady Explorers.* London: Basil Blackwell, 1989.

Birkett, Dea, and Julie Wheelwright. "'How could she?' Unpalatable Facts and Feminists' Heroines." *Gender and History* 2 (Spring 1990): 49–57.

Bourdieu, Pierre. *Distinction: A Social Critique of the Judgement of Taste.* Translated by Richard Nice. Cambridge: Harvard University of Press, 1984.

Buckler, William E., ed. *Prose of the Victorian Period.* Boston: Houghton Mifflin, 1958.

Buckley, Jerome. *The Triumph of Time: A Study of the Victorian Concepts of Time, History, Progress, and Decadence.* New York: Oxford University Press, 1980.

Buzard, James. *The Beaten Track: European Tourism, Literature, and the Ways to "Culture," 1800–1918.* New York: Oxford University Press, 1993.

Caine, Barbara. "Beatrice Webb and the 'Woman Question.'" *History Workshop Journal.* 14 (Autumn 1982): 23–43.

Callaway, Helen. *Gender, Culture, and Empire: European Women in Colonial Nigeria.* London: Macmillan, 1987.

Cantalupo, Catherine. "Alice Meynell." In vol. 19 of *Dictionary of Literary Biography*, edited by Donald E. Stanford, 313–24. Detroit: Gale Research Company, 1983.

Christ, Carol T. "'The Hero as Man of Letters': Masculinity and Victorian Nonfiction Prose." In *Victorian Sages and Cultural Discourse: Renegotiating Gender and Power*, edited by Thais E. Morgan. New Brunswick, N.J.: Rutgers University Press, 1991.

Clifford, James. *The Predicament of Culture: Twentieth Century Ethnography, Literature, and Art.* Cambridge: Harvard University Press, 1988.

Clifford, James, and George Marcus, eds. *Writing Culture: The Poetics and Politics of Ethnography.* Berkeley: University of California Press, 1986.

Colby, Robert. "'Rational Amusement': Fiction versus Useful Knowledge in the Nineteenth Century." In *Victorian Literature and Society: Essays Presented to Richard Altick*, edited by James R. Kincaid and Albert Kuhn, 46–73. Columbus: Ohio State University Press, 1984.

Conrad, Peter. *Imagining America.* New York: Oxford University Press, 1980.

Cotsell, Michael, ed. *Creditable Warriors, 1830–1876.* Atlantic Highlands, N.J.: Ashfield Press, 1990.

Crais, Clifton C. "The Vacant Land: The Mythology of British Expansion in the Eastern Cape, South Africa." *Journal of Social History.* 25 (Winter 1991): 255–75.

Crawford, Martin. *The Anglo-American Crisis of the Mid-Nineteenth Century.* Athens: University of Georgia Press, 1987.

Dale, Peter Allan. *The Victorian Critic and the Idea of History.* Cambridge: Harvard University Press, 1977.

David, Deirdre. *Intellectual Women and Victorian Patriarchy.* Ithaca: Cornell University Press, 1987.

———. "'Getting Out of the Eel Jar': George Eliot's Literary Appropriation of Abroad." In *Creditable Warriors*, edited by Michael Cotsell, 257–72. Atlantic Highlands, N.J.: Ashfield Press, 1990.

Diamond, Arlyn, and Lee R. Edwards, eds. *The Authority of Experience: Essays in Feminist Criticism.* Amherst: University of Massachusetts Press, 1977.

Edelstein, Debra. "Vernon Lee." In vol. 57 of *Dictionary of Literary Biography*, edited by William Thesing, 158–67. Detroit: Gale Research Company, 1987.

Eisler, Colin. "Lady Dilke (1840–1940): The Six Lives of an Art Historian." In *Women as Interpreters of the Visual Arts, 1820–1979*, edited by Claire Richter Sherman and Adele Holcomb, 147–80. Westport, Conn.: Greenwood Press, 1981.

Elshtain, Jean Bethke. *Public Man/Private Woman: Women in Social and Political Thought.* Princeton: Princeton University Press, 1981.

Foucault, Michel. "Intellectuals and Power: A Conversation Between Michael Foucault and Gilles Deleuze." In *Language, Counter-Memory, Practice: Selected Essays and Interviews*, edited and translated by Donald F. Bouchard, 205–17. Ithaca: Cornell University Press, 1977.

Frank, Katherine. *A Voyager Out: The Life of Mary Kingsley.* Boston: Houghton Mifflin, 1986.

Frawley, Maria. "Desert Places/Gendered Spaces: Victorian Women in the Middle East." *Nineteenth-Century Contexts* 15, no. 1 (1991): 49–64.

———. "Fair Amazons Abroad: The Social Construction of the Victorian Adventuress." *Annals of Scholarship* 7, no. 4, Edited by Nikki Lee Manos (1990): 501–22.

———. "Harriet Martineau: Gender and the Discourse of Sociology." *Victorian Newsletter*, no. 81 (Spring 1992): 13–20.

Fredeman, William E. "Emily Faithfull and the Victoria Press: An Experiment in Sociological Bibliography." *The Library* 29, no. 2 (June 1974): 139–64.

Fussell, Paul. *Abroad: Literary Traveling Between the Wars*. New York: Oxford University Press, 1980.

Gendron, Charisse. "Images of Middle-Eastern Women in Victorian Travel Books." *The Victorian Newsletter*, no. 79 (Spring 1991): 18–23.

———. "Lucie Duff Gordon's 'Letters from Egypt.'" *Ariel: A Review of International English Literature* 17 (April 1986): 49–61.

Gilbert, Sandra, and Susan Gubar. *No Man's Land: The Place of the Woman Writer in the Twentieth Century*. Vol. 1, *The War of the Words*. New Haven: Yale University Press, 1988.

Green, Martin. *Dreams of Adventure and Deeds of Empire*. New York: Basic Books, 1979.

Hall, Catherine. "Private persons versus public someones: class, gender and politics in England, 1780–1850." In *Language, Gender and Childhood*, edited by Carolyn Steedman, Cathy Urwin, and Valerie Walkerdine, 10–33. London: Routledge and Kegan Paul, 1985.

Hamalian, Leo, ed. *Ladies on the Loose: Women Travellers of the Eighteenth and Nineteenth Centuries*. New York: Dodd, Mead, 1981.

Heineman, Helen. *Three Victorians in the New World: Interpretations of the New World in the Works of Frances Trollope, Charles Dickens, and Anthony Trollope*. New York: Peter Lang, 1992.

———. *Mrs. Trollope: The Triumphant Feminine in the Nineteenth Century*. Athens: Ohio University Press, 1979.

Holcomb, Adele. "Anna Jameson: The First Professional English Art Historian." *Art History* 6 (June 1983): 171–85.

———. "Anna Jameson (1794–1860): Sacred Art and Social Vision." In *Women as Interpreters of the Visual Arts, 1820–1979*, edited by Claire Richter Sherman and Adele Holcomb, 93–121. Westport, Conn.: Greenwood Press, 1981.

Homans, Margaret. *Bearing the Word: Language and Female Experience in Nineteenth-Century Women's Writing*. Chicago: University of Chicago Press, 1986.

Israel, Kali. "Writing Inside the Kaleidoscope: Re-Representing Victorian Women Public Figures." *Gender and History* 2 (Spring 1990): 40–48.

Jameson, Frederic. *The Political Unconscious: Narrative as a Socially Symbolic Act*. Ithaca: Cornell University Press, 1981.

Jann, Rosemary. *The Art and Science of Victorian History*. Columbus: Ohio State University Press, 1985.

Kenyon, John. *The History Men: The Historical Profession in England Since the Renaissance*. London: Weidenfeld and Nicolson, 1983.

Kerber, Linda. "Separate Spheres, Female Worlds, Woman's Place: The Rhetoric of Women's History." *Journal of American History* 75 (June 1988): 9–39.

Klein, Viola. *The Feminine Character: History of an Ideology*. New York: International Universities Press, 1949.

Kroller, Eva-Marie. *Canadian Travellers in Europe: 1851–1900*. Vancouver: University of British Columbia Press, 1987.

Levine, Philippa. *The Amateur and the Professional: Antiquarians, Historians and Archaeologists in Victorian England, 1838–1866*. New York: Cambridge University Press, 1986.

————. *Feminist Lives in Victorian England: Private Roles and Public Commitment*. Oxford: Basil Blackwell, 1990.

Lewis, Jane. "The Place of Social Investigation, Social Theory, and Social Work in the Approach to Late Victorian and Edwardian Social Problems: The Case of Beatrice Webb and Helen Bosanquet." In *The Social Survey in Historical Perspective, 1880–1940*, edited by Martin Bulmer, Kevin Bales, and Kathryn Kish Sklar, 148–69. Cambridge: Cambridge University Press, 1991.

Lipset, Seymour Martin. "Harriet Martineau's America." In *Society in America*, edited by S. M. Lipset, 5–42. New Brunswick, N.J.: Transaction Books, 1981.

Lonoff, Sue. "Charlotte Brontë's Belgian Essays: The Discourse of Empowerment." *Victorian Studies* 32 (Spring 1989): 386–409.

Manganaro, Marc. "'The Tangled Bank' Revisited: Anthropological Authority in Frazer's *The Golden Bough*." *The Yale Journal of Criticism* 3 (Fall 1989): 107–26.

Marks, Patricia. "Harriet Martineau: *Fraser's* 'Maid of [Dis]Honour.'" *Victorian Periodicals Review* 19 (Spring 1986): 28–34.

McCleod, Dianne Sachko. "Art Collecting and Victorian Middle-Class Taste." *Art History* 10 (September 1987): 328–49.

Melman, Billie. *Women's Orients: English Women and the Middle East, 1718–1918*. New York: Macmillan, 1991.

Middleton, Dorothy. *Victorian Lady Travellers*. New York: Dutton, 1965; Chicago: Academy, 1982.

Mills, Sara. *Discourses of Difference: An Analysis of Women's Travel Writing and Colonialism*. New York: Routledge, 1991.

Moers, Ellen. *Literary Women*. New York: Doubleday and Co., 1976.

Morgan, Susan. "An Introduction to Victorian Women's Travel Writings about Southeast Asia." *Genre* 20 (Summer 1987): 189–207.

————. "Victorian Women, Wisdom, and Southeast Asia." In *Victorian Sages and Cultural Discourse: Renegotiating Gender and Power*, edited by Thais E. Morgan, 207–24. New Brunswick, N.J.: Rutgers University Press, 1991.

Murray, Janet. *Strong-Minded Women: And Other Lost Voices from the Nineteenth Century*. New York: Pantheon Books, 1982.

Myer, Valerie Grosvenor. *A Victorian Lady in Africa: The Story of Mary Kingsley*. Southampton, England: Ashford, 1989.

Nevins, Allan. *America Through British Eyes*. New York: Oxford University Press, 1948.

Newton, Judith. "History as Usual? Feminism and the 'New Historicism.'" *Cultural Critique* 9 (Spring 1988): 87–121.

Nitchie, Elizabeth. "Mary Shelley, Traveler." *Keats-Shelley Journal* 10 (Winter 1961): 29–42.

Nord, Deborah Epstein. "'Neither Pairs Nor Odd': Female Community in Late Nineteenth-Century London." *Signs: Journal of Women in Culture and Society* 15 (Summer 1990): 733–54.

Ortner, Sherry B. "Is Female to Male as Nature is to Culture?" In *Women, Culture, and Society,* edited by Michelle Zimbalist Rosaldo and Louise Lamphere, 67–87. Stanford, Calif.: Stanford University Press, 1974.

Park, Jihang. "Women of Their Time: The Growing Recognition of the Second Sex in Victorian and Edwardian England." *Journal of Social History* 21 (Fall 1987): 49–67.

Pemble, John. *The Mediterranean Passion: Victorians and Edwardians in the South.* London: Clarendon, 1987.

Peterson, Linda H. "Harriet Martineau: Masculine Discourse, Female Sage." In *Victorian Sages and Cultural Discourse: Renogiating Gender and Power,* edited by Thais E. Morgan. New Brunswick N.J.: Rutgers University Press, 1991.

Petrie, Sir Charles. *The Victorians.* London: Eyre and Spottiswoode, 1960.

Pichanick, Valerie. *Harriet Martineau: The Woman and Her Work, 1802–76.* Ann Arbor: University of Michigan Press, 1980.

Poovey, Mary. *The Proper Lady and the Woman Writer: Ideology as Style in the Work of Mary Wollstonecraft, Mary Shelley, and Jane Austen.* Chicago: University of Chicago Press, 1984.

———. *Uneven Developments: The Ideological Work of Gender in Mid-Victorian England.* Chicago: University of Chicago Press, 1988.

Pratt, Mary Louise. "Fieldwork in Common Places." In *Writing Culture: The Poetics and Politics of Ethnography,* edited by James Clifford and George Marcus, 27–50. Berkeley: University of California Press, 1986.

Robinson, Jane. *Wayward Women: A Guide to Women Travellers.* Oxford: Oxford University Press, 1990.

Rosaldo, Michelle Zimbalist, and Louise Lamphere, eds. *Women, Culture, and Society.* Stanford, Calif.: Stanford University Press, 1974.

Rosaldo, Renato. "Imperialist Nostalgia." *Representations* 26 (Spring 1989): 107–22.

Rossi, Alice S. "Harriet Martineau: The First Woman Sociologist." In *The Feminist Papers: From Adams to de Beauvoir,* edited by Alice S. Rossi, 118–24. New York: Columbia University Press, 1973.

Russell, Mary. *The Blessings of a Good Thick Skirt: Women Travellers and Their World.* London: Collins, 1986.

Said, Edward. *Orientalism.* 1978. Reprint. New York: Vintage Books, 1979.

Shattock, Joanne. *Politics and Reviewers: The Edinburgh and the Quarterly in the Early Victorian Age.* London: Leicester University Press, 1989.

———. "Travel Writing Victorian and Modern: A Review of Recent Research." *Prose Studies: History, Theory, Criticism* 5 (May 1982): 151–64.

Shattock, Joanne, and Michael Wolff. *The Victorian Periodical Press: Soundings and Samplings.* Leicester, England: Leicester University Press, 1982.

Sheppard, Francis. *London 1808–1870: The Infernal Wen.* Los Angeles: University of California Press, 1971.

Sherman, Claire Richter, and Adele M. Holcomb, eds. *Women as Interpreters of the Visual Arts, 1820–1979.* Westport, Conn.: Greenwood Press, 1967.

Showalter, Elaine. "Feminist Criticism in the Wilderness." *Critical Inquiry* 8 (Winter 1981): 179–205.

———. *A Literature of Their Own: British Women Novelists From Brontë to Lessing.* Princeton: Princeton University Press, 1977.

Siltanen, Janet, and Michelle Stanworth, eds. *Women and the Public Sphere: A Critique of Sociology and Politics*. New York: St. Martin's Press, 1984.

Sklar, Kathryn Kish. "Hull-House Maps and Papers: Social Science as Women's Work in the 1890s." In *The Social Survey in Historical Perspective, 1880–1940*, edited by Martin Bulmer, Kevin Bales, and Kathryn Kish Sklar, 111–42. Cambridge: Cambridge University Press, 1991.

Smith, Valerie. *Hosts and Guests: The Anthropology of Tourism*. Philadelphia: University of Pennsylvania Press, 1977.

Steegman, John. *Consort of Taste, 1830–1870*. London: Sidgwick and Jackson, Limited, 1950.

Stevenson, Catherine Barnes. *Victorian Women Travel Writers in Africa*. Boston: Twayne, 1982.

Sunstein, Emily. *Mary Shelley: Romance and Reality*. Boston: Little, Brown, 1989.

Thomas, Clara. *Love and Work Enough: The Life of Anna Jameson*. Toronto: University of Toronto Press, 1967.

Tinling, Marion. *Women into the Unknown: A Sourcebook on Women Explorers and Travelers*. New York: Greenwood Press, 1989.

Treves, Giuliana Artom. *The Golden Ring: The Anglo Florentines, 1847–1862*. Translated by Sylvia Sprigge. London: Longmans, Green, 1956.

Tuchman, Gaye, and Nina Fortin. *Edging Women Out: Victorian Novelists, Publishers, and Social Change*. New Haven: Yale University Press, 1989.

Vicinus, Martha. *Independent Women: Work and Community for Single Women, 1850–1920*. Chicago: University of Chicago Press, 1985.

———. *A Widening Sphere: The Changing Roles of Victorian Women*. Bloomington: Indiana University Press, 1977.

Walling, William. *Mary Shelley*. New York: Twayne, 1972.

Webb, R. K. *Harriet Martineau: A Radical Victorian*. New York: Columbia University Press, 1960.

Weiser, Marjorie, and Jean Arbeiter, eds. *Womanlist*. New York: Atheneum, 1981.

Williams, Raymond. *Culture and Society, 1780–1950*. New York: Columbia University Press, 1958.

Woodham-Smith, Cecil. *Florence Nightingale, 1820–1910*. New York: McGraw-Hill, 1951.

Yaeger, Patricia. *Honey-Mad Women: Emancipatory Strategies in Women's Writing*. New York: Columbia University Press, 1988.

Index